A DISTANT LIGHT

Kentucky's Journey
Toward Racial Justice

by
Bill Cunningham

Book design by Asher Graphics
Cover illustration by James Asher

Manufactured in the United States of America

All book order correspondence should be addressed to:

McClanahan Publishing House, Inc.
P.O. Box 100
Kuttawa, KY 42055

270-388-9388
800-544-6959

www.kybooks.com
books@kybooks.com

Dedicated to the beloved people of west Kentucky.

"But the path of the just is as the shining light, that shineth more and more unto the perfect day."

Proverbs 4:18

A distant light does not brighten the way.
It does not warm the frigid night.
But a distant light offers hope.

Contents

CHAPTER 1

THE LINGERING DARKNESS

*T*welve-year-old Melinda Cunningham slipped into her father's bedroom on a cold December morning in 1865. She stood quietly in the corner and watched. The darkness from night was just falling away from the shaded windows. Dancing flames from the fireplace cast flickering shadows along the wall. The high drama about to unfold before her would be forever etched upon her young mind.

Her father, Alexander Cunningham, was a tall, raw-boned farmer who lived in the Goose Hollow area near Rock Castle in Trigg County, Kentucky. Only 51, he looked much older, with his lined face and shock of white hair. The War Between the States, drawing to a bloody conclusion that past spring, had taken its toll.

His wife, Cynthia, had lost a brother and his sister, a son, both fighting for the South. His own son Zan, a fun-loving prankster, had also served for the losing cause, but made it safely home. Throughout the long ordeal, Alex's farm had been ravished by marauding Union troops: his crops trampled, live-

stock and chickens slaughtered, smokehouses raided, his own home ransacked and violated. One slave had run away with the Yanks. He was near economic ruin. Even his family, consisting of ten children, had been terrorized and threatened by the invaders from the North. Several times Alex had narrowly escaped capture, constantly eluding their reach in order to avoid being compelled to take the "loyalty oath." His oldest son, William, known as "Sir," was abducted on one occasion when a company of tired and frustrated Yankees discovered his name. "Another Cunningham!" the young captain had exclaimed in disgust. "The woods are full of 'em, and every one a damn Rebel! "

 On the day before, word of momentous import had reached this far-flung part of Kentucky. At the store just two miles up the road, where men gathered to whittle, talk, and exchange the news of the day, Alex had learned what he knew was inevitable. The slavery issue was over. The 13th Amendment to the United States Constitution had just been ratified. Slavery was officially abolished "within the United States or any place subject to their jurisdiction."

 Upon arriving back at the house the previous evening he had conferred briefly with Cynthia. Little Melinda, inquisitive and precocious, had caught part of the conversation.

 She knew what was coming.

 Early the next morning, Alex moved toward the fireplace and sat down in the cane-bottom chair. Cynthia stood at his side. Their house slave, Bell, plump and much younger than she looked, came in from the kitchen where she had been feeding breakfast to the horde of kids.

 Alex motioned for her to sit in the chair facing his. Bell nervously wiped her hands on her apron and studied the face of her master and his wife, discerning keenly that they were about serious business. Their faces were solemn, even ashen, like people attending to the grieving and knowing not what to say.

 As soon as she was seated, Alex got straight to the point.

 "Bell, you are free," he spoke in a voice so low that his little daughter watching a few steps away could barely hear him, "you and your children."

It was not a totally unexpected message for Bell. The word had been coming since the spring.

Nevertheless, the proclamation came heavy and with tremendous power.

For a long moment she sat quietly. What thoughts ran through the head of this servile creature of toil, were known only to God. Whether she pondered frightening consequences or the exciting prospects of liberation is not known. Neither did her demeanor or expression give it away. But surely she must have wondered, if only for a fleeting moment, about the uncertain road which lay ahead.

Finally she spoke.

"Thank you. Thank you Marse Alec and Miss Cynthia."

These words, expression of gratitude to whom no expression of gratitude was due, came deep from within the mingled and complicated soul of a slave. This sacred right seemingly afforded by her erstwhile master was merely a reaffirmation of what the bleeding wounds of Antietam, Shiloh, and Sharpsburg had so profoundly acquired. Two human beings unwittingly played out a rite of passage presaged by the ages. Surfacing from within her came the recognition that her plight could have been much worse–stories of beatings and floggings, families busted asunder, refractory darkies sold "down river"–the harrowing yet routine nightmares of all members of this docile mass of involuntary servitude. Even within that simple response was the endearing gratitude of a loyal friend, grateful in some kind of indescribable way, for this formal pronouncement, this benediction, which gave not only closure to the journey, but also absolution, and at last, the final blessing of the master.

The room was deathly quiet, with only the crackling of the fire and the doleful ticking of the battered old clock on the mantel breaking the eerie silence. Then a rooster, with its ancient trumpet, proclaimed the dawn.

Alex nodded.

Bell arose from her chair. After a quick glance at Cynthia, the former slave departed the room. Not knowing what else to do, she left the house and went to her cabin.

Slavery was slow to give up the ghost in Kentucky.

This was due mostly to the peculiar place of this state during that grand struggle between North and South.

While "officially" remaining neutral at first, and then loyal to the Union, it was a Southern state which actually seceded from itself. It had its own Confederate capital at Bowling Green and elected its own representatives to the Confederate Congress in Richmond. This commitment to the secessionist movement was good enough to earn the state a star on the Confederate flag. But there wasn't much for Kentucky's Confederate state government to do but to fight.

So fight it did. Kentucky's Confederate Governor, George W. Johnson, was killed at Shiloh in 1862.

Early on, President Abraham Lincoln considered the prospects of Kentucky actually leaving the Union and joining its Southern brethren as a dreadful possibility. "I think to lose Kentucky is nearly the same as to lose the whole game," he said. But all that the split in loyalties served to do was to make a militarized zone where both camps struggled for ground, and more critically in the west, for control of the rivers.

Lincoln had made a tactical mistake on April 15, 1861. On that day he issued the command for the conscription of troops from all of the states except those which had seceded. The draft extended to Southern states which were still hanging by a thread to the Union. While the deep South of cotton states had pulled out early, the eight northernmost slave states remained loyal. Delaware, Maryland, Virginia, North Carolina, Kentucky, Tennessee, Missouri, and Arkansas were all poised on the brink. In issuing his call for the conscription of troops to put down the rebellion, he did not exempt the Southern states which had not yet defected. In essence, he was calling upon Southerners to make war against Southerners. Historian Shelby Foote reports the response, "Telegram after telegram arrived from governors of the previously neutral states, each one bristling with moral indignation at the enormity of the proclamation, rather as if it had been in fact an invitation to fratricide or incest."

Kentucky's Governor Beriah Magoffin was among the indignant. He flat refused President Lincoln's call for Federal troops from the Bluegrass state. Magoffin stated that he would not draft Kentucky boys to take arms against their "Southern brethren."

Tennessee, which had just previously voted not to secede, changed its mind, moving quickly to part ways with the North. Virginia, North Carolina, and Arkansas were also lost to the Union.

Kentucky still held on. But Governor Magoffin, unable to swallow that bitter pill as well as some other pro-Union measures being asked of him, would resign his office. Later on in regard to emancipation of the slaves, President Lincoln did not want to make the same mistake again and antagonize the state of his birth.

He withheld his freeing of the slaves until January 1, 1863 so as not to unduly offend Kentucky and other states still in the Union where slavery was practiced. Also, when it was penned, it specifically excluded these states from the Proclamation.

Slavery remained legal in Kentucky. And it did so through the balance of the bloody war, and all the way up until December 18, 1865 when the 13th Amendment to the United States Constitution was ratified. Only then—almost three years after The Emancipation Proclamation, eight months after Appomattox, eight months after the Great Emancipator's death—did slavery finally gasp its last breath in Kentucky.

Interestingly, the 13th Amendment was not approved by the Kentucky legislature until 1976—over 110 years later!

So, one wonders, what happened to all the Kentucky slaves in that time warp between the time when guns were being fired and people killed "trampling out the vintage where the grapes of wrath are stored" and the quiet and peaceful passage of the 13th Amendment near Christmas of 1865?

When we search out that question, we shall find a peculiar answer as to the peculiar institution within a most peculiar state.

First of all, the Civil War in Kentucky wreaked havoc on the property of its citizens. Fortunes were lost; homes destroyed;

crops obliterated and foodstuffs stolen.

Slaves were property. When the guns fired upon Fort Sumter on April 12, 1861 to begin our nation's bloodiest war, there were approximately 211,000 slaves in Kentucky.

Almost immediately after the war began, a good number escaped to the North, across the Mason-Dixon Line to freedom. There was no longer any legal authority to retrieve them.

Others, over 28,000, were enlisted in the Union ranks as soldiers.

This recruiting of slaves and free blacks from Kentucky had been an explosive issue. It was a good thing for Lincoln's intention of keeping Kentucky in the Union that it began late in the war. When conscription of blacks was first ordered by the Union in 1864, it was an after-shock in Kentucky to the original secession movement. It was rumored that two thirds of the members of the Kentucky Legislature favored the state's belated secession in response to the Emancipation Proclamation and the subsequent drafting of blacks. Even the loyalist Kentucky Governor, Thomas Bramlette, scolded the president in a letter to him in September 1864. "We are not willing to sacrifice a single life or imperil the smallest right of free white men for the sake of the Negro...to permit the question of the freedom or slavery of the Negro to obstruct the restoration of national authority and unity is a blood-stained sin."

Small wonder that Kentucky was never considered a full-fledged, dues-paying member of the Union cause.

In March of 1865 the United States Congress took care of those former Kentucky slaves who had donned the Yankee blue. It passed a law whereby all slaves serving in the Union Army, their wives and children were free.

Near the bitter end, even Jefferson Davis authorized the recruitment of slaves to help supplement the military manpower shortage of the South. They would be offered their freedom in exchange for their service.

In a letter from President Davis to Governor William Smith

of Virginia dated March 25, 1865 he stated:

> *You have probably noticed that the order issued from the Adjutant General's office, for the organization of colored troops looks only to the acceptance of volunteers, and, in a letter received this evening from General Lee, he expresses the opinion that there would be no compulsory enlistment in the first instance. My idea has been that we should endeavor to draw into our military service that portion of the negroes which would be most apt to run away and join the army of the enemy, and that this would be best effected by seeking for volunteers for our own army.*

It was so late in the game that nothing much came of it.

Suffice it to say, except for these Kentucky slaves somehow made free, there were still thousands of slaves in Kentucky in bondage at the war's end when the long walks home began. The Kentucky Legislature in 1865 had soundly defeated the 13th Amendment proposed for the state's ratification. Just three days before the 13th Amendment was finally ratified by the requisite number of states–Kentucky's highest court had held illegal the Federal release of wives and children of black Union soldiers.

What happened to those hapless, uneducated, penniless, and destitute men, women and children of color, cast from the bonds of slavery onto the social and economic landscape of Kentucky?

First was cold, hard reality.

The black man and woman were free. And that was it.

No property. No resources. No jobs. No laws to protect them. The 13th Amendment to the U.S. Constitution is short and sweet: "Neither slavery nor involuntary servitude except as punishment for crime where of the party shall have been duly convicted, shall exist within the United States, or any place subject to their jurisdiction."

It would be over three years later in 1868 before the 14th Amendment–affording the ex-slaves citizenship–would go into law.

In the South of course, the laws were not applied equally to blacks. Most placed them at a severe disadvantage. At first, they did not have the right to own property, to vote, to even testify in court. The Freedmen's Bureau, established under the U.S. War Department was set up to protect and care for ex-slaves adrift in the former slave states. Once again, Kentucky resisted this effort by the federal government as an unwarranted and unwelcomed intrusion into state affairs. Judge Wiley P. Fowler of Smithland even ruled it as an unconstitutional infringement into local concerns. Therefore, to some degree, the Bureau's effectiveness was thwarted.

Consequently, many former slaves did what other blacks had done during the war, except now with greater ease, and moved across the Ohio River and disappeared into what they probably thought was the vast promised land of the North.

Many, exuberant over their freedom, immediately left the farms and plantations in droves for the cities of Louisville, Nashville, Lexington, Memphis, St. Louis, and Cincinnati. There they huddled in dense, low rent squalor, trying desperately to root out a living as hired servants, factory workers, or menial laborers. The black population of Lexington, for example, increased 130 percent between 1860 and 1870. It was not an easy life. Not only did they live in dilapidated housing with inadequate food and fuel, which led to widespread disease, but they also suffered the slings and arrows of outraged whites who saw the former slaves committing crimes to survive.

Many men and women of previous bondage made desperate and poignant searches for husbands, wives, and children, long scattered by the savagery of slave trading. To the great credit of this struggling race, a large number succeeded in not only reuniting families, but solemnizing their marriages under the law. Many Negro families heroically survived the devastating wreckage of slavery. By 1880 for instance, 70 percent of black children in Louisville lived with both parents-a figure comparable to whites.

While the morally riddled package of slavery was ugly from any angle, it is denying history not to recognize that some sides

14

were less evil than others.

By the best accounts possible, it appears that the plight of former slaves in west Kentucky was less drastic and disruptive than in most other places throughout the South.

To understand this, one must consider the nature of slavery in this far end of the state.

Unlike the large cotton plantations of the deep South with hundreds of slaves laboring under overseers and tenders, most of the slaveholdings in west Kentucky were by less substantial farmers. While cotton-still grown in this area-and tobacco were labor-intensive crops conducive to slavery, the planters themselves were not of the affluence of the grand plantation owners further South. Therefore, the family slaveholdings in far west Kentucky and even Tennessee were much smaller. In 1860, for instance, the average number of slaves per slaveholding family in the large cotton and tobacco growing counties of Graves, Calloway, and Fulton in west Kentucky was less than six.

Because of this smaller number of slaves owned by white families, the relationship between them was generally much closer. Many were house slaves and field hands who worked side by side with their owners during the day and were in close proximity to them all the time. There were constant and direct associations between the races without the intercession of overseers and farm foremen found on the sprawling rice and sugar cane plantations of the lower South.

The labor-intensive crop of tobacco, grown throughout west Kentucky, had a lot to do with this. It required numbers–ma, pa, kids of all ages and sexes in a perpetual movement of bending backs and elbows–and slaves. It was a crop requiring year-around attention and pursuit. From the burning of plant beds in late winter, to the many hours of seeding, drawing plants, setting row after row, hoeing constantly, topping, suckering, worming, and on and on. The bondsmen of the soil were of both colors, bending, stooping, reaching, lifting all together from the sharp winds of February through the stifling heat of August, on into the crisp autumn evenings as the leaf hung smoldering in the barn; they labored together. And those who spend hour upon hour together in tedious, back breaking toil get to know each other intimately. Exchanging casual grunts of conversation along the row of corn or tobacco or engaging in reflective discourse in the noon-time shade, sharing sweat and bleeding blisters, or moving frantically to beat a gathering summer squall–all of it tends to bring mortals closer together. In the mind numbing and ancient ritual of physical labor and screaming muscles, the lines of master and slave became blurred.

Many of the slaves stayed with the white families for a lifetime, and in many instances were passed down through their owners' estates to succeeding generations. Consequently, close familial relationships developed between the masters and the enslaved. Young white children loved their black "mammies" intensely and the matronly slaves were as protective of them as they were of their own children. And while there was always that knowing and rigid divide, steeped in the ages, they moved together with ease and affection. For many of the poorer whites who had inherited family slaves, there was not a great bit of difference in the standard of living between the owners and the slaves. They were poor whites owning poorer blacks. Both races, toiling in the hot sun of summer, shared much of the same grueling pain of labor and poverty. In short, it is safe to say that slavery in west Kentucky, generally speaking, was a kinder, gentler form of involuntary servitude. This provided the groundwork for the ongoing paternalism many whites felt for blacks long after the latter were free.

But of course there was a down side to this close knit community of slavery. Because of the limited number of slaves on one farm or plantation, they usually had to look elsewhere for mates. Therefore dual ownership of a slave couple made it more likely that the pair would be split up by the business dealings of the owners. Also, some historical studies have reflected that miscegenation between masters and slaves occurred more frequently on small farms in Kentucky where whites and blacks lived closer to one another than on the large plantations of the lower South.

Many slaves in west Kentucky, even when liberated, still turned to their old masters. Most always they were not found wanting. Some former owners even pleaded with ex-slaves to stay, for they were in dire need of their labor. Many, perhaps most, did stay, working on for their masters for hire, living in the same old cabins in which they had lived as slaves.

Generally speaking there were three types of labor arrangements between the former bondsmen and white landowners.

The sharecropping setup was probably the most popular, at least during the first days of the Reconstruction era. The black farmer would be provided land, house, necessary tools and working animals. At harvest he would pay his white landowner a certain percentage of the crops which were usually tobacco, cotton or corn. The ex-slave's take was usually two thirds.

Just a straight out wage-earning arrangement was another means by which blacks worked the farm to survive. The emancipated worker's lifestyle was not too far removed from the days of his bondage. In some instances, he continued to live in his former cabin. Average monthly wages for males in the state in 1866 were $14.00. For females, it was slightly over half of that.

Lastly there was the practice of apprenticeships. Although this concept was closely linked to slavery in the minds of many blacks, it became a standard working procedure, especially for children. The law required that the apprentice receive humane treatment, medical care, adequate food, and general upkeep in exchange for his labor. Of course the idea was for the worker to learn a skill or trade, and for the keeper to receive much needed labor. Upon completion of the agreement, usually when the apprentice reached the age of eighteen, the laborer would be released from his obligation. Usually his "graduation" was celebrated with a new suit of clothes.

It was the fortunate black indeed who was able to acquire property of his own. And this was done more times than one might think. Usually it would be sold, or even given to the former slave by a former owner. Some former slave owners would leave land for their former slaves in their wills. Once again this was most likely to occur where there had been a more casual and friendly relationship between master and servant during enslavement.

Faint evidence of friendly relations between white owners and black slaves, during slavery and immediately afterwards can still be detected in Trigg County. There exist, even today, large families in that county, both black and white, who bear the same last names. Just to name a few, such families as Redd, Wadlington, Cunningham, Wallace, Bacon, Rogers, Alexander and Thomas–both black and white–are descendants of the same soil, the same farms.

Bertie Gingles, in her exhaustive mid-1950s history of the Caucasian Cunningham family, felt moved to include a section on "Colored Families."

Those blacks who suffered cruelties and injustices during enslavement, most often departed to parts unknown with their emancipation, and would never adopt the names of their former owners.

At Hurricane Baptist Church, near Rock Castle in that same Trigg County community, blacks and whites worshipped together for several years after the Civil War.

Some have argued that the former slave owners in west Kentucky were more considerate, protective and compassionate of their former slaves after their freedom than any other group of whites.

There's no way to prove or disprove this proposition. But it makes sense.

The blacks deserved little if any credit for their freedom. Their liberation was not born of slave insurrection. So they could not be blamed by the former owners for the latter's economic loss. "It's not their fault that they are cast penniless upon the land," was the general sentiment of thoughtful whites. This lack of rancor would in most instances be complemented by their knowledge and familiarly with their former servants. Feelings of good will toward the Negroes were most likely nurtured by those who knew them most intimately.

But tragically, these bonds of friendship and decency between races were not the rule, and neither did they last.

If mankind could search out the poisonous root from which the insidious bile of racism flows, we could hack it out of our human existence. But alas, that awesome task is still before us.

In those days following our deadliest and most divisive war, the social climate was ripe for upheaval.

In 1865, as thousands of liberated blacks flowed out into the South, free and unencumbered, the violent prejudice raised its ugly head and spewed its venom over the region.

There was a myriad of emotions brought to bear upon this fractious time.

There was the boiling resentment of the lower and middle class whites who were not too far advanced in education, skills and knowledge from the liberated slaves.

These white tenant farmers, yeomen, menial laborers made up a large part of the population in the rural South. Almost overnight a competing labor force came into being, seeking to survive along with the lower income whites. The majority of white Southerners felt their very livelihoods threatened by the freshly freed blacks.

Perhaps most importantly was the element of fear–fear by the white population of the Negro.

Generally speaking, with the exception of inheritance, slave ownership had not been for the poor. It was costly, requiring large investments and heavy ongoing expense. In 1850 only 23 percent of the white males in Kentucky owned slaves. Those who did not have slaves living on their farms or plantations really did not know the black population well– their ways, their culture, and their seemingly strange African heritage. What people do not know and understand, they are inclined to view with suspicion, and ultimately fear. In Kentucky, as throughout the South, most citizens had viewed slavery ambivalently. There had been serious movements throughout the region over the years for its abolition. Many saw it as morally indefensible and economically doomed. Yet any hope of willing emancipation ended with the bloody and deadly uprising by Nat Turner in Virginia in August of 1831 and John Brown's ill fated insurrection at Harper's Ferry some 28 years later. These disturbances, along with others less deadly, scared the living daylights out of white Southerners. It made them believe that in slavery they had a "tiger by the tail." That if freed, the black population, which at one time in Kentucky reached almost 25 percent of the population, would turn upon their former masters and all other whites in a bloodletting frenzy of retribution and death. Many believed that the post-war emancipation would invite racial attacks by the blacks upon the whites. This was especially anticipated in light of the fact the former slaves would be desperate for means to survive and hungry for the white man's land, property, and means.

And then of course there were the sore losers.

For many of the whites who had held so strongly to the losing cause of the South, the free blacks reminded them of this bitter defeat. A special enmity was felt toward those ex-slaves they knew had taken up the cause of the Union as soldiers. Returning home from the war, their weapons were taken, while white Confederate veterans were allowed to retain theirs. Many were then beaten, abused, and run out of the community. In the late 1860s, a U.S. Congressional report described their plight as follows: "Having served in the Union army, they have been the special objects of persecution, and in hundreds of instances have been driven from their homes." Because of this violent persecution, Union veterans of color left Kentucky in droves.

And then there was of course sex.

Nothing inflamed the emotions of white Southerners more than the thought of the blood of their race being mixed with the African descendants. The purity of Southern womanhood somehow became a powerful and destructive cause for many Caucasian men. It must be left to the psychologists and sociologists to digest and analyze the primal fear, passions, and violence the prospects of interracial sex engendered. But it was there, at many midnight visits, burning fire brands, and hooting mobs with faces contorted with hate. No other crime invoked the uncontrollable vengeance of the lynch mob more than the rape of a white woman by a black man.

It should be noted in passing, however, research indicates that while such atrocities were always appalling in their demonic frenzy, the number of killings because of sex offenses was not as great as for other perceived wrongdoing. In fact most of the interracial sexual assaults were white men against black women.

Records show that most lynchings of blacks were of those accused of murder or attempted murder. It really didn't take much of a reason though. In November 1872, three blacks in Fayette County and one in Hopkins were lynched "for being Republicans."

So alas, one must sadly recognize that for the most part, man's most hideous acts are borne within the talons of devils not yet mastered nor understood. Suffice it to say that from the beginning of their pilgrimage out of bondage, the black man and woman became the targets of racial violence.

West Kentucky was not spared this perfidy.

CHAPTER 2

NEGRO CHASERS

"The Negro who committed the outage on Mrs. Benson, in McCracken Co., last week was taken out of the Paducah jail on Monday night, and on Tuesday morning his body was found suspended in midair about a mile from the city."

This cheery bit of news was reported in the August 19, 1869 issue of *The Jackson Purchase* newspaper published in Mayfield, Kentucky. It was hidden away on the second page, sandwiched between short notes on the number of postage stamps sold daily in New York City and the state of crops in Mississippi.

Lynching of blacks in Kentucky had become almost too routine to report.

One hundred years ago distinguished writer and historian James E. Cutler defined "lynching" as the practice whereby "mobs capture individuals suspected of crime, or take them from the officers of the law, and execute them without any process at law."

That description will suffice.

Cutler points out that these unlawful "executions" were not always by hanging, though that was the most common method used. There were other cruelties inflicted in the process including bludgeoning, shooting, burning and torture.

Between the Civil War and 1920 there were 344 reported lynchings in Kentucky. Almost one third of them–110 to be precise–occurred in far west Kentucky, that area roughly west of a straight line drawn between Owensboro and Bowling Green. Of those victims, 94–or eighty-five percent–were black.

Regrettably that is a conservative number. Many of these atrocities were never reported. The one mentioned at the beginning of this chapter for instance did not make the list. And the figures do not include those outright murders of blacks by whites, falling outside the narrow definition of lynching, that never were investigated. Frequent occurrences were shootings across a fence row or into a house in the dark of night; fatal blows in a fight, when the white killer would simply lay low or maybe leave town for a respectable period, never answering to the law for his act.

While the statistics might indicate that some communities were worse than others, it was a social malignancy eating away at the very soul of the entire region.

Marshall County, Kentucky is an enigma when it comes to race relations.

Today it is a thriving, bustling county with a healthy blend of a sizable industrial complex at Calvert City, river trade, farming, vibrant small businesses, deeply solvent banks, and a vigorous tourism trade with a big chunk of massive Kentucky Lake within its boundaries. The county seat of Benton, and smaller burgs of Calvert City to the north and Hardin to the south, are blessed with an outstanding educational system, active and dynamic churches, strong community spirit, and people–many of whom are new to the county–that are magnanimous and friendly.

The estimated population of the county as of 1997 was just

under 30,000 people.

There were no blacks.

Not unless you put stock in the U.S. Census Bureau Report which recorded 13 living there.

Today there may be a few but you would have to go door to door canvassing to find them. Most people living there would tell you there are none. One at Wal-Mart or the grocery store will turn heads. The few who are there are most likely mixed race, and Negro children residing temporarily in foster homes in the northern part of the county.

There is probably no other county in the South with such numbers.

The reason for the lack of blacks in Marshall County is steeped in its history.

First of all, there have never been many people of color in this community.

In 1850 there were 6,114 slaves in the Jackson Purchase area of far western Kentucky. There were only 249 in Marshall County.

While that number was up slightly by the end of the Civil War, there were still only a handful of slaves in Marshall County to be emancipated in December 1865.

Many people have speculated as to this island of slave scarcity in a sea of servitude.

Generally speaking it can be laid at the feet of poverty. This was largely attributed to a poor agricultural base. Only with the advent of soil enhancement, herbicides and pesticides, over the last 100 years has this county been able to increase its agricultural yield. Its red clay and wooded ridges sloping away from the Tennessee River bottom provided rough going for the hardscrabble farmers of that era. Much of the county was, and still is, taken up by the Clark's River basin of wetlands and swamp forest, totally incapable of being cultivated. It's astonishing to learn, in light of its current prosperity and vibrant economy, that even as late as 1940 Marshall County had the lowest per capita income in the state.

Since it was a poor county, its people simply could not afford many slaves.

Therefore, there were not many blacks to be disseminated into the white population of roughly 7,000 in 1865. Many left, and by the turn of the century there were only a handful of blacks scattered throughout the county in small pockets.

As to the question of what happened to them, many local historians point to one tragic night in March of 1908.

Birmingham, Kentucky is no more. Like the legendary continent of Atlantis, it has sunk beneath the waters. Only "Birmingham Island" can be seen today arising out of Kentucky Lake in far western Kentucky.

It was located 12 miles from the seat of Benton on the Tennessee River right across from the "Between the Rivers" section of neighboring Lyon County. During prohibition, its little ferry would haul "government men" across the stream, searching for moonshine stills. Their searches were usually thwarted, however, by secret signals by the helmsman of the ferry, giving advance warnings to sentinels on the opposite shore.

The town's founding in 1849 was built upon the dream that it would prosper well into the future with the iron smoldering pits and mills which were firing slag across the river. It hoped to be another Birmingham, England–thus its name.

By 1867, with the bustling iron mills silenced and tumbling into ruin, the village peaked at 476 residents. It boasted three "white" churches and two "colored" as well as a "white" school and a "colored" school.

The village settled into a sleepy existence, satisfied to make its way with the river trade of packets and excursion boats which regularly made their stops.

But it was a nice little town, Birmingham, except for that one night which still lives in infamy.

On the evening of March 9, 1908, the world was purring along at a rather easy pace.

West Kentucky Republicans were wrangling around trying

to select delegates to the upcoming national convention in Chicago.

The Kentucky General Assembly had just appropriated 75,000 dollars for the construction of a new tuberculosis sanitarium.

In far western Kentucky the weather was bright, calm, almost spring like.

The population of the little Tennessee River town of Birmingham had settled into around 300 people. This included a handful of blacks who not only owned property, but farmed some of the prime Marshall County land along the Tennessee River bottom. Their economic advantage was resented by many of the less resourceful whites.

Around midnight on this early spring night, about 100 irritated and jealous white men raided the Negro settlement, shooting into their homes. Seven men were shot, and five others whipped. Negro John Scruggs and his family, for some reason, seemed to have been the main target of the attack. Three women of his family were wounded when their house was lacerated with gunfire and Scruggs and his infant granddaughter were killed. Eight to ten blacks were escorted down to the river bank where they were whipped severely. All the blacks in Birmingham were given warning to sell their land, and get out of town.

There was a pitiful rush of these victims onto the passenger packet boats as they made their escape to Nashville and Paducah. The Louisville *Courier Journal* reported "Only six blacks remain since the notices to leave town were posted. A steamer from Marshall County brought in seventeen black families and their household goods. In all about 100 blacks got off the steamer when it arrived in Tennessee."

Soon, the white band of racists pushed to oust the entire county of blacks by posting, near a railroad station, a clear and ominous message of impending doom for those people of color who dared to stay in Marshall County: "Niggers Don't Let the Sun Set on You."

The message got through.

By 1910, two years after the Birmingham raid, the number of blacks in the county had dwindled from 348 to 135. By 1930, there were only 62. And finally, as the century drew into its final decade, and the bright sunshine of prosperity shone upon its people, blacks had vanished altogether. The descendants of slaves, who had labored in the broiling sun to hack out a living for their masters from the unyielding loam and clay, would be denied the journey across Jordan into the land of milk and honey.

A little historical house cleaning is needed here.

In the early years of the 20th century, a farmer's revolt broke out in west Kentucky and Tennessee. It was spawned by the consolidation of the American Tobacco Company into a price strangling trust, driving the tobacco farmers into severe economic straits. The farmers formed the Dark Tobacco District Planters Protection Association for the purpose of pooling their crops and holding them off the market until the "trust" offered them a reasonable return on their investment and hard work. It cost about six cents a pound to grow the tobacco, but they were being offered only three cents.

They were growing desperate and hungry.

While membership in the Association grew to large numbers, many independent farmers refused to join, and sold their tobacco to the Trust. This weakened considerably the effectiveness of the farmers' boycott.

Therefore in 1906, a group of "Opossum Hunters" were formed as the militant arm of the Association. They visited recalcitrant farmers at night urging them to join. Things got nasty, and soon farmers were being beaten and their plant beds and barns destroyed. It wasn't long before these militant farmers were given the name "Night Riders" as their methods spread out all over the "Black Patch"—those counties in west Kentucky and Tennessee growing "dark fired" tobacco. They also became superbly organized with ranks, secret signs, masked identities, and ritual, under the leadership of David Amoss, a little country doctor from Cobb, Kentucky.

The "Silent Brigade," as it also became known, grew in popularity and though lawless in their tactics, garnered the support of the populace, most of which were tied indirectly to the farm economy. Towns of Eddyville, Princeton, Russellville, and Hopkinsville were raided with military precision and warehouses sated with Trust tobacco burned and destroyed.

By 1908, the Night Rider movement was beginning to wane. Casualties mounted, and lawsuits began to fall upon their heads. Most importantly, they began to lose their Robin Hood image, and public support eroded. The state militia was deployed to various places in west Kentucky to quell the lawlessness.

The image of this farmers' union was severely tainted by groups of hoodlums, vigilantes, racists, and criminals who replicated the Night Rider nocturnal ways, by disguising themselves and under the cloak of darkness, committing atrocities throughout the area like the Birmingham raid. Soon the lines blurred and historians even now refer to all of these acts of lawlessness as the doings of the Night Riders.

This is an injustice to the forces of Dr. Amoss.

The Night Riders were surely not a group without racists. But it was not a racist organization.

The Dark Tobacco District Planters Protection Association had a higher number of black members per capita than whites. Black tenant farmers were among the most severely affected by the despised Trust of James B. Duke. There was even a handful of black Night Riders.

Their leader, Dr. Amoss, was known within the black community as a kind, compassionate doctor, who provided his services to people of color with the same energy as he did the whites.

Therefore, it should be noted, that while some blacks were undoubtedly beaten by the Night Riders for their errant ways of selling to the Trust, Amoss and company did not sanction, sponsor, nor participate in any raids or attacks which were not directly related to their chief grievance–the vilified Trust and the independent farmers selling their tobacco to it.

The dastardly raids against blacks, personal vendettas, and vigilante raids of other kinds–now well known for the brutality and criminality–were simply hordes and mobs of criminals, taking advantage of the Night Rider popularity. It is no more apt to call the perpetrators of these raids and crimes "Night Riders" than to apply that term to solitary burglars or murderers simply because they plied their evil ways after dark. The tobacco uprising of 1904-09 gave rise to the Night Riders. Their tactics and means are questionable in and of themselves, and they should not be unfairly besmirched with those crimes which they did not commit.

The very night that the racist gang visited Birmingham, the "real" Night Riders were up to mischief all over the area.

Near Clarksville, Tennessee a wheat thresher owned by an independent farmer was destroyed by Night Riders.

Not far away from this criminal activity, and at the same time of the racist attack upon Birmingham, about 30 Night Riders took over the little town of Port Royale, Tennessee and wreaked havoc. They rode into an ambush by local law enforcement, however, as they made their escape; one Night Rider was killed and another wounded. Two horses lay dead in the road.

On this same night of violent activity, way up in northeastern Kentucky, the town of Brooksville in Bracken County was taken over by disgruntled tobacco farmers. About fifty of them captured the town in buggies and horses and destroyed 15,000 pounds of tobacco belonging to one of the wealthiest planters of the area who was dealing with the despised Trust.

The outlaws who raided the black section of Birmingham at that March midnight hour were part of a gang called both "Negro Chasers" or "Whitecaps." Their openly avowed purpose was rooted in racial bigotry.

In fairness to the people who resided in Marshall County at that time, there is strong evidence to suggest that a sizable number of the marauders were from across the river in the adjoining county of Lyon.

Said the Paducah paper the day after the atrocity, "The raid had nothing to do with the tobacco situation."

No, it was not about tobacco. Not about the ongoing struggle of labor against capital. Not about the noble struggle of the impoverished bondsmen of the soil. It was about evil. Unfortunately David Amoss and his Silent Brigade have been saddled with much of the blame for many of these racial atrocities.

Two weeks after the Birmingham tragedy, a group of the same ilk vented their venomous prejudice by whipping and fatally wounding a black man by the name of Tom Weaver from the Golden Pond area of Trigg County. This attack was part of a pronounced crusade to run all of the Negroes out of "Between the Rivers."

In the long history of violence in the South against the black man and woman, perhaps there is none so incredibly cruel and cowardly as that which occurred in Fulton County in the fall of the same year as the Birmingham atrocity.

On the evening of October 5, 1908, David Walker was living in Hickman with his wife and five children. Walker, a "surly Negro," had reportedly gotten into an argument with a white woman and threatened to shoot a man who came to her defense. This aroused the anger of some local whites. Late that evening about fifty men made their way to his house and ordered him to come outside.

He refused, and fired a gun into their midst.

Then the vigilantes poured coal oil on the house and proceeded to set it afire. When Walker opened the door to come out he was immediately cut down with a deadly barrage of gunfire.

His wife begged for mercy, then proceeded out with a small infant in her arms. Once again the mob opened fire, killing the baby first, and then the mother as both fell together on the ground.

Three more children attempted in vain to escape the burning inferno, only to be cut down like animals by the merciless gunfire from the murderers. The oldest son was either not at home or seeing such carnage and the slaughter of his entire family, chose to remain in the house and die in the flames and smoke rather to confront the deadly gunfire of the mob.

A white neighbor, Tom Bowan, heard the shots and attempted to lend assistance to the Walkers. He was driven off, however, by the fusillade of bullets from the attackers.

The next morning six members of the Walker family, including the pitiful remains of a mother and her small infant, lay dead or dying near and in the charred ruins of their home.

The Mayfield Daily Messenger gave this unbelievably sad account of the whole matter:

For sixteen hours the victims of a raid made on the Walker home by night riders lay unsheltered and without the necessary provisions being made for their disposal. Three of the family were killed outright, three others are mortally wounded and one has disappeared.

All day Sunday the dead and wounded lay side by side without being attended by any one except a Negro doctor, Dr. Overby, who made a short visit to the living and then refused to return, saying that he feared for his life.

Walker, who was an overbearing and shiftless Negro, had been in several scrapes which put him in bad odor with the people in his vicinity. Not heeding several warnings, he overstepped the bounds and tongue-lashed a white woman, calling her bad names and making insulting remarks regarding her husband's treatment of his stock.

At midnight Saturday a mob was formed and proceeded to the cabin of the Negro, where they called upon him to come out. Several shots were fired from the window and the riders set fire to the house, driving the inmates out. As they rushed across the open space in front of the door they were mercilessly shot down and left on the spot. Tom Bowan, a white man, heard the shots and attempted to reach Walker's house but was driven back by the fusillade of bullets from the mob.

Very little excitement is felt here, and although there is a great deal of street talk, the usual quiet prevails. So far there have been no orders issued for the arrest of anyone, and it is generally thought that the matter will not be deeply investigated.

Late yesterday the bodies were placed in coffins by the white residents of the neighborhood and turned over to Charles Walker, brother of the dead man, who was the first to investigate the condition of the victims. He found that the three wounded were going to die and his verdict was sustained by the doctor.

As it turns out, Kentuckians may not have been guilty of this dastardly atrocity.

It was apparently the work of the murderous band of Night Riders of the nearby Reelfoot Lake area in Tennessee.

This group of masked marauders was totally divorced from the tobacco militants of west Kentucky and Tennessee. They were formed ostensibly to protest the private control of Reelfoot Lake by private corporate interests to the detriment of the local fishermen and trappers. But unlike the noble intentions of the tobacco warriors, they also championed less noble causes as well as inflicting racial violence upon "trouble making niggers."

As if the killing of the Walker family wasn't horrible enough, the heartless gangsters also perpetuated a cruel crime upon a local white citizen. Reports historian Paul J. Vanderwood in his book, *Night Riders of Reelfoot Lake:*

A Mrs. Keith revealed that her teenaged son had been taken from their home near Hickman and forced to accompany the Riders in their attack on the Walkers. When Walker returned the rifle fire of the intruders, the boy had been killed and buried in a nearby forest. Because the Riders had threatened to punish her if she complained about the death of her son, the mother had remained silent until the militia could assure her of protection.

The militia Vanderwood writes about was most likely the

Tennessee detachment of Forrest Rifles of Memphis detached by Governor Malcolm R. Patterson to capture and punish the Reelfoot criminals who were committing scores of crimes including other assaults and murders. This military detachment was encamped near Samburg, Tennessee. However, just across the line near Hickman, Governor Augustus Wilson had deployed a company of the Kentucky militia to curb any further violence.

While some of the Reelfoot murderers were brought to trial for some of their crimes committed in Tennessee, no one was ever prosecuted for the demonic butchering of the Walker family.

By 1916, half a century had passed since the Civil War. Kentucky had moved with the rest of the nation into the automobile age. The wonderful invention of telephones was now a part of many households. Labor laws were liberating children from the sweat shops of industry. Kentucky's farm production was highest in the South outside of Texas. Women were on the verge of earning the right to vote. And Kentucky had just elected a progressive and enlightened governor by the name of Augustus Owsley Stanley.

But in our treatment of the Negro, it was business as usual.

On the morning of October 13 of that year, 45 year old Elita Rose was alone at her home on Pool Road in Paducah. Mrs. Rose, wife of a car repairman at the Illinois Central railroad shops, was ironing clothes in her kitchen when she heard the front screen door open and slam shut. Suddenly a black man with a pistol in his hand was upon her demanding money. Mrs. Rose ran for a shotgun in the corner and the intruder shot at her. Abandoning that idea, Mrs. Rose ran out the door. The Negro caught her on the back porch and dragged her back into the house. There he proceeded to club her about the head with his pistol. He grabbed the small coin purse which she carried and ran out of the house. It contained 60 cents.

At least that was the news report. However, the fact that the assailant would be subsequently charged with rape, and the delicate manner which the press dealt with her "nervous" injuries, are strong indication that things much more serious went on in the Rose home.

A Negro woman passing by heard the cries for help inside the house and found the victim battered and bloodied on the floor. The alarm was sounded, and Mrs. Rose was rushed to Riverside Hospital for medical care.

A massive manhunt ensued all over western Kentucky. Mrs. Rose gave a description of her assailant as "a stranger in Paducah, colored, five feet and eight inches tall, weighing between 175 and 185....around 25 years old, brown skinned." He had a "hole" or scar in his cheek.

Thousands of angry men gathered for the search. All the roads leading in and out of Paducah were guarded throughout that day and night to prevent law enforcement officers from slipping the Negro out of the city for safe-keeping once he was apprehended.

The mayor of Paducah immediately shut down all of the saloons in order for the infuriated crowd not to be further inflamed by intoxicating liquors. Commonwealth Attorney Jack Fisher from Benton heard about the hysteria and immediately took a train to the city. After visiting Mrs. Rose at the hospital, the prosecutor went downtown and confronted the mob at the corner of Fourth and Broadway, about two blocks from the courthouse. There he tried to calm the throng by assuring them that if the Negro was caught, a grand jury would be summoned immediately and he would be prosecuted, convicted and sent to the electric chair. The mob seemed to listen patiently, if unconvinced. "That's all right" one of the men yelled, "we'll be able to stand all the electric shock that Negro gets."

Blood hounds had been called out and they led the search team to a discarded bloody sweater which was found near the railroad tracks south of town. The victim's purse was also found nearby. This led most of the pursuers to believe that the fugitive had caught a train out of town. By nightfall the crowd had ballooned even more, with men getting off work for the day and joining the belligerent forces. At about 7 p.m., a report was received in Paducah that the Negro had been captured at Wingo, in Graves County, and was being brought back on the "Whiskey Dick"–a passenger train due to arrive at the Littleville Union Station at 7:20. A rowdy and eager crowd was at the terminal when the much anticipated train pulled in. Some carried rifles and shotguns. To their great disappointment the suspect was not aboard the train, and the report of his capture was revealed as false.

On the evening of October 15, a black woman, Miss Katie Pitman, and her twelve-year-old daughter went to bed in their home at 1006 Husbands Street. At about 3:30 in the morning she heard someone raise her window, slip into her room and crawl under her bed. The intruder apparently fell asleep. She carefully slipped from her bed, quietly rousted her daughter from her slumber and sent her for help.

City police officers soon arrived and found Brack Kinley, a Paducah Negro and former convict, still under the bed, dressed only in his under clothing.

He matched the description given by the victim, and he was immediately arrested. Just before sunrise Paducah Police Chief J.W. Eaker and other officers took Kinley to the home of Mrs. Rose, where she had returned from the hospital the night before. She made a positive identification of the black man. Her husband became so angered by Kinley's presence that he tried to kill him with a pistol, but the police intervened.

Even though the hordes of vigilantes were roaming the streets at that early hour, the police got Kinley to the jail.

By 7:30 in the morning, news of the prisoner's capture had spread all over the city and hundreds descended upon the jail. They were led by George Rose, who was determined to vindicate his wife's injury by unlawful means. The jailer, C.B. Whittemore, and other officers pleaded with Rose and the mob to let the law take its course. This seemed to have some effect, for Rose agreed to leave and go and consult with his wife about the matter.

But soon the awaiting crowd once again grew impatient

and demanding. After a while they grew out of control, overcame the officers and at a little before 10 a.m. broke open the door to the jail. But, they did not have the keys to the cellblock and the jailer had disappeared.

They headed for the courthouse to look for Whittmore. There they were confronted by Circuit Judge William M. Reed. Surrounding the jurist, the mob demanded that he order the jailer to turn over his keys. The courageous judge held his ground.

"I will not be a party to your mob, gentlemen, and I will say that everyone who participates in this mob will be indicted," he boldly declared. "I'll tell Whittmore to die before he gives up those keys. The law must take its course."

The insatiable rabble was not deterred.

One angry voice yelled, "The Negro took his course. Now we will take ours."

Reed pushed his way through the crowd in an attempt to find the jailer and instruct him to stand fast.

Suddenly the barrel of a 44-caliber pistol was thrust into the judge's side by one of the hoodlums and the hammer pulled back.

Deputy Sheriff Doc Allen lunged at the attacker and grabbed the gun before he could fire it. Other members of the mob immediately seized Allen and a melee ensued with the life of Judge Reed and others hanging in the balance. It came to a halt when Allen hollered over the din, "I'm not trying to hurt him (meaning the attacker). I just don't want to see a white man killed over this Negro!" The plea seemed to sober them, and relative order was restored.

Then someone saw an unidentified person with a camera taking pictures from the second floor of a dwelling across the street from the jail. The possibility of their lawlessness being captured on film caused panic.

"Take that camera away!" one of them pointed. A small group broke loose from the larger gathering and headed across the street and into the house. The camera man was grabbed and the plates from his camera smashed against the floor.

It was then that the large gathering moved from the courthouse back across the street to the jail. The jailer still courageously stood his ground, but the horde summoned a foundry man to cut the prisoner out of his cell. This took time. One newspaper reported one hour. Another reported three. Yet another report was that it took five hours for the persistent gang of outlaws to break loose their prey. It would have been plenty of time for the police to have come to his aid.

But none came. Alas, they had given up.

To the loud applause and approval of the crowd, Kinley was at last brought forth from the jail—understandably dazed with utter terror and fear. His coat and vest had been left in the cell. He was bareheaded and his shirt was almost torn from his back. The prisoner was hand-cuffed to one of the leaders who with some kind of perverted sense of fair play, suggested they take the prisoner once again to the Rose home for identification.

The law had conducted its investigation. The mobsters would conduct theirs.

They started to push the poor soul into a car for the trip, but the throng evidently thought it would be more humiliating to make him walk the full three miles to the victim's home.

Along the way on Seventh Street, a drunken black by the name of Luther Durrett stumbled into the goings on. It was a horrible twist of fate for him.

Packing a 44-pistol, Durrett ill-advisedly decided he was going to be a hero for his stricken brethren. Pulling his weapon and waving it in the air he yelled, "I'm going to shoot every white son of a bitch in town. Somebody ought to shoot into this mob and if they try to hang this Negro I'm going to do it!"

Confronting the moving mass of angry white faces now numbering close to a thousand, one has to wonder, "What was he thinking?"

Durrett was easily overcome and disarmed and thrown into step behind the accused. It quickly sobered him and he began to pitifully plea for mercy and release. His cries went unheeded.

At about two hundred yards from the Rose home, the men evidently grew tired of fooling with Durrett. There was some debate as to what to do with him. A rope was put around his neck and a tree picked out. One of the members of the mob came to his defense. "Let's whip him and turn him loose," he argued to the relief of the Negro now petrified with fright. "He hasn't done much. And he's drunk. Let's whip him and turn him loose."

A drop of mercy seemed to have fallen from the October sky upon a gathering of merciless men. The rope was removed from his neck. But one solitary voice in the rear suddenly pierced the interlude of compassion: "Let's hang the black son of a bitch."

It was enough to reignite the flames of murderous passions. Men in a crowd are like birds on a wire. When one flies, they all fly.

William Faulkner spoke of the mass mentality of a lynch mob in his work *Intruder In the Dust*. Said Faulkner,

....the men who his uncle said were in every little Southern town, who never really led mobs nor even instigated them but were always the nucleus of them because of their mass availability.

Such a man on this night in Paducah, Kentucky sealed the fate of Luther Durrett.

So the noose was returned to the poor man's neck. Over his pleas for mercy, they heaved the rope over the limb and swung him into the air.

There he dangled and kicked until death took him home.

Kinley was not to last much longer. Mrs. Rose, who seemed to be enjoying all of the attention of the masculine crowd, quickly and without relish identified the Negro once again. Now rushing through the floor of lawlessness and murder, the gang quickly moved Kinley back to the same tree from which Durrett's warm body was still hanging. There, Kinley too was strung up to kick his way into eternity.

After a few moments, everyone was directed to stand back. A fusillade of bullets was then sent into the bodies of the two Negroes. Altogether two hundred bullets were fired.

As the shots were fired, Mrs. Rose, who had just hours before supposedly had been in very bad shape physically and emotionally, arrived on the scene.

"Burn him! Burn him!" she screamed.

Reported the paper the next day:

Coroner May N. Trice held a double inquest over the charred remains of the two Negroes yesterday morning at 9 o'clock. The few remaining bones were dug out of the ashes of the fire in which they were cremated after the hanging, and a coroner's jury returned a verdict of death by burning and hanging at the hands of a mob, composed of unknown persons. The bones of both Negroes were then placed in a single coffin and buried in the county cemetery. Souvenir hunters haunted the spot all day yesterday cutting bits of the tree out for mementos of the occasion. Some even dug about in the ashes for bits of the Negroes' skeletons to keep to remember the double lynching. The rope with which the Negroes were hung was early cut into bits by eager spectators.

Mrs. Rose expressed gratitude for such a strong show of murderous support. "I did not know I had so many friends," she announced.

The unspeakable brutality of the carnage stirred anger and resentment in the Negro section of Paducah. Rumors began to circulate in the white community that blacks were preparing to arm themselves and set out en masse to extract revenge. The city commissioners met and directed that all the saloons in the city be closed. Also, the various hardware stores in town refused to sell guns and ammunition to Negroes.

Any real threats of retribution from the black community soon subsided.

In spite of death threats, the gallant Judge Reed summoned a grand jury ten days later to investigate the lynching and mutilation of the two Negroes. On November 3, 1916 the special grand jury returned no indictments, even though it had heard the testimony of over 100 witnesses.

In his play *The Merchant of Venice,* William Shakespeare wrote, "In law, what plea so tainted and corrupt but, being seasoned with a gracious voice obscures the show of evil?"

Sometimes the "shows of evil" took place in broad daylight, and even under the guise of a totally perverted justice system.

At sundown on a muggy July evening in 1906, twenty-two-year-old Ethel McClane of Mayfield was making her way home from work. She was employed as the day operator of the Cumberland Telephone Company and lived with her mother just outside town, having lost her father some six years past. Ethel was supporting herself and her mother with the money earned from the telephone company.

Near a gravel pit on a railroad track she was attacked by a black man. He threw her down the embankment, savagely tore away her clothes, and raped her. It was in an isolated area and her screams at first went unheard. However, Riley Kelso, another Negro, was walking the same way and heard her cries for help and rushed to her aid. As he did so, he met the assailant as he ran passed him. Kelso found Miss McClane hysterical, bruised, and bleeding. Tenderly he helped her up and led her home.

Immediately the Mayfield city police chief was notified and a large and angry posse was formed to hunt for the culprit.

Riley Kelso not only saw the rapist fleeing the scene. He knew him.

Allen Sievers was a 30-year-old black man who had come to town with the circus earlier in the summer. He had stayed around and was suspected of several thefts. He sometimes went by the name of Allen Mathias.

The next morning near noon he was apprehended four miles south of town by a group of railroad workers who held him for the authorities. With the sheriff home sick, City Police Chief Charles McNutt and a large group of sheriff deputies rushed Sievers back into town through the angry mob to the courthouse. There, in the courtroom, he confessed to the crime as well as a similar rape in Carlisle County earlier in the summer.

This incensed the throng of 1,000 men and his lynching appeared imminent. County Judge Ed Crossland courageously threatened the would-be attackers with criminal prosecution and order was restored.

After Miss McClane positively identified Sievers, he was then whisked off to the McCracken County Jail in Paducah for safekeeping.

The very next night, over 50 men from Graves County moved upon the jail in Paducah in an attempt to take possession of Sievers. The group was leaderless and mostly intoxicated. The McCracken County jailer and the Paducah police easily stood their ground and not only was the effort repulsed, but the visiting marauders came close to being charged themselves.

The next day, afraid that other attempts might be made upon their prisoner, the McCracken County authorities took him to Louisville by train for safe keeping.

It was decided by the Graves County prosecuting attorney that the hapless black would be immediately charged and tried. Governor J.C.W. Beckham was no dummy. He had to have known he was playing into the hands of the deadly conspiracy when he ordered Mathias returned to Mayfield within a week for trial.

Only six days after the alleged rape, on a sultry Tuesday morning, August 1, the criminal defendant who had absolutely no hopes of a fair trial left Louisville under escort for west Kentucky and almost certainly a terrible fate.

Before the defendant reached the Green River, the Mayfield citizens began constructing the scaffold for his hanging.

On that train ride, Sievers was cajoled by his guards to plead guilty to the crime. This was not as incredible as it may now seem. It is a terribly sad thing to now learn, during this time, many of the victims of hangings of black men in the South agreed to plea guilty to hopefully assuage the vehemence of their keepers who in turn might give them a "lawful" and more humane execution, and not throw them into the ravaging and crazed jaws of the mob.

Understandably the young captive was terrified, almost to the point of collapse as his train pulled into Mayfield at 6:58 that evening. An estimated four thousand people were reportedly on hand at the depot to witness the arrival of the train–the largest gathering in the history of that community.

Two companies of soldiers of the state militia–one from Hopkinsville and one from Madisonville-had accompanied Sievers from Princeton to Mayfield. At the train station in Mayfield they were joined by the local militia. When the train reached the train station, one of the crazed crowd attempted to break through the line and stab Sievers. He was halted by a bayonet thrust from a Hopkinsville soldier.

What happened during the course of the next hour or so is one of the most astonishing events in our nation's judicial history.

The criminal defendant was ushered to the Graves County Courthouse where he immediately pled guilty. At 7:12 a.m., the local newspaper reported the next day, a jury of all white men went out to deliberate with the scaffold ready in the yard, and the throng of thousands milling about outside. Twelve minutes later–at 7:24 p.m.–the farce continued with the jury returning to the courtroom with a sentence of death. It is reported to have taken twelve minutes for all the men to affix their signatures to the verdict sheet.

To the sound of loud cheers and applause, the judge announced that the sentence would be carried out immediately. At 7:40 that night, less than an hour after arriving in town for his trial, Allen Sievers arrived at the scaffold and had the hangman's noosed fastened around his neck.

The crowd tore down a wooden stockade that surrounded the jail in order that all might witness the execution. Men and boys hung from nearby trees and on telegraph poles. Women held their small children up to witness the fate of this friendless black man standing on the brink of eternity.

At 7:50, as the peaceful summer twilight fell upon the

vengeful and blood thirsty throng, the trap was sprung to the thunderous roar of the crowd. Some of the onlookers sprung forward to cut the body with knives. In order to assure the crowd that the rope had done its job, the body was allowed to fall through the trap four separate times.

The sheriff was cutting the body down at 8:00 o'clock sharp.

It was one of the shortest "legal" trials and execution in the history of the country's judicial system.

But the mob wasn't through with Allen Sievers.

The account of *The News-Democrat* of Paducah related, with a want of sensitivity, in the next day's newspaper what happened next:

"The body of the dead demon was carried through the streets in a coffin. The handcuffs were still upon the dead black arms and the crowd of Negroes standing by were called upon to witness the fate of Allen Sievers and take warning there from.......The carcass was hauled out of the coffin and dragged through the streets until 10:30 o'clock when the coroner once more took possession of it."

One Negro in attendance, however, was given a different type of treatment.

As the paper reported, "Lee Kelso, the gallant colored man who aided Miss McClane when she needed it most, was carried about the city by the whites and cheered for the part he performed."

The statements of the state's prestigious news organ, the *Courier Journal*, reflect the distorted notion of justice which infected such a process. In recounting the event the next day it wrote that while the process might have been a bit hurried, "The fact, however, that Kentucky was saved the mortification of a lynching by an indignant multitude, bent upon avenging the innocent victim of the crime, is a matter for special congratulation."

Strange times indeed.

CHAPTER 3

DECEMBER BLOOD

The year 1916 was very strange in Calloway County, Kentucky.

A six-foot alligator showed up at the Murray Hospital, as part of an exhibit of exotic zoo animals put together by Dr. Will Mason, Jr. to entertain the patients.

Joe Bates, 96-year-old, fathered his 25th child.

A 75-year-old Confederate veteran and his 54-year-old wife became the proud parents of their first-born offspring.

The first-ever malpractice lawsuit against a local doctor was filed in the Calloway Circuit Court and actually resulted in a judgment for the plaintiff in the amount of $2,500.

Night school began at Temple Hill and Hazel in an attempt to wipe out adult illiteracy. Other "moonlight schools" soon followed.

On May 31, with more than 1,500 people present, magnificent old Confederate Captain J.N. Williams gave a stirring farewell speech at the Murray Depot to departing Company L of the Calloway County State Militia. Trouble was brewing on the Mexican border as revolutionary Pancho Villa was leading raids across the Rio Grande against American settlements. Kentucky's State Guard was being mustered for duty in southern Texas.

And for the first time ever, more people left the county than came. The automobile not only took over the roads of Calloway County from the horse and buggy, but caused the beginning of a steady exodus north, to Detroit City, for work in the auto manufacturing plants.

Most of the people went about their business trying to ignore the gloomy news constantly hovering over the national scene.

War in Europe dragged into its third bloody year, with over two million casualties suffered at the battles of Verdun and the Somme alone. America looked on nervously.

On November 7, Woodrow Wilson won re-election as President of the United States by such a thin margin that most Calloway Countians sadly went to bed that night thinking that Republican Charles Evan Hughes was their new president.

December 9, 1916 was a Saturday. The weather was cold, in the low 20s, and mostly overcast. The coal scuttles in town were getting a good workout, and the pungent smell of soot hung in the air.

Just past noon, 60-year-old Guthrie Diuguid was making his way along what was then Curd Street, now Fourth Street. He was on his way to town from his home on a small farm just north of town. The former town marshal was the member of a highly-respected family of Murray, one brother a leading banker in town, one a lawyer in Paducah and a third was on the Murray City Council.

Guthrie Diuguid was a man of intrigue and dark secrets; two bitter enemies were destined to meet on that Murray street.

Coming along Curd Street from the opposite direction was a 32-year-old, light-skinned Negro named Lube Martin. With him were two of his brothers and a friend from out of town.

45

When Diuguid and the group of blacks met, he and Martin became involved in a heated conversation. Threats were made. Then a scuffle ensued.

The much younger and stoutly-built Martin pulled a pistol and shot four times at Diuguid. Two of the bullets hit the mark—one in the chest and the other in the victim's left shoulder.

Martin and his confederates split, going north up Curd.

Incredibly, Diuguid stayed on his feet. At first, the small caliber bullets in his body seemed to have minimal effect upon his movements.

Knowing that he had been shot, and in need of medical attention, he made his way south toward town. Moving along the side of the street, he waved down an approaching delivery wagon

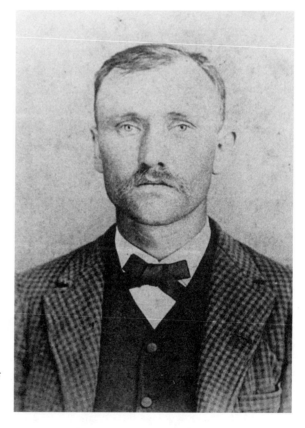

Guthrie Diuguid
Photo compliments
of Chuck Shuffett

driven by Curt Owen. He climbed into the wagon without assistance. Upon learning of Diuguid's plight, Owen immediately turned the wagon around and headed toward the office of Doctors Rob and Will Mason which was located uptown over Sexton's hardware store.

By the time the rig pulled up to the curb at Dr. Mason's office on the northeast corner of the square, the victim had begun to fade and grow weak. It took three or four bystanders to remove him from the wagon and take him upstairs to the doctor's office.

Dr. Will Mason was out on a house call. But his brother, Dr. Rob Mason, was in and quickly attended the victim and gave him a shot of opium to ease his pain.

On a Saturday afternoon in the winter time, in 1916, Murray was a crowded place. Farmers from all points in the county–Kirksey, New Concord, Almo, Coldwater, Knight and Hazel–all converged upon the burg of 3,000 to buy needed supplies and staples as well as to swap and exchange gossip. Christmas was already in the air and talk of war in Europe cast a shallow pall upon their visits, hanging there like the blue film of coal smoke which floated in the sharp winter air. On sidewalks and around piping hot stoves, in the court house yard, these leather-faced yeomen gathered in small clusters. There they pulled on handmade cigarettes, spat amber onto the frigid ground, spoke and listened in the simple idiom of the hereditary bondsmen of the soil.

If a black man had to shoot a white man, he couldn't have picked a worse time than in Murray on a winter Saturday afternoon.

By the time Guthrie Diuguid was hauled up the steps into the care of Dr. Mason, word was spreading like a flash of lightening throughout the Saturday gathering.

With Lube Martin at that fateful encounter with Diuguid were two of his brothers, Sylvester and the other with the unusual nickname, Ann. Also in the group was Ann's friend, Ed Jordon. Immediately after the shooting, the foursome scattered and fled for their lives.

Reports around town immediately named the shooter, and a large crowd of angry men quickly formed on the court square to assist in the manhunt.

Soon it was a mob.

Sheriff W. A. "Will" Patterson tried to take charge and put some order into the search.

It was rough going, however, as the Christmas spirit of good will, which had permeated the town just minutes before, now turned bitter with anger and acrimony.

Various accounts of the shooting were making their way around town, each one more dastardly than the last. Suffice it to say, it was a white official, from a prominent family, shot down in cold blood by a man of color–or a gang of colored ruffians–if that version was to be believed.

Before long, as many as a thousand men fanned out over town searching for the fugitives.

It wasn't long before Lube Martin's companions were taken into custody. But Sheriff Patterson and his deputies had little trouble protecting them from the mob and moving them safely to the jail on the corner of Third and Walnut.

It was Lube Martin, the shooter, who raised the ire of the mass and became the solitary prey of this vengeful crowd.

And Martin had given them the slip.

Bloodhounds had been brought in and led Sheriff Patterson and the other pursuers northerly out Curd Street and in the direction Martin had fled. Soon they were out of town and into the open countryside.

Unknown to the avenging horde, Martin had run out to the edge of town to the corner of Chestnut and Curd. There at the Rowlett Tobacco Factory, located on the northeast corner of the intersection, he turned right and down the street toward the railroad. From there the fleeing Negro had doubled back south, through the black section of town. While Patterson and his expansive posse had followed the howling hounds out Curd Street, Martin was coming back in the opposite direction only a couple of blocks to the east.

Martin knew that his only escape was to the south, along the railroad track, either by foot or hopefully by train, to Tennessee. He was able to move quickly through his own neighborhood, under the silent gazes and tacit protection of his own people.

Lube made it to the southern edge of town, and finally out of hearing of the barking hounds and yelling men. He retreated to whatever cover the naked winter woods could afford him and traveled just off the railroad toward Paris, Tennessee. From there he hoped to catch a train to Memphis and get lost in the teeming black population of that large city.

As night began to fall upon Murray, it became evident to the frantic man hunters, many of them now armed, that Lube Martin had most likely escaped their hot pursuit.

Their numbers dwindled as many from out in the county had to get back to their homes and families. It is very likely that some had wives and children patiently waiting in their wagons, or motor vehicles, on the court square.

Tension was still running high, however. But as the short December day began to give way to twilight and darkness, the search for Lube Martin was left primarily to Sheriff Will Patterson and his deputies.

The seriously wounded Guthrie Diuguid had been moved to the Murray Hospital. Slowly the town began to close up and shut down as the cold winter night moved in.

The next morning, Sunday, December 10, the town was quiet, except for the tolling of church bells under the gray winter skies. Reports from the hospital on Diuguid's condition were not good.

Conversations at most of the Sunday morning church services in the county centered upon the Saturday shooting. More than one theory was bantered around concerning the whereabouts of Martin.

Will Patterson and a handful of men kept up the search, primarily working the phone out of his office. The name and description of the fugitive were put on the wires to law enforcement agencies and newspapers in the area. Patterson stayed in touch with other sheriff offices and police stations in both western Kentucky and Tennessee.

Then, just as dusk was falling upon the second day of their search, word came by telephone from Humboldt, Tennessee.

Lube Martin had been apprehended.

An alert conductor on the L&N Railroad somehow recognized Lube and took him into custody on the train near the little town of Henry, Tennessee, just south of Paris. For some reason–perhaps train connections–the captive was taken all the way down to Humboldt, which was about halfway between Murray and Memphis. There he was lodged in the local jail.

This stirring news livened up the Sunday night in Murray. It was too late for Patterson to leave for Humboldt that evening. Plans were made to leave the next morning.

Forty-six-year-old Will Patterson looked like a lawman from the Wyatt Earp era. Handsome, with a large mustache, his broad shoulders made him appear larger than his frame of less than six feet.

The father of eight children, Patterson had been elected sheriff in 1913 after serving several years as magistrate from the southeastern part of the county. Having grown up on Shannon Creek near the Tennessee line, Will was a prominent businessman, owning 1500 acres and two sawmills. He also operated a busy country store at New Concord and had been active in the timber business. His logging enterprise consisted of cutting large amounts of timber, and constructing log rafts which were floated the remaining length of the Tennessee River and sold on the banks of the Ohio near Paducah and Metropolis, Illinois. It was a tricky business–collaring the loose slippery logs, most times in the dead of winter upon frigid waters. They were fastened together into "barges" by the use of "chain dogs" which were spiked clamps hammered into place with a pole ax. The lean and muscular men would move upon the

Sheriff Will Patterson
Photo compliments of Chuck Shuffett

floating timbers with the agility and dexterity of cats. If a log ever went to spinning, you knew you were going into the brink—not a pleasant experience on a cold November morning. "If she starts spinning on ya," a seasoned old salt of logging would deadpan to a fresh recruit, "jump just as high as you can, to stay out as long as you can."

Will Patterson was a tough cookie. Once he endured stomach surgery performed by Dr. Will Mason without anesthesia.

He was also from a tough section of the county called "the Bluffs" on the Tennessee River. The area drew its name from the popular gathering place known as Pine Bluff on the river. Though the massive white cliff itself was in Tennessee, there was a country store, picnic area, horse shoe pits, and baseball field on the Kentucky side of the river. There, large numbers of country folks would gather in the shade of the towering cottonwoods for various festivities such as picnics, barbecues, music making, and watching baseball games. Some of the players who played there on Sunday afternoons, on the banks of the Tennessee, became legendary throughout the county and are still talked about to this day.

There was often an ample supply of Kentucky "shine," made locally as well as from across the stream in the "Between the Rivers" area which was well known for its top-notch whiskey.

Patterson had narrowly lost the race for sheriff in 1909. O.J. Jennings, editor of the *Murray Ledger and Times* had written that "Squire Patterson would have probably been elected had it not been for the 'rougher elements' of the river bottoms that supported him." This comment so angered and energized the proud citizens of southeastern Calloway County that Patterson won by a landslide four years later. The voters turned out in mass from the remote settlements of Pottertown, New Concord, Knight, and Hamlin.

On Monday morning, December 11, 1916, Sheriff Patterson chose his biggest, toughest deputy, Felix Davis, to go with him to pick up the prisoner. Davis, at six feet two, was all muscle and totally fearless.

Patterson and his deputy boarded the train in Murray that morning, leaving behind a seething and restless gang of vigilantes anxiously awaiting the return of their prey. As the two lawmen headed south on that winter day they had plenty of time to talk.

Both of them agreed. There was no way they could bring Lube Martin back to Murray.

If they did, they would be faced with three dreadful possibilities. They would have to shoot some of their fellow citizens, maybe even friends. They would be killed themselves. Or they would have to surrender their prisoner to the mob, or worst of all, maybe all of the above.

Of course Will Patterson was not above shooting people.

At one Fourth of July picnic at "the Bluffs," the lawman had been confronted by a gang of intoxicated ruffians from across the river, in Tennessee. He arrested one, and the others moved in to attack the out-manned sheriff. Patterson pulled his pistol, and after his would-be assailants ignored his warnings, he wounded one in the leg. That caught their attention and made true believers out of the rest. Hurriedly the sobered roustabouts packed their wounded friend onto the ferry and headed back across the river. Patterson proceeded to Murray with his prisoner in his buggy.

But a lynch mob is a sheriff's worst nightmare.

Duty and honor go to war with fear and self-preservation. At the midnight hour one is suddenly thrust upon the threshold of sudden death, as the heat of the hooting mob drives one to the critical moment of decision. Does one offer their life for one who not only may be a stranger, but one who is unseemly, friendless, and is likely guilty of some despicable crime?

In almost every instance, the law officer cannot win. Contrary to wild western movie lore, he is not routinely possessed of the powerful eloquence of a Mark Antony, able to turn back the swelling tide of emotions with mind-bending oration. Neither is he a Gary Cooper.

He either gives up the prisoner, along with his honor, or he gives up his life. Once he inflicts the first injury in defense of his prisoner, he—outnumbered and outgunned—will be savagely engulfed by the maniacal mob, trampled and destroyed.

So as Will and Felix rolled along on the way to Humboldt, they devised a plan.

They would take Lube Martin to Hopkinsville for safe keeping.

It was a logical choice given the geography and logistics of far west Kentucky at that time.

Paducah, the largest town in the area, less than fifty miles to the north of Murray, would ordinarily have been the most convenient. But there was no good way of getting there from Humbolt without going back through Murray. Also, neither Will nor his deputy were convinced it was a safe enough distance away. It was an easy train ride for angry citizens gone awry. Also, some awful nasty stuff had gone on there just that past October. The social climate in that city was uncertain at best. The McCracken County

Grand Jury was just completing its investigation into the Kinley-Durrett lynchings and burnings. No indictments had been returned.

Taking Lube to Paducah for safe keeping might be like having your dog keep an eye on your chopped liver.

The two west Kentucky towns of Murray and Hopkinsville—though 54 miles apart—had a lot in common in 1916.

Both were county seats, located close to the Tennessee line and steeped deeply in the Southern cause. The President of the Confederacy, Jefferson Davis, was born only a dozen miles east of Hopkinsville. In 1916, grand designs were on the drawing board for the construction of a giant obelisk at Fairview to commemorate the spot.

Calloway County had its own Confederate Fort Heiman on the Tennessee River which General Nathan Bedford Forrest had used as a staging area for his successful assault on Johnsonville, Tennessee. Rebel enlistments in the county had been four to one over the Unionists.

While Hopkinsville was larger, both cities were railroad towns. The Louisville & Nashville and Illinois Central Railroads intersected at Hopkinsville. Murray's depot was on the Paducah, Tennessee & Alabama line.

But the cultural cord which linked these communities more than any other was tobacco—especially the dark fired which was smoke-cured leaf requiring tender care and traditional artistry. Calloway and Christian were the two leading dark fired tobacco growing counties in the entire South. By the turn of the century, seven tobacco warehouses selling from 15,000 to 21,000 hogsheads of export tobacco annually were located in Hopkinsville. Murray was also home to several warehouses.

These two sister towns both suffered through two civil wars: first, the War Between the States; secondly, the Black Patch War fought between 1904-1909.

On the night of December 7, 1907, the tobacco Night Riders raided and took over Hopkinsville, burning the tobacco warehouses and inflicting thousands of dollars worth of damages upon the city. The Kentucky State Militia was sent in immediately afterwards to put down the lawlessness. The Night Riders then took aim on Murray and its holding of tobacco tucked away in the buildings of the despised Trust of James B. Duke's American Tobacco Company. But fiery Calloway County Judge A.J.G. Wells, a tough and courageous opponent of the militant farmers, managed to get Governor Willison to move the state militia into Murray just in time to save the city.

So both towns–Hopkinsville and Murray–had been occupied twice by "foreign troops" within a fifty year period. And neither time were they welcomed by most of the population. Wrote Murray newspaper publisher O.J. Jennings at the time of the tobacco war occupation, of some of the unruly troops, "Hell, we'd rather have the Night Riders!"

Lastly, and most significantly, as far as Sheriff Will Patterson was concerned, both towns shared the same circuit judge, and commonwealth attorney, in the same Third Judicial District, which consisted at that time of Calloway, Christian, Lyon and Trigg counties.

Yet as similar as the county seats of these two counties were, there was a significant geographical gulf between them. Smack dab between the middle of the fifty mile trek from city limit to city limit ran two of the most prominent rivers in the Southeast. The Cumberland River tracked through the western portion of Trigg County heading to its rendezvous with the Ohio River at Smithland. The wider Tennessee, just a short distance to the west of the Cumberland, was not only the boundary between Calloway and Trigg counties, but marked the eastern edge of the Jackson Purchase. This eight county portion of extreme western Kentucky did not join the state until 1818, when Governor Issac Shelby and General Andrew Jackson were able to wrestle these lands away from the Chickasaw Indians by a treaty signed in northwestern Mississippi on October 18 of that year.

These two resourceful streams served as vibrant economic

arteries into west Kentucky and ready means of transportation for new citizens moving into the area, especially downstream from the east. But, even in 1916 the twin waterways posed natural barriers to land movement from east to west.

Early on ferries went into operation at various places to bring land travelers across the two rivers. In fact, they were quite numerous. Usually they marked river settlements and served as connectors to well-traveled roads and highways. By 1916 there were river crossings as such small towns as Smithland, Pinckneyville, Tilene, Dycusburg, Iuka, Eureka, Kuttawa, Eddyville, Rock Castle, Canton and Linton on the Cumberland. The Tennessee River was crossed at such places as Ledbetter, Gilbertsville, Birmingham, Egner's Ferry, Pine Bluff and others.

Going by road from Murray to Hopkinsville at that time, either by motor car or horse carriages, one had to use ferries at Egner's Ferry and Canton. But it was a hard trip, the roads rutted and sometimes impassable, especially in the muddy bogs of winter. Flooding of the two rivers, at times, virtually isolated the Jackson Purchase area from the rest of the state.

So it was not an easy trip overland between the county seats of the Third Judicial Circuit. Judge Bush and Commonwealth Attorney Denny Smith—both from Hopkinsville—would come to stay during the court terms, lodging and taking their meals at the local hotels, maybe making it home on weekends, weather permitting.

But there was an easier but longer route between Murray and Hopkinsville in 1916.

In 1872, the Elizabethtown-Paducah Railway was completed and for the first time these historic old streams, which had been the pathways for the Union army into the heart of Dixie, were bridged. The railroad bridge crossed the Cumberland at Eureka in Lyon County, roughly at the location where Barkley Dam is today. The Tennessee was bridged at Gilbertsville near the location of today's Kentucky Dam.

Only then could the Jackson Purchase, and these towns

within its borders, be reached by rail from the east with speed, convenience and comfort.

But even this mode of travel between Hopkinsville and Murray was a zigzag affair. To Murray by train from Hopkinsville, one had to travel on the Illinois Central through Princeton to Paducah. There, one switched trains and rode the N.C. & St. L. south to Murray.

So Sheriff Patterson and Deputy Davis had to carefully plot a way to get Lube Martin to Hopkinsville from Humboldt, without returning through Murray. It would require bringing their prisoner back from Humboldt, just north of Jackson to Paris. From there they would have to take the Louisville & Nashville line to Clarksville, Tennessee and then the Illinois Central to Hopkinsville. As far as Patterson was concerned, the two men had little choice.

The politically astute sheriff also knew that his decision not to bring Martin back to Murray would be a very unpopular one. Even then the city waited for their public officials to bring their bounty home so that the will of the crowd could replace the majesty of the law.

Will Patterson was no stranger to the light-skinned, muscular and intelligent Negro who would soon become his prisoner.

Lube Martin was the son of a former slave who had migrated to Murray with his wife and fourteen children in 1902 from North Carolina. Discarding his slave name of Cherry, Lube's family first worked at farming until the children grew old enough to find jobs in town. The five Martin boys were known as hard working, and law abiding, except for occasional fighting in the black section when the local concoction of "corn beer" would make its presence felt. They were not known to start trouble, but were always ready to finish it once it started.

Lube eventually got a job as a laborer for the railroad, married and began to raise a family. His dusky-colored wife, the former Bettie Jones, turned the head of every man she passed.

Patterson also knew Lube's victim, Guthrie Diuguid.

Interestingly, the elder brother, Edwin (Diuguid), had also

played a pivotal and fateful role in the town's partial destruction during the War Between the States.

As a ten-year-old boy, Edwin and another young friend had one night climbed to the top of a large sycamore tree which was a highly visible landmark on the court house square.

There they had hung the Confederate flag.

The next morning the local populace poured into the streets, charged with excitement thinking the Confederates had retaken the town. Droves of people came into town from out in the county, cheering and singing "Dixie" as they quickly gathered at the sycamore tree under the stars and bars. A local merchant who was a Yankee sympathizer sent word to the Union command at Ft. Anderson, in Paducah, that the Rebs had moved in to occupy Murray. Adding credence to the report was the fact that a few days before some of General Nathan Forrest's recruiters had been in town signing up volunteers for his Confederate Cavalry.

Four days later, all hell broke loose.

A company of Union troops came rampaging into town on horseback, crazily shooting up the place and retaking the village from what was in reality a phantom enemy. The Yanks set up camp just south of town. That night they recklessly stormed into town and set fire and burned down a row of buildings on the east side of the court square. One must assume it was simply a show of force to intimidate the rebellious town.

Ed Diuguid's distant past was not on Will Patterson's mind as he and his deputy made their way south on that Monday morning. What was more relevant to the current crisis was the fact that Edwin S. Diuguid, Sr., was a big man in Murray.

There was another troublesome side of the influential Diuguid family that lawman Will Patterson had to think about. Guthrie had sometimes been where he should not have been, doing things he should not have been doing.

At the time of the shooting, Guthrie was serving as deputy county constable in charge of the work detail for the prisoners in the county jail. He had been relegated to this rather inglorious job because of his past actions: he had been messing around with Lube Martin's pretty young wife while serving as deputy police chief for the city of Murray.

From that day until the deadly encounter on December 9, Guthrie Diuguid hounded and threatened Lube Martin. It became so bad that Martin finally had to leave Murray, moving to Paris, Tennessee to work. He would slip back into town to visit his wife and family, getting off the train in the little settlement of Tobacco, just south of town, and walking the rest of the way so as not to draw attention to himself and to avoid being detected by Diuguid. Even when Lube's mother died in the summer, he had to sneak to the funeral and back out of town as quickly as possible.

All of this was surely known to both Sheriff Patterson and Davis as they sat and talked to the hypnotic clicking of the rail. One thing was crystal clear. They had a monumental crisis on their hands which would test their mettle before it was over: a Negro killing a white man, a member of the most influential family in town; however, the Negro perhaps having good cause, or at least one worthy of hearing. Yet there was a mob at their back, wanting to lynch their prisoner, before the accused would ever have a chance to tell his story.

It was a story that Guthrie Diuguid would never have to hear.

On Sunday afternoon, December 10, he died at the Murray Hospital from his gunshot wounds.

CHAPTER 4

SETTING THE STAGE

I f the town folks were put out with Sheriff Will Patterson for not bringing their prized prey back to within their clutches, they were placated somewhat by the swift action taken by the Calloway County Circuit Court.

On Wednesday night, December 13, in response to the request of many of the leading citizens, Circuit Judge Charles H. Bush of Hopkinsville came to Murray. He met with a large number of citizens at the courthouse to discuss their urgent demands for calling a special term of court to try Lube Martin in January.

At the conclusion of the meeting, Judge Bush, fresh from his easy win in the November election, signed and entered an order calling a special jury to convene on Monday, January 8 to both indict and to try Lube Martin. Judge Bush could sense the electrifying tension in the air and felt tremendous pressure to bring the prosecution of the black defendant for trial as soon as possible. Otherwise, even Hopkinsville might not be a safe place for Lube Martin.

Sixty-year-old Charles H. Bush was a highly

respected jurist who had a wealth of legal experience under his belt.

In a 1904 biography from a western Kentucky book on prominent citizens, the following was conveyed:

Charles H. Bush is a prominent lawyer of Hopkinsville and enjoys a large practice in the town and county. He was born in Montgomery County, Tennessee, October 28, 1856. His grandfather, Zenas Bush, is supposed to have been of German descent. His father, Howard B. Bush, was born in North Carolina and emigrated to Tennessee in the early part of the nineteenth century...He married Panthea B. Ellis, a native of Tennessee...

Charles Bush was the only child and son of his parents, and he lost his mother when he was four months old and his father when he was six years of age. He was reared in the family of an uncle till he was fifteen years old, and at that age started out on his own responsibility. He clerked in a country store and attended school at what odd times he could find. He was a student in a West Virginia college for two years, and then entered the law office of Henry Bennett, of Paducah, where he read law for one year and was then licensed to practice. He remained in Paducah for about a year after being admitted to the bar, and while there was married to Miss Jennie Gary, of Christian County. He soon afterward located in Hopkinsville, where he has been engaged in constant practice for twenty-two years....He made the race for the Democratic nomination for circuit judge, which resulted in one of the closest contests within the party ever known in western Kentucky. He is a director in the Bank of Hopkinsville and is interested in the Crescent Milling Company, and has been as successful in his business enterprises as in his legal career.

Mr. Bush has been a member of the Christian church for twenty-nine years, and holds the office of deacon. He lost his first wife after they had been married about six years, and in 1888 he was married to Miss Mattie M. Rives, of Montgomery County, Tennessee. Of the first marriage there were three children: R. Howard, of Texas, and Lillian and Lucile, at home. The children of the present marriage were Jennie and Florence, and Sarah, deceased.

Judge Charles H. Bush who presided over the trials of Lillian Walters. Reared as an orphan, he became a highly respected lawyer and jurist. Bush dealt with many controversial cases with great poise and competence.   Photo compliments of William Turner

Bush made his greatest mark as a lawyer in 1911 when he led the defense team representing the charismatic Night Rider leader, Dr. David Amoss, against criminal charges in Hopkinsville. Amoss had been indicted for his part in leading the 300 hooded and armed members of the Silent Brigade in their daring raid upon that town in December, 1907.

It was the trial of the century for west Kentucky, a trial that every barrister of the day would have savored. For this drama, played out under the guise of a criminal trial, was the closing chapter of a violent and sensational era of agrarian unrest which had raged through west Kentucky and Tennessee between 1904-1909.

The Night Rider trial took place in the old Circuit Court room on the top floor of the handsome and colonnaded court house in downtown Hopkinsville. The trial began on March 6, 1911–less than six years before the death of Guthrie Diuguid on the streets of Murray.

Even to this day the subject of the Night Riders brings forth peculiar reactions of intense ambivalence among natives of the battle ground of that epoch struggle. It was the Civil War all over again, tearing communities apart, neighbor against neighbor, brother against brother. There was no right without a tinge of wrong. No wrong without a wisp of virtue. There were few totally bad guys and even fewer fully good. Today, descendants and kin of the outlaw gang which plied their clandestine ways against the hated tobacco trust of James B. Duke, will relate the crimes of the lions of their blood with pride and fierce intensity in their eyes. Others, who descend from the other camp, the so-called Hillbillies, the independent victims with hearts of steel, will recount their family stories with equal ardor and glory.

Just like the War Between the Sates.

The movement had also split the law and the courts–the lawyers and the judges.

County Attorney Walter Krone of Lyon County–a county whose own governing body had voted to pay off civil judgments obtained against the Night Riders of that county–had fought them so hard that he had been threatened and ran out of the state. While the sheriff of that same county, Sam Cash, was an ardent supporter of the nocturnal marauders.

The Cadiz Record was the unofficial news and editorial paper in total support of the Night Riders. Next door, Hopkinsville Mayor Charles Meacham's *The Kentuckian* was a newspaper seething in invective against David Amoss and his soldiers.

It was a mess.

Some tobacco farmers with friends on both sides simply threw up their hands, and their tobacco. They quit growing their cash crop and turned to the scraggly timber on their ridges, and the tortuous labor of hewing cross ties for the railroad in an effort to mitigate their loss.

During the peak of the Night Rider movement, it was impossible to either criminally prosecute, or to obtain civil judgments against the outlaws in the courts of west Kentucky. If a victim was able to get a lawyer foolish enough to take the case, or an independent sheriff to investigate the wrong, then several members of the Night Riders–or at least fervent sympathizers–would show up on the jury.

By 1911, however, the dust had settled, tobacco prices restored, the Night Riders disbanded, and peace returned to the Black Patch. The popular appeal of Dr. David Amoss and the Silent Brigade had run its course.

Now the political powers and business interests of Hopkinsville wanted the old Night Rider leader's head on a platter for the destruction he had inflicted upon their town. Even if was for a crime committed on December 7, 1907-over three years before.

And Commonwealth Attorney Denny Smith of Cadiz was, by that time, willing to do their bidding.

He was running for attorney general of Kentucky.

Smith had walked through the political land mines of the days when the Night Riders had popular and political support. He did this by giving the impression, at least, that he sympathized, even applauded their cause and tactics. More importantly, he absolutely refused to prosecute them.

Until 1911.

Charles Bush and David Amoss were almost the same age. Dr. Amoss had made his living caring for the sick in body while Bush had ministered to the woeful lives of the rural poor in need of his legal acumen.

The Lord God hath given me the tongue of the learned, that I should know how to speak a word in season to him that is weary.

Bush and Amoss had been good strong Democrats, and both in sympathy with the hereditary bondsmen of the soil who were members of the larger working class; involved in a death struggle with the abuses of centralized capital. Among the farming communities of the time, nationally acclaimed labor leader Eugene Debs–Socialist as he was, and a terror to the rich–was a hero to those who suckered the gummy green plant in the searing heat of summer.

While this doctor and this lawyer fought the cause of the humble tobacco farmer on the back roads and court houses of west Kentucky, their friend, Congressman A.O. Stanley, was fighting for them in the marbled halls of Washington, trying desperately to get the onerous tobacco tax repealed to increase both consumption and prices.

So with David Amoss, his client, at his side, Charles Bush fought the battle of his lifetime through that historic week in Hopkinsville. A full house of spectators and scads of newspaper reporters watched as Bush and Smith, along with other attorneys lined up on each side, slugged it out over the guilt or innocence of the Night Rider commander.

In the end, it was Bush and his defense team who won. Denny Smith withdrew from the race for attorney general as his political stock fell.

Bush, on the other hand, had played the right card politically, at the right time. There is an age old axiom in Kentucky politics which players in the political game violate at their own peril: "Win with your friends, and lose with your friends–good days and bad."

Bush did just that, even when their popularity was on the wane. He stood by their leader, Amoss, in his hour of maximum need.

And in the summer of 1916 when Circuit Judge J.T. Hanberry died in office, Charles Bush was named as his replacement. The appointment was made by his friend and political ally, the Democratic Governor A.O. Stanley. Commonwealth Attorney Denny Smith, holding a position which usually served as heir apparent to that position, was passed over.

He was a decent man–Charles H. Bush.

Not perfect for sure, and not above bending to the give and take of partisan politics. The office of circuit judge was very much still in the fiery mash of political intrigue and passions. And it was a rough-and-tumble time in politics just as it was in all aspects of life. Public officials had to take an oath, even as they do to this day, that they had never engaged in a duel.

The days of dueling to satisfy the great questions of honor were not that far in the past.

But Charles Bush's heart was in the right place. In his short time on the bench he had garnered the reputation as being an even-tempered, and fair-minded judge. He was a "lawyer's judge"–meaning that he remembered what it was like out in the trenches and handled lawyers and parties with understanding and respect.

The quick and decisive action by Judge Bush and Commonwealth Attorney Denny Smith reassured the citizens of Murray for the time being.

Christmas was upon them. It was time to put away this ugly piece of reality lurking at them through the tinsel and mistletoe and think in terms of the holiday spirit of peace on earth and good will toward men.

At least until January.

Murray House Hotel renamed here as New Murray Hotel.
Photo compliments of Don Henry

Christmas 1916.

United States of America.

It was a time when the country stood upon the threshold of manhood.

Fighting continued in the bloody trenches of Europe. And while many possessed a sense of foreboding about the distant storm clouds of war, most felt reassured by their newly re-elected president who had promised to "keep us out of war."

It was a time when our presidents were still taken at their word.

Those concerned with the war raging in Europe watched with interest as President Wilson made a formal plea for all of the belligerents to put down their arms and come to the peace table.

News had seeped into the U.S. that the mysterious and highly-influential Russian monk Grigori Rasputin had been murdered, his body dumped into the icy Volga River. Czarist Russia was about to fall.

But for the most part, the news of Europe was just a distant rumble and America was enjoying one of its most prosperous years ever.

It was the heyday of the silent movies and Charlie Chaplin was a giant of the silver screen in blockbuster productions "The Rink" and "Love's Toll." Actress Gretchen Hartman starred in the movie "The Love Thief."

In west Kentucky, times were thought to be good. Tobacco prices were up. More and more people had telephones in their homes. Henry Ford had made the automobile affordable to such a large number of people that their coughing and sputtering along the rural roadways was a common sight. Kinfolk in Detroit wrote back glowing reports of high wages, 8-hour shifts, and good working conditions.

Come on up.

There were some concerns about the Third Kentucky Infantry still skirmishing with the Mexican snipers on the Mexican border. But even that news failed to dampen the festive holiday spirit.

No one was particularly interested during this season of peace and good will that fifty-four persons had been lynched in the United States during 1916. Fifty were Negroes.

There were many who were more concerned with losing their nightly brandy than matters of life and death, as the strong winds of prohibition were sweeping across the nation. A mid-December report out of New York proclaimed that the lack of liquor was turning men to other habit-forming drugs.

Closer to home, things were so good that Kentuckians were thinking about tax reform. Pressure was being brought to bear upon Governor A.O. Stanley to call a special legislative session for that purpose. "When I am convinced," responded the Governor, "if I ever am, that the representatives of the people from the hundred districts of Kentucky will meet, talk business, pass the act and adjourn, I will call a special session."

Beloved old Confederate veteran, Uncle "Pink" McCuistion, of the Pottertown and Hamlin part of Calloway County entertained his family, friends and neighbors at his annual Christmas dinner in his stately old antebellum home. Bright lights and cheerful fireplaces warmed the cold night, as sumptuous food and spirits were consumed amidst laughter and lively conversation. Fiddle music, singing and dancing celebrated the season late into the night until these hard-working country folks finally and happily made their way home in time to milk.

So, Christmas morn 1916 dawned bright and serene over Calloway County and all west Kentucky.

After the festivities, the last belts of spiked eggnog and pecan pie, people turned their eyes toward the new year and promising plans, hopes and designs.

Then on a cold Sunday night, 1916 began to fade away–as all years do, good or bad–into the darkening hills, meadows, naked woods and hollows of west Kentucky. Down the rivulet corridors of the ancient Cumberland and Tennessee, passing and paying farewell through the dimly-lit streets of small towns, past frost-covered wooden benches and empty porches, from the hilltops of Cadiz and Benton to the steep and arching streets of Hickman, from flat Paducah to the brown, rolling meadows of Lamasco and Joy, the year faded.

Near midnight on December 31 most houses in village, farm and dale slept. From the silently-moving Ohio on the north–to the flinty cliffs of Pine Bluff nestled in the crook of Tennessee, darkness descended, first to lively suppers and then to sleeping homes. Infants in cradles; towhead boys entangled in dreams of Christmas still; flannelled young maidens, fresh and clean; gray and gnarled old grandmas swallowed by feather beds; tender moms snuggled under hefty, colorful, quilts- one part asleep another part listening for children in need; exhausted men, big and small, good and bad, lying dead to the labors of the day.

They slumbered away as Father Time inched them one year

closer to their graves. Clocks ticked into the night, the clicking cadence of their pendulums keeping pace with human hearts. Mercifully these mortals at rest did not know of the bloody and tumultuous days 1917 would bring. It was the eve of America moving upon the stage as a world power with its entry into the bloody conflict in Europe. These were our last nights as a nation before leaving home.

It was the last New Year's Eve America would ever have as a child.

The year 1917 was exactly seven days old when the case of Lube Martin went back onto the front burner in Murray, Kentucky.

To the buzz of the entire community, Judge Bush and Commonwealth Attorney Denny Smith were in town to em panel a special grand jury on Monday morning, January 8. They arrived on Sunday afternoon by train, and checked into the Murray House Hotel, only a short distance from the courthouse on Main Street.

Though excitement ran high, it was a fairly routine day at the office.

The courtroom was full of prospective jurors—"honest and sagacious" men pulled from all corners of the county.

The justice system in Kentucky was still a "men's only club." Although a strong delegation from the women's group called the Kentucky Equal Rights Association had attended the Democratic National Convention in 1916, they were still four years away from voting for the first time.

Consequently the only women in the courtroom on this cold winter morning were spectators. Even the court reporter was a man—future Commonwealth Attorney John C. King.

The law in 1917 concerning felony cases and grand juries was the same as it is today. Circuit court had exclusive jurisdiction over felony prosecutions. And before a felony could be tried in that court, there had to first be an indictment—or a charge—returned by the grand jury.

Actually this body is somewhat of a misnomer. Its function is not to determine guilt or innocence, but to investigate crimes and determine if there is probable cause to charge someone with a felony. It is required to hear only one side of the case, and it takes just nine of the sitting twelve members to indict.

Twenty-four Calloway County citizens had been summoned by Judge Bush to appear on January 8, from which the names of 12 grand jurors would be pulled. A separate pool of 36 citizens were summoned to appear to be petit jurors–jurors to try the case of Lube Martin. On Monday morning, January 8th, Judge Bush called the names of 12 citizens at random, and they were sworn as grand jurors. The circuit judge then instructed them as to their duties, and sent them to work.

In the Lube Martin shooting of Guthrie Diuguid, it was over in a matter of minutes.

An indictment for murder was returned against Martin. Almost as an afterthought, his sidekicks on that day–brothers Sylvester and Ann, as well as his friend Ed Jordon–were charged as accomplices. They were all jailed with Lube in Hopkinsville. In open court, and to the great satisfaction of the waiting mass, Judge Bush set Lube Martin's trial for the following Wednesday, January 10.

A young Murray lawyer of Irish descent, Pat Holt, was the attorney assigned by Judge Bush the unenviable job of defending Martin.

No one knows what Will Patterson was thinking in the early morning darkness of January 9, 1916 as he strapped on his sidearm and pinned on his badge. But he had to be deeply concerned, if not downright worried.

He and three deputies were about to depart for Hopkinsville by train to pick up Lube Martin and his three accomplices, and return them to Murray–Martin for trial; the others for arraignments.

Over the past two days, the town had once again come alive

with the excitement and anticipation of the Lube Martin trial.

Patterson may have thought that the gods had laid the case at his door at the worst possible time of the year.

While the farmer's work is never done, January is the one month of the year where he worked the least. With the exception of the daily chores of feeding, milking, and maybe killing hogs, most of his work was laid by–waiting for those few perky days in February when spring would send the message to burn their tobacco beds.

So, the idle time meant time to go to town. And it meant time to get in trouble, if trouble came calling.

And now, farmers from out in the county were in town, scenting the mass gathering of manhood for the cause of justice, one way or another. And of course they were joined by town people, some of them with honest jobs, others upon the vagrancy list, hovering mighty close to the line of being on the wrong end of court themselves.

But one individual who rolled into town probably bothered Will Patterson more than all the others–Guthrie Diuguid's lawyer brother, George, from Paducah.

The Diuguid family consisted of nine children, with George being the oldest of seven boys. In his late 60s, he undoubtedly considered himself the leading avenger of the clan.

Arriving in town shortly after his brother's death, the barrister had talked a mean line and was joining the prosecution team to make sure that the family was well represented in the trial of Lube Martin.

He was an agitator. And one thing Will Patterson and the city of Murray did not need on this day was another agitator–an educated and articulate one, at that–sparked by the emotional fire of grief.

Undoubtedly another young man, not particularly looking forward to the latter part of the week on this Tuesday morning, was defense lawyer Pat Holt.

If there was one man with a more difficult job than Sheriff

Patterson's, it was Holt.

Both the Sixth Amendment to the United States Constitution, and Section 11 of the Kentucky Constitution guaranteed the right to counsel in a criminal trial. At that time the right to counsel guarantee of the U.S. Constitution was considered only applicable to federal courts. But the Kentucky Constitution made it mandatory for state judges to appoint legal counsel for the poor.

In 1917, it was usually thin gruel for poor and indigent defendants.

There were no state-paid public defenders with staff and investigators at their beck and call. In fact, it meant a lawyer was chosen by the judge from the local bar to do the job for nothing–or pro bono. Usually the judges chose young, inexperienced lawyers in the community who were just getting started, and who not only needed the experience, but would not lose much in the way of shorting other clients in the process.

With decent, fair-minded judges, however, the competency and ability of the lawyers appointed for this rock pile task depended upon the gravity of the case. The more serious the charge, the more the defendant had at stake. And the more at stake, the greater need for good legal representation. Death penalty cases obviously demanded competent counsel.

In Pat Holt, Judge Bush had made a solid choice. He was the son of the revered Confederate colonel, G.A.C. Holt. Pat's father had distinguished himself mightily with his exploits in the ranks of the legendary Nathan Bedford Forrest. A 1931 Calloway County history books reports:

Colonel Holt was with General Forrest's left wing at Fort Heiman. He always rode a magnificent horse and dressed in the picturesque uniform of his rank, booted and spurred and with gleaming sword he was as splendid a picture of the typical and storied and romantic soldier as was ever put on canvass.

After the Civil War Colonel Holt became Lt. Governor of

Kentucky.

By 1917, Pat Holt's prosperous practice had allowed him to build one of the nicer homes in Murray. Respected in the community for his deep Southern heritage, Holt would serve well two concerns of the moment: first, to provide Martin with able counsel; secondly, to thrust someone into the breach, who on the surface at least, would appear to be "one of them."

It is unlikely that anyone noted the historical irony: a son of a Confederate colonel, representing the son of a former slave.

It is not known for sure, but it is highly unlikely that the appointment of Holt as the defendant's lawyer came as a thunderbolt out of the blue only after Martin had been indicted on January 8.

Everyone knew when Guthrie Diuguid drew his last breath on that Sunday afternoon in December that there was going to be a trial. And with the immediate and angry reaction to the shooting by the people of the community, there would have to be a trial soon.

Judge Bush and Commonwealth Attorney Denny Smith, who rode the four county circuit together, no doubt discussed the case at length. They rode the train together, slept in the same hotel, and took their meals at the same table. And herein lies the peculiar relationship of these two office holders-one a prosecutor and the other a judge. The judge is expected to maintain at all times his detached and neutral perspective in regard to the person accused of a crime. At the same time, he is charged with the responsibility of running his court system in a dignified and orderly manner. In addition to wearing the hat as a judge, he is also an administrator. And in this role, he must rely to a large extent upon his prosecutor who is responsible for moving and disposing of the criminal docket. And when dangers lurk which might disrupt this process, both a judge and a prosecutor are remiss indeed not to confer and plan for the troublesome possibilities lurking on the horizon. While the substance of guilt or innocence and the attending motions and rulings may be improper points of discussion between judge and prosecutor, matters of procedure where security is at risk must be talked about seriously in detail.

And the subject of counsel for Lube Martin must have come up between the time of Guthrie Diuguid's death on December 10, and the convening of the grand jury almost a month later.

It is furthermore highly likely that these three men–Judge Charles H. Bush, Commonwealth Attorney Denny Smith, and Pat Holt–at some time, at least once before the special term of court began, sat down together and discussed the appointment of Holt to represent the beleaguered Lube Martin.

Bush may well have broached the prospects with Holt when the judge came to Murray on December 13 to put the restless citizens at ease concerning an early trial date.

Of course lawyers appointed by the court to defend poor defendants had no choice but to obey the judge's command. However, in high visibility cases such as the one then before the bar, it would have been a judicial courtesy to ask a lawyer of Holt's professional standing and experience before officially appointing him to the task.

Why would a lawyer like Holt willingly accept such an unwelcomed responsibility fraught with dire legal and social problems? Why would a lawyer, comfortable in his practice, and held in high esteem in the community of his birth, risk his reputation, his peace of mind, even his own safety, for such a hazardous mission?

It is possible that Holt simply assumed, perhaps correctly, that he had no choice. But there was another consideration which no doubt played a major part in the acceptance this challenge.

A sense of duty.

Someone had to do it.

Not unlike the gallantry and sense of duty of a young corporal who steps forward when his commanding officer asks for a volunteer to undertake a dangerous mission on behalf of the safety and survival of the rest of the men–his friends, his fellow soldiers.

Pat Holt, when asked by Judge Bush, showed similar courage, no doubt out of respect for the judge and the crying need of the court system and the law, but on behalf of his community as well—most of which would have strung Lube Martin up, and his lawyer too if the time and place became safe for them to do so.

Even though Holt was up to the task, he was still at a severe disadvantage.

First, it was 1917 in west Kentucky, and he was representing a black man who was charged with murdering a white man.

Secondly, the white victim came from one of the most prominent and respected families in town.

If these circumstances were not intimidating enough, the logistics of his job were daunting. He had no investigators, no law clerks, no assistance from the state. And to compound his problem even more, his client was being housed fifty miles away, making it impossible to confer with him with any regularity.

But while Pat Holt lacked a cadre of investigators and clerks, and was without the deep resources of the state, he possessed an army of sorts of an entirely different ilk.

For the Negro settlement, strung out on both sides of the railroad in the northeast part of town, had eyes and ears. There were hundreds of them, including family and close friends of Lube Martin and his brothers, Sylvester and Ann.

The Negro neighborhood of Murray was typical of the thousands of settlements throughout the South where former slaves and their descendants had managed to survive under the rigid and oppressive social code of Jim Crow segregation. Tar shacks, lean-tos, unpainted frame houses with hogs rooting in the front yards; cinder block churches and honkytonks; privies, open sewers and pot-holed streets; a community of stout-hearted souls, still reeling from the economic and social hangovers of slavery, but with lives made bearable by their faith, their families, and their irrepressible spirit of music and laughter. Here they retreated nightly from menial jobs in the white man's world as field hands in the searing heat, workers in the tobacco factories, railroad laborers, and domestics. In the evenings and on Sundays their streets, front porches, and yards would come alive with the sounds of a resilient and durable people–the squealing of small children, low bass notes of a Negro spiritual, a gleeful cry of delight and the taunting jive of friends having fun.

Their nightspots came alive with jazz and blues, cheap whiskey, "corn" beer and flashing blades, fights and killings. Food spots like The Blue Heaven served up soul vittles of catfish, barbecue and chitlins both to blacks, and carry-outs for whites.

Sunday churches rocked with the spirit, well into the late afternoon, washing away the sins of their passions.

They were a happy but melancholy people; a people exuding mirth from the dark pits of despair.

These sable faces in exile had heard and seen plenty of Guthrie Diuguid. They had seen him at the home of Lube Martin, as deputy police chief attempting to become intimate with Lube's wife, Bettie. Since March of 1916, he had been in their neighborhood regularly, looking for Martin himself, who had escaped the officer's wrath by going to Paris, Tennessee. They had heard his threats. They were witnesses.

There was Lube's brother, Clarence, who could report that Diuguid had told him to tell his brother he would kill him when he laid eyes on him.

Neal Williams had seen Guthrie Diuguid on that past September 21 pull his gun on Lube and tell him, "Come on with me to the council and change that affidavit you made, you damned black son of a bitch, or I will shoot the top of your head off. I have been looking for you all the year and you have been dodging me."

And there was Avey Rose, Lube's neighbor. Late one afternoon in the past summer she had been outside her house. Guthrie Diuguid had come by with a gun in his hand looking for Lube. Not finding Lube at home, he made some threats and left.

But Holt had also learned from his sources that these crucial witnesses were all out of town and unable to be reached in time for the trial. Williams was reportedly in Memphis. Clarence was working for the railroad somewhere deep in west Tennessee. Avey Rose had disappeared, reportedly in Paris, Tennessee. The street talk was that this critical Negro witness had been spooked by the prospects of getting involved and fled. It might require Holt to actually have her arrested, or "attached" as was the legal term to apprehend unwilling witnesses.

Pat Holt desperately needed time.

And time was growing short when on the afternoon of January 9–one day before the trial was scheduled to begin–Sheriff Patterson and his deputies arrived in Murray with their prisoners.

Because of the limited security at the jail, located two blocks away, Patterson decided that he and his deputies would literally live with Martin until the trial. Therefore, he brought him to the courthouse.

The three other defendants, whose trial would be scheduled for a later time, but might be needed as witnesses, were lodged in the jail. There had been no real threat against them.

The petit jury which had been called in for orientation on that day had already gone home, instructed to return the next day for the murder trial of Lube Martin. Pat Holt then met with his client–most likely for the first time–in the anteroom to the upstairs courtroom with the sheriff and his deputies standing nearby.

It was then he learned of another missing witness–even more critical to the self defense claim of his client than Avey Rose.

His name was Lum Blanton.

The law in Kentucky was basically then as it is now when it comes to missing witnesses and the need for continuances:

A motion by the defendant for a postponement on account of the absence .....of a witness may be made...by affidavit which shows what facts the affiant believes the witness will prove.......and that the affiant believes them to be true.

Frantically Holt put together the affidavit upon which Lube Martin put his mark as the affiant. It said in part that if Lum

Blanton was present:

> .....*he would testify that he was present at or near by the scene of the shooting in which the deceased Guthrie Diuguid was killed.....and that he saw said Diuguid stop the affiant and say a few words to him, the import of which he did not hear or understand, and that he saw said deceased draw his pistol from his pocket from beneath his clothing and snap or fire same at the affiant, and that after he had so drawn and fired or snapped his pistol, the affiant drew his pistol and fired at the said Diuguid. And that said affiant only drew his weapon and fired at said Diuguid after said Diuguid drew and fired his at affiant.*

Holt also made sure to include in the affidavit that the attendance of the witness could not possibly be assured by the time of the trial scheduled to begin the next day.

One can only imagine the frantic and desperate actions of defense lawyer Pat Holt, assisted by his law partner, J.D. Thompson, on that Tuesday afternoon. Staring down the barrel of a death-penalty trial to begin the very next day, they had just met with their client for the first time. A jury, no doubt tainted and contaminated by intense public sentiment, would be returning within hours. There might even be an old-fashioned lynch mob waiting in the wings for good measure.

Their predicament was desperate enough to send shivers down the spine of modern day defense lawyers.

But these were men of mettle in their marrow, of an age when very few things came easy.

And they had the advantage of a circuit judge and commonwealth attorney who were not going anywhere. Court was virtually in continuous session since they would be housed for the duration just a block away in the Murray House Hotel.

So, as the weary day wore on into the night, as Murray and Calloway County braced for the trial of the century, lawyer Pat Holt went to the commonwealth attorney with his dilemma.

Denny Smith was a capable prosecutor and an affable personality. Extremely political, he was swayed substantially in his decision making by public opinion. Like most all office holders, Smith always had at least one eye on the next election, for either that office or another.

The 50-year-old commonwealth attorney was a native of Trigg County, born on October 9, 1866. He earned his college degree from the University of Kentucky, and like most lawyers of his day, acquired his license to practice law by "reading" law and passing the bar examination.

As a Democrat, he won the first political race in 1899 by being elected county attorney of Trigg County. Four years later he won his race for commonwealth attorney for the counties of Calloway, Christian, Lyon and Trigg. At the time of the Lube Martin trial, Denny Smith—like Bush—was fresh off his successful re-election campaign and just beginning his second term as chief prosecutor of the district.

Smith had a patrician look about him with his high forehead, fair complexion and thin, chiseled features. Affable and reasonable, his mild manner would easily transform into fiery indignation when prosecuting a criminal and addressing a jury.

He was married to the former Susie Evelyn White of Cadiz, and had one daughter, Martha, and one son, Ben.

In 1911, he had announced his candidacy for the state's attorney general. However, after his unsuccessful prosecution of David Amoss, the Night Rider leader, that same year, he changed his mind about his state-wide aspiration and withdrew from that race.

After the Lube Martin trial he moved to Hopkinsville where he was subsequently elected to the Kentucky General Assembly as state representative.

While Smith was sensitive to the pull and sway of public pressure, he was also a lawyer. That meant that he not only had deep appreciation of the dire straits of Pat Holt and his client, but also knew that ethically and morally he had an obligation to do the right thing to assure a fair trial for Lube Martin—even if he was "colored" and even if he had shot and killed a white deputy constable.

The highest court in the state has spoken to this awesome duty held by the people's lawyer:

One of the finest offices the public can give to a member of the legal profession in this state is that of commonwealth's attorney. Its very status becomes a mantle of power and respect to the wearer. Though few are apt to wear it lightly, some forget, or apparently never learn, to wear it humbly. No one except for the judge himself is under a stricter obligation to see that every defendant receives a fair trial, a trial in accordance with the law, which means the law as laid down by the duly constituted authorities, and not as the prosecuting attorney may think it ought to be.

So, Smith listened sympathetically to Holt's plea for a continuance. Although Holt knew Judge Bush would make the final call, the judge would give great weight to the position of the Commonwealth and the recommendation of the commonwealth attorney. He needed Smith in his corner.

In Kentucky, the law allows the commonwealth attorney a rather peculiar and powerful option in those cases where continuances are requested by the defense because of missing witnesses.

The law says:

If the attorney for the Commonwealth consents to the reading of the affidavit on the hearing or trial as the deposition of the absent witness, the hearing or trial shall not be postponed on account of his absence.

In other words, if the prosecutor agrees to let the defense lawyer read the affidavit of the expected testimony to the jury, as the expected testimony of the missing witness, the defendant—in theory at least—is not denied use of that evidence and the request for continuance may be denied.

This lawful alternative always places the prosecutor in a quandary. Does he want the testimony to go to the jury without cross examination, or does he want to agree to the continuance?

It always goes to the nature of the testimony.

On this day, Denny Smith might well be able to live with the unchallenged affidavit of expected testimony of an Avey Rose, or Neal Williams or Lube's own brother Clarence—all Negroes simply talking about threats that may have been made. The jury would know they were "colored," friends of the defendant, and choose what weight to give their credibility, which in that day and age would likely be minimal.

But the proposed testimony of Lum Blanton dealing with the actual shooting itself was dramatic and extremely exculpatory.

He would have been remiss in allowing the defense to put in this testimony by affidavit, unchallenged, untested, and unquestioned without the cleansing exercise of truth—cross examination.

So, Smith agreed with Holt. A continuance of the trial was needed.

Judge Bush agreed with both of them.

On the evening of January 9, 1916, it was decided that the trial set for the next day would be continued, and the prisoners would be returned to the Hopkinsville jail the next day.

Sheriff Will Patterson was so informed.

It was late. All was quiet. But Patterson knew his people. He was of the opinion that the next morning when news of the postponement hit the streets, Murray, Kentucky would not be a very good place to be for black men accused of murder.

He had seen the anger and temper of the crowd and community in December, and knew that the tense situation had only been diffused by the prompt action of Judge Bush setting the matter for quick trial. Tomorrow morning the mood of the community might once again turn nasty.

So, on the dark, cold streets of Murray just before 5 a.m. on January 10, Sheriff Patterson and three of his deputies made their move.

Calloway County Courthouse, circa 1965.
Photo compliments of John Ed Scott

Stealthily they escorted Martin quickly down the back stairway from the courtroom, and out the side door of the courthouse into the predawn quietness. Just four hours before the trial had been scheduled to start, the town was still sound asleep.

East, down Main Street, by the Murray House Hotel where Judge Bush and Denny Smith lay slumbering, and then north on Third Street to the jail. There, to the sounds of jangling keys and low murmurs they picked up Ann and Sylvester Martin, and Ed Jordon. Back toward Curd Street, the rapid-moving lawmen hurried on foot with their string of shackled prisoners. There they turned north as they began their four mile trek on foot to Almo.

It was a plan that Patterson had devised to avoid detection of their leaving with the prisoners. He had concluded that taking them to the train station in Murray, just three blocks away from the courthouse, would draw attention–even at that early hour. Also, when the word did get out of the continuance and movement of prisoners, they wouldn't be sitting ducks waiting for the train at the Murray Depot. Only a select few knew of the Almo plan.

So, the Patterson express would walk–hopefully unnoticed–all the way out to the small village to the north and catch the N.C. & St. L. train to Paducah, and from there to Hopkinsville.

They silently crossed the small stream at the foot of the hill near the intersection of Curd and Olive Street. Even at that early hour, lights in some of the houses gave evidence of people beginning to stir. Quickly they passed the fateful spot where these same four men, now chained, had met Guthrie Diuguid on that cold Saturday, one month before.

Soon they were near the edge of town, passed the Rowlett Tobacco Factory at the corner of Chestnut and Curd, and then into the secure darkness of open country.

The plan went off without a hitch.

By 9 o'clock when jurors began to arrive at the Calloway County Courthouse to hear the case against Lube Martin, he was safely on a train pulling out of Paducah heading for Hopkinsville.

CHAPTER 5

A MIDNIGHT RIDE

O n the night of January 10, 1917, the Seelbach Hotel in Louisville, Kentucky was aglow with all of its regal splendor.

Built in 1903 by the Bavarian brothers Louis and Otto Seelbach, it was one of the most elegant and magnificent hotels in the South, standing on Fourth Avenue, just a few blocks from the Ohio River and the Mason-Dixon Line.

Its grand lobby bustled with activity under the soaring ceilings which were supported by marble columns imported from Switzerland, Italy and Vermont. Huge murals ran along the high walls, depicting scenes from Kentucky history, including several images of Daniel Boone.

It was pretty much an exclusive club for men at that time. Female guests were provided with a separate entrance and waiting room, and most of the hotel's parlors were reserved for men only. Dark mahogany, bronze and leather mingled with the scent of expensive cigars to give the place an opulent and cozy feel on this cold winter night.

The dining room, richly adorned with linen table

cloths, crystal glassware, and silver, murmured with the sound of light banter and laughter, serenaded by the soft melodic sounds of a piano.

Its 350 rooms and facilities provided a meeting place for the rich and the powerful of that time.

On this particular evening, one of the large banquet halls was full of some of the leading moguls of the South and Midwest.

They were railroad executives attending the annual dinner of the prestigious Transportation Club of Louisville. Over 300 of the most prominent leaders in transportation were in attendance, to include representatives from several of the nation's leading railroads. Sumptuous food was being served at the long tables, the wine glasses constantly refilled by the Negro porters dressed in starched whites.

But there was another powerful group of men staying at the Seelbach that evening.

Governor A.O. Stanley and his aides, friends and some fifty leading Democrats of the general assembly were meeting in anticipation of a special session of the legislature expected to be called later in the month to consider revision of the state's tax code.

The 49-year-old chief executive had been skewered by the Louisville Courier Journal that very day for the paroling of Tom White, an aged convicted murderer out of Jackson County. Stanley had just come from Frankfort where he had met with the widow of White's victim who had complained of his action.

"I am quite sure," he later wrote, "that the governor and the prison board did exactly the right thing in conditionally liberating a poor wretch in the last stages of tuberculosis, broken in spirit, and decrepit in body, that he might not live–but die–in a cabin on a mountainside, breathing the pure air so essential to his comfort during the bitter little of his life that remains."

That behind him, the ebullient Hendersonian moved through the Seelbach, back slapping and shaking hands with friends and colleagues, enjoying the warmth of fine bourbon, good friends, humorous stories, all weaved into an evening of politics and governing.

By 8 p.m. the railroaders were heavy into their cups and speeches. Upstairs in the suite of Governor Stanley, he and several aides and legislators were heavy into the business of state craft.

It was about this time that the governor received a mysterious telephone call from Paris, Tennessee.

The caller's name was Barrard, and he appeared to be intoxicated.

Over the crackling line he conveyed an incredible message.

He said that there was big trouble in Murray, Kentucky. The caller reported that Judge Bush was being held hostage, and that the judge's life was in great danger. As a result of threats to his life, Barrard stated, Judge Bush had ordered Lube Martin be returned to Murray.

Click.

Astonished, Stanley related the message to those with him. Senator Seldon Glenn, from Lyon County and John Chilton, warden at the Kentucky State Penitentiary, were among those present. Both of them knew Bush well. They were his constituents. They had just helped to vote him into office. They insisted that the judge would never do such a thing, that the caller had to be some kind of crank, and the phone call should be ignored.

But the telephone call bothered Stanley.

He had it checked out, directed that calls be made out west to see if anything was happening.

Then the governor received this dramatic telegram from Circuit Judge W. M. Reed in Paducah:

Judge Bush and Commonwealth Attorney Smith are prisoners of a mob at Murray whose intention is to hang both tomorrow morning unless a Negro prisoner taken away today by the sheriff is returned by morning train. If you can command any power to save them it is necessary.

The courageous Judge Reed, fresh from the Paducah atrocity, knew trouble when he saw it.

The message hit the gathering of state leaders like a thunderbolt.

Suddenly all plans for tax revision, legislative nose counting, and political strategy discussions came to a halt. The atmosphere changed from busy, lighthearted work to crisis mode.

Stanley and the rest of the group were incredulous. Other reports were coming now from their own canvassing of western counties which corroborated the unbelievable news.

"My God! Would they hang a circuit judge?" Stanley kept repeating.

Then the chief executive took charge.

First he telephoned the state adjutant general of Kentucky, General J. Tandy Ellis, to confirm what he already grimly knew.

Every single unit, every single man, in the state militia had been "federalized" and were on the Mexican border chasing after Pancho Villa. It would take an act of Congress and days to get them back.

Stanley had no state militia.

He advised Ellis to check with the state's attorney general about the legality of deputizing special agents to assist him.

Next, he attempted to reach Judge Bush by telephone at the Murray House Hotel. He had great difficulty in making the connection.

Telephone service in 1917 was common and available throughout the Commonwealth. However, over long distances it was still unreliable, and depended entirely upon the proficiency and competence of local switchboards and their operators.

Finally, he got through to Judge Bush.

The old man was shaken, and distressed.

"Governor, it is worse even than that," he gravely reported.

Over the long distance wire, strung out to the far western part of the state, the beleaguered jurist faintly but distinctly related to the governor what had transpired.

An angry crowd packed the courthouse that morning,

Governor A.O. Stanley
Photo compliments Kentucky Historical Society

already having heard that the trial was postponed and Martin removed from the city.

When Judge Bush officially announced the action from the bench, the mob–and by that time it had turned into a mob–went ballistic.

Led by Guthrie Diuguid's brother, George, they demanded that Lube Martin be returned and the trial commence at once.

Bush tried to explain the reason for the delay. But there was no placating the growing crowd, which by now spilled out of the courthouse and onto the court square.

Again, with Diuguid taking the lead, they persisted upon the return of Martin forthwith. Bush refused, adjourned court, and tried to leave the courthouse with Commonwealth Attorney Smith. The press moved in upon them, some of them armed, making their case noisily. The sheriff and three of his deputies were somewhere between Murray and Hopkinsville. The remaining bailiff was no match for the crowd.

The terrified judge and prosecutor managed to make their way down the narrow back steps behind the courtroom and through the west doors of the courthouse. But still the mass followed after as they made their way back down Main toward the hotel. Ominous threats to hang the judge if he did not bring Martin back began to rise from the ranks. Only some less volatile tempers interceded to keep the two men from being physically attacked and mauled. Even so, Judge Bush was pushed and shoved about.

Miraculously they made it back to the hotel. But there was no safety here. Into the lobby the throng poured, with Bush and Smith able only to escape to their room.

As the morning wore on, the protest grew in size and vehemence. There were over 1,000 men inside and outside the hotel.

After all, it was cold, and mid-winter. Not much going on at their farms. So, hearing of the disturbance, some of the country folk wondered into town to see what was going on. Still, men of town made up most of the mob.

Representatives of the uprising visited Bush's room period-
ically, carrying the same ultimatum–return Martin for your life.
The frightened judge wore down, became almost moribund.

At one stage a doctor had to be summoned to check on
him.

There were preachers, even some friends in the crowd,
beseeching him to relent, to give in to their demands.

His commonwealth attorney even seemed to be leaning
toward trading out their lives for the defendant's.

There was growing talk of two dreadful possibilities: hanging the judge or dynamiting the hotel.

Of course the wrathful stampede did not have the approval
of all Murray citizens. Wiser and more reasonable heads, including
many of the community leaders, were appalled by the developments.

One of these was Rainy T. Wells, lawyer and highly respected citizen. He was also politically connected, a good friend of
Governor Stanley. He had been one of those Stanley had called to
confirm the early and alarming reports of the trouble.

Wells was a forceful, take-charge-type of guy. He did not
walk into a room without taking over the room. But now, he sober-
ly recognized, he had his hands full. There was little which could be
done against the surging tide of angry humanity.

Both the Civil War and the Night Rider violence were still
very much in the memory of many Calloway Countians. Grizzled
and bearded old Confederate survivors still gathered for their regular reunions. There were also veterans of the gun-toting, lash-bear-
ing Silent Brigade of Night Riders among the numbers now storm-
ing the Murray House Hotel.

The point was not lost on Wells. Buildings, even towns,
going up in smoke were not particularly strange notions to these
people.

And the hanging of a circuit judge and the dynamiting of
hotels were not topics likely to make chamber of commerce
brochures–if such things existed at that time.

Rainy T. Wells had dreams of a college coming to town.

George Diuguid, one of the leading advocates of Martin's immediate return, had to be brought under control. Undoubtedly with the quiet assistance of older brother and banker, Ed, this was accomplished–to a point.

After about four hours a delegation of some of the leading citizens of the community, including Wells, along with attorney George Diuguid, came to see the circuit judge and commonwealth attorney.

Although this small group of emissaries did not realize it, they were participating in one of the most effective means of persuasion in criminal interrogation. It's called the "good guy-bad guy" technique.

Compared to the murderous and enraged mob outside their doors, this "come let us reason together" tone of these seemingly friendly men was overwhelming to the two weary hostages.

Order Lube Martin back for trial, they proposed, and there would be no bloodshed–no hanging, no dynamiting, no town going up in smoke. They in turn would assure not only the safety of the judge and prosecutor but Lube Martin's as well. If need be, they would assemble one hundred men, armed to the teeth to protect the Negro. They had the power and influence to do so within the time it would take to get Martin back.

These were men Judge Charles Bush knew, some of them quite well; men he trusted, men who represented the strong pillars of a good and vibrant community of decent and law-abiding citizens. Some no doubt had strongly supported him in the November election. Their leader, Rainey Wells, exuded the confidence of a tornado.

To a weakening and broken old man, it seemed like a respectable way out–like a thin line of rope tossed his way in a raging torrent. It was all too much.

He agreed to do it.

It was a fateful decision that would haunt the aging magistrate for the rest of his life. Time and time again, the circumstance, the pull and draw, the words spoken, the threats, the long moments of that dreadful winter day would be written, talked about and debated. In a flash, in the heat of combat–moral or otherwise–under the fire of awful options and life and death choices–it's where men are sometimes crushed by events swirling beyond their control, pressing down upon their fragile frames.

For through that lonesome valley of decision, each man treads alone.

Multitudes, multitudes in the valley of decision; for the day of the Lord is near in the valley of decision.

It was an outrageous choice.

First, how could this meager handful of men assure Judge Bush of anything in light of the seething cauldron of violence and discord rumbling just past the portals of his own room? If they could not control them now, what made them think they could summon sufficient help to contend with them later?

Their bravado totally ignored reality.

"I can call spirits from the vastly deep," bragged Glendower in Shakespeare's *Henry IV.*

"Why, so can I, or so can any man," was the practical retort of Hotspur, *"but will they come when you do call for them?"*

Secondly, what kind trial could possibly be given to Lube Martin, once he was safely back in Murray–assuming he lived to be tried–amidst a billowing sea of hate, recrimination and prejudice?

All of it decries rational thought, bereft of any common sense, and hints more at the deranged thinking of a crazed prisoner deprived of his senses, than it does of a decree of a competent judge.

But mitigation might be brought to bear upon a sick and badgered old judge, in dire risk of losing his life. One has to wonder of the motives and reason of the "leading citizens," who clear headed and free of life-threatening duress and coercion came up with such a preposterous plan. Maybe they were just desperately buying time.

But the die was cast.

The order went out.

Bring Lube Martin back to Murray.

It was a little before 3 o'clock in the afternoon on January 10 when the order caught up with Sheriff Will Patterson and his prisoners.

They were in Princeton, preparing to switch trains to Hopkinsville.

One can only imagine the consternation and dread with which Patterson received this awful news.

Sleepless, tired, and drained from two days of transporting and protecting Lube Martin and company, he was now faced with the foreboding task of backtracking with his prisoners to Murray and whatever conflagration awaited him there. He directed two of his deputies to continue on to Hopkinsville with the three accomplices. He and Deputy Felix Bailey would return to Murray with Lube.

At 3:50 p.m., Sheriff Patterson, Deputy Bailey and his bewildered and frightened prisoner wearily arrived back in Paducah. The last train of the day for Murray had departed on the N.C. & St. L. shortly before they arrived. Just as the January night began to fall upon the city, the lawmen deposited their human cargo in the Paducah City Jail.

This was, in essence, the startling tale related by Judge Bush to the governor of Kentucky by telephone.

Stanley listened in rapt wonder and amazement. Finally, after Bush had finished, the governor exclaimed, "My God Judge Bush! You mean to tell me that at the insistence of this mob you have ordered the return of the prisoner to Murray?"

"Yes," came the feeble response of Judge Bush. "I had to do it to save my own life; if I had longer refused they would have hung me."

Governor Stanley paused, taking in what had just been said, and the enormity of the crisis.

Bush then informed the governor that the prisoner was due the next morning from Paducah on the 9 o'clock train.

There was silence, as Stanley pondered the situation, the open line humming and snapping across the miles.

Then the governor of the Commonwealth of Kentucky felt his ire begin to rise. With a tinge of anger lingering just below the surface he spoke slowly and deliberately, "That Negro will never be on that train. And you can tell that mob that they won't have to settle for hanging a circuit judge. They will get their chance to hang the governor of Kentucky first. I'm on my way to Murray."

Bush expressed hope that he would get there before further violence ensued.

And with that, the telephone conversation was ended.

"My God! Would they hang a circuit judge?" Stanley looked at his friends with continual amazement.

This time, the question took on new meaning.

If a person had to be some place in Kentucky in a hurry on that night, they could not have been in a better place than the Seelbach Hotel in Louisville.

By the time Stanley concluded his phone call with Judge Bush, the situation in Murray, Kentucky was the topic of all hotel conversation.

The mighty "wheels" of the railroad industry were just breaking up, many of them loitering around the lobby, puffing on cigars, and becoming enthralled with the growing crisis confronting the governor.

He needs to get to Murray?

No problem.

The frocked-coated big wigs of the Illinois Central and the N.C. & St. L. lines huddled briefly, made a phone call or two, and it was done.

At nearby Union Station in Louisville, frantic activity ensued in the cold winter night. Coupling began to take place for a special train with a plush executive car and berths for the governor. Dispatchers sent out the train orders to operators along the way.

Clear the rails for a special express.

It was close to midnight on that Tuesday night, and the streets of Louisville were nearly deserted. Governor Stanley and a small cadre of companions left the splendor of the Seelbach and made their way into a waiting Model T, which noisily sputtered off to the train station.

No doubt there were many left behind who had, in excited tones, discouraged his going. After all, even with the aid of telephone and telegraph, they had only been able to get a general idea of what was going on in Murray. The wild west scared them—distant, isolated by distance and unpredictable rivers. Why the farthest part even appeared cut off the map from the rest of the state, like it had started to sink into the state of Tennessee. Smoking towns and hooded horsemen, slashing through the night; killings, maiming, barbaric lynching and mob violence were all a part of the perceived culture of this far-flung piece of statehood. If the mountains had their bloody feuds, the west had its outright insurrections and universal lawlessness.

At least that was the perception which much of the rest of Kentucky held for most of the counties west of the Green River.

For a governor, single-handedly without troops or numbers, to strike out into the night toward this cauldron of unrest seemed suicidal to most.

"Would they hang a circuit judge?" was a foolish question to most of the legislators and politicians left standing at the Seelbach.

Yes, and a damn foolhardy governor too.

And probably anyone who was just as foolish to be with him.

Everyone should have friends like A.O. Stanley had with

him on that night.

While others fell away, either by their own design or at his direction, at least three brave men made a steely decision.

They were going with their governor.

State Fire Marshall Tom Parnell, Prison Commissioner Henry Hines, and Fred LaRue, administrator of the West Kentucky State Hospital–the insane asylum in Hopkinsville–were the gallant three who elected to make that midnight ride toward an uncertain dawn.

Even under more serene circumstances, A. O. Stanley vibrated with energy. With the adrenalin pumping, and the fateful decision made, he was the picture of a man in motion, with a purpose.

Quickly he set the pace, as the delegation was disgorged at station and made its way toward the waiting train.

Like some slumbering dragon, the giant locomotive sat idling, hissing steam out into the frigid air. Hooked to its rear were the coal tender and the special coach. Engineer, fireman, conductor, and flagman conferred as Stanley and company made their hurried way to the open door of the coach. Stanley bounded up the steps, his fellow travelers on his heels.

The conductor moved up onto the bottom step, grabbed the handle, leaned back and waved up the track. Then, he too ducked inside and slammed the door shut.

Slowly, ponderously, the locomotive began to shuffle out of the terminal.

No one knows what was said, what was thought, what was discussed on that midnight train.

We can only guess.

We can make an educated guess only if we knew the people.

Little is known of Henry Hines, Tom Parnell, and Fred Larue.

The fact that these three men were on this train, heading

into the darkness of unknown perils and possibilities, says a lot in and of itself. Their mettle alone is laudable enough to earn their names a place in print.

But we know much about the governor who was on that train.

If he was not the greatest of Kentucky's governors, he was, to use the colorful Dizzy Dean terminology, "amongst'em."

And without a doubt he was the most colorful.

Augustus Owsley Stanley was born on May 21, 1867 at 301 Washington Street, Shelbyville, Kentucky. His father, William, was a Confederate veteran, having served as a captain in the famed Orphan Brigade. Later his father served as editor of the Shelby County Sentinel newspaper, and then as a Christian Church minister.

A. O.'s mother, Amanda, was the niece of Kentucky's 16th governor, William Owsley.

Stanley was named Nudicutt Owsley at birth. Later at age ten, he had the foresight to persuade his parents to rename him Augustus Owsley, so that he would not be called "NO" Stanley.

It was as a 19-year-old student at the Kentucky Agricultural and Mechanical College—now the University of Kentucky—that he first displayed a flair for oratory.

Stanley was very popular with his fellow students. He possessed a lively and effervescent personality, full of good cheer and merry mischief. Friendly and considerate of everyone, he enjoyed participating in the rowdy life of college boys, especially in pranks and practical jokes.

He ended up graduating from Centre College in Danville in 1889, after which he taught school for four years.

But his love for public speaking and the law were his great passions and he read law during this time. In 1894 he was admitted to the practice of law, and began his legal career in Flemingsburg.

For some reason his practice faltered there, and Stanley turned his eyes west to a little river town on the Ohio River.

Henderson, Kentucky in 1898 was a picturesque village in western Kentucky just coming into its own. Near the confluence of the Green and Ohio Rivers, it was an ideal river town–sitting high upon a bluff above the flood plain, it serviced the tobacco industry of the western end of the state. A considerable distance upriver, and to the east of the larger town of Paducah, it only had to compete with larger Owensboro for the river trade.

By the time A. O. Stanley arrived on the scene, there were eighteen tobacco factories located there along with some distilleries and a brewery. Not only was it a chief river port, at a time when the river industry was booming, but it was a railroad center as well. Several of the major lines ran through Henderson, and a railroad bridge connected Henderson with Evansville, Indiana.

All of this created a climate for a bustling economy, and no doubt attracted the ambitious young lawyer.

It was here in Henderson where the 31-year-old lawyer hit his stride, and made his mark.

Stanley almost immediately came under the influence and tutelage of Circuit Judge John L. Dorsey and the mayor, Irvin Thompson. They liked this energetic, gregarious and bright young man who had a gift with words.

Within a few years, the future governor was in the midst of a thriving law practice.

But politics was becoming the love of his life. He became an avid Democrat and a devout disciple of another grand orator, national figure, William Jennings Bryan. In 1900 he became an elector for Bryan in his unsuccessful presidential bid.

In 1902, at the age of 35–and reportedly upon the dare of his new bride–A. O. Stanley jumped into the congressional race for the Second Congressional District of Kentucky and won.

He had just married a Henderson girl by the name of Sue Soaper, who was the daughter of a successful tobacco agent. In a few short years, they would have three sons.

By this time Stanley's political philosophy had solidified. And it remained consistent, oft times to his great detriment, throughout the rest of his life.

As a strong Democrat, he was also a strong believer in individual rights. While a supporter of state's rights, he advocated strong government involvement on behalf of the "have-nots" in curbing the abuses of the privileged rich. It was an era of an emerging struggle between capital and labor, and Congressman Stanley took off after the large business trusts almost as soon as he arrived in Washington.

In racial matters, he was a champion of social justice regardless of color. In a Chicago speech on April 9, 1967, he eloquently stated, "Today, Southern in every fiber, the son of a rebel captain, I declare that, from the depths of a grateful heart, I reverently thank the God of Hosts that there is not a manacle or a chain on one mute and cowering slave under the protecting folds of my country's flag."

A more unique and interesting friendship has never been struck as that between A.O. Stanley and Edwin P. Morrow, ten years his junior.

For some unexplainable reason, these two men of opposing political parties were drawn to each other like brothers. They were kindred spirits, sharing the same nutmeg sense of fun and zest for life and politics.

Most likely they first met during the U.S. Senate campaign of 1912 when the Republican Morrow took on Stanley's good friend and fellow congressman from the First Congressional District, the promising Democrat, Ollie James, of Marion. James, a rising star in state and national politics soundly defeated Morrow.

Politics was much different in those days. While the candidates were ruthless and vicious in their attacks upon each other from platform and print, they became intimately familiar with each other in their campaign travels–riding the same train, staying in the same hotels, and even taking meals together.

It was in this environment, in the campaign between Morrow and Stanley for governor in 1915, that their spectacular friendship became legendary.

Politically, they were not as far apart as they liked to proclaim. Morrow, former U.S. attorney from Somerset ,was, like Stanley, a progressive. He fully supported women's suffrage, and tolerance—strongly opposing the influential Ku Klux Klan. And Morrow was no slouch of a public speaker himself.

The two campaigned against each other in that epic governor's race of 1915 like two young boys out on a frolic. It was if neither one took themselves or the issues that serious, but were simply and thoroughly enjoying the game.

One time Stanley and Morrow were campaigning in the mountains of east Kentucky, which was strong Republican country. Morrow was pretty much taking it for granted. Stanley saw an opening, however, when he learned that his Republican opponent had refused to go into Knott County by mule from the end of the C & O's Beaver Creek Railroad line. A. O. grabbed his mule and took to the hills, telling all good Republicans along the way that Ed Morrow was too good to ride a mule.

He would loudly exclaim, "He doesn't want to see you as badly as I do. He thinks he's got you in the bag. He didn't think I'd come over here on a mule either. But here I am. Where's Ed? He's only speaking where he can ride on a train."

The voters loved it. Later, after the election, Morrow shook his head in disgust, "Owsley has gone into the governor's mansion on a mule." To mark out their differences, the two progressives often had to jump onto trivial, if intriguing issues.

One was the "free ole ring" anthem of the Morrow camp. He promised that if elected he'd repeal the dog tax that had been voted by a Democratic legislature.

This had been a very unpopular act by the general assembly, and Stanley had a hard time defending it. With tears pooling in his eyes, Morrow proclaimed in great oratorical flourishes from one end of the state to the other, "no man has a friend so true as his dog, so faithful and loyal." Once the two were speaking in the same courthouse at the same time before large partisan crowds. Stanley waited till he was told Morrow was onto the "free ole ring" issue in the upstairs courtroom, and then he commenced baying like a dog to deride his opponent.

It was all great fun at a time when grown men knew when not to take themselves too seriously.

Both candidates liked to imbibe, but Stanley often did so in excess.

His biographer Thomas W. Ramage reported about one hot summer day at a political picnic when A.O. had too much to drink:

On one occasion, Morrow and Stanley shared the same platform. Speaking first, Morrow thrilled the crowd with his brilliant oratory. Stanley, who had drunk too much bourbon prior to the engagement, managed to sit quietly during Morrow's address, but when he rose to make his own speech, 'his head swam and his knees buckled.' Nauseated, he staggered to the back of the platform where he vomited. Then, embarrassed but not at a loss for words, he returned to the speaker's stand where he said: 'Gentlemen, I beg you to excuse me. Every time I hear Ed Morrow speak, it makes me sick at my stomach.'

Their rhetoric whereby they tore into each other was mostly tongue-in-cheek.

The story comes down that they met each other on a street in a central Kentucky town one day and Morrow refused to speak to his Democratic nemesis.

"What's wrong with you Ed? You mad at me?" Stanley pulled Morrow aside.

"You're damn right I'm mad at you," came the response.

"Why?" inquired the startled Stanley.

"Because," Morrow intoned in mock anger, "you've been going up and down this state telling lies on me and that didn't matter. But now, you're going around telling the truth.....and it hurts like hell!"

So this was the essence of the man rolling through the night; through a darkened tunnel of doubts, fears, and frightening possibilities. As minutes turned into hours, the conversation waned, and the calming mace of fatigue overwhelmed the traveling troupe.

Averaging 50 miles per hour the iron horse and its cargo tore through the night on a heavy mission to the west.

Rolling, rolling, rolling–the gargantuan machine of power and steam huffing and puffing along rails of steel. But the man himself–Augustus Owsley Stanley-was being borne along on the wings of conscience.

Most likely he remained awake, peering out the window at the passing towns, sleeping farms and villages, one-gallus stations and remote crossings. The mournful whistle regularly sounded the urgent knell, as the express flashed past road crossings and station platforms, with sleepy keepers inside, signs of these places lightened only briefly to the governor's eyes.

Litchfeld. Spring Lick.

Roscine. Where little five-year-old Bill Monroe, destined for immortality as the founder of bluegrass music, lay sleeping in his father's home.

Over the Green River. The names taking on old familiarity.

Beaver Dam. Rockport and Greenville.

Through the heart of his old congressional district.

Depoy. Nortonville and IIsley.

Across the Tradewater and into the heart of far west Kentucky.

But places are not places really. They are people. With each passing town, each darkened landmark came the names of people flowing over his cluttered mind like a steady stream through a dense wood. Friends and enemies. Men and women. Good and bad. Some long dead, and some who should be dead. Rogues and saints; workers and slackers; the congregate body of the flesh to which Stanley regularly turned, not only for surcease but for purpose: their needs, their pains, their sins; his most beloved being those who had fallen upon the thorns of life and bled.

Princeton. The Night Rider capital of the world.

Eddyville. The prison town. Where even at these most

silent moments of the infant morn, men lay awake soaked in their sins.

At around 3:30 in the morning between Eddyville and Kuttawa, the cold rail bent slightly more westward, running at the eastern edge of the Cumberland River. There the churning and charging locomotive passed directly in front of Mineral Mound, the magnificent plantation, home of Willis B. Matchen, a man of great wealth and influence who had been the Confederate congressman to Richmond from west Kentucky during the Civil War. The stately edifice still stood as a lordly sentinel on the hill overlooking the narrow Cumberland River just below. At this moment as the governor hurried by on his urgent mission, darkness hid the scarred facade where the replacement brick had never matched the original after a Union gunboat had sent a cannon ball through the Matchens' upstairs bedroom in answer to the Confederate flag waving tauntingly above its roof.

And then, as night began to give way to morning, across the Cumberland and the Tennessee rivers into the Jackson Purchase–ancient lands of the Chickasaw.

Calvert City. Little Cypress.

Paducah.

He had departed from Union Station in Louisville and he arrived at Union Station in the Littleville area of south Paducah.

Although the winter morning was still pitch black, a sizable number of people were at the station to meet him as the train chugged in around 4:20 a.m.

The situation in Murray had captured the attention of all west Kentucky.

Members of the press, local politicians, friends and supporters, and the downright curious hovered around him as Stanley bounced off the train-his energy and dynamic personality unaffected by a night on the rails.

While the engine was being switched for the N.C. & St. L. railroad tracks which led to Murray, the governor moved with his followers into the lunch room for a quick breakfast. After ordering

Union Station in Littleville section of Paducah as it appeared
around the time of the Lube Martin trial in Murray.
Photo compliments of the late Barron White

coffee, two eggs and toast, the affable chief executive leaned back to answer questions from the curious gathering.

"Are you here on your own initiative, or did citizens or officials of Murray appeal for your assistance?" barked a reporter from the local *Paducah News-Democrat.*

"I came because I wanted to," he answered emphatically.

"When are you going to Murray?" came another inquiry.

"As soon as I can get a train out of here," said Stanley.

"What do you intend to do after you get there?" came undoubtedly the best question of the day.

Unblinking, the golden-tongue orator exclaimed, "I am going to appeal to the people for justice."

Governor Stanley and his friends were only in Paducah for about forty minutes on that critical trek.

During that short span, however, he made some crucial decisions which would prove pivotal in the course of the new born day.

First, as to the main question at hand: Lube Martin.

Unbeknownst to Stanley, Martin had not been lodged in the McCracken County Jail the night before as he had thought. So, his order to the county jailer not to send Martin back to Murray was misdirected.

The prisoner instead had been deposited by Sheriff Patterson in the Paducah City Jail, and neither that jailer, nor the county lawman, knew of the governor's edict.

At the time Stanley's train pulled into Paducah, Patterson and Deputy Felix Bailey were already up and had Martin at the train station, planning to catch a taxi to take their prisoner back to Murray.

It was a close call. Had Stanley not arrived in Paducah when he did–had his train been a few minutes later, or he had decided not to leave Louisville until later–Martin would have been on his way back to Calloway County and the awaiting lynch mob. Stanley immediately countermanded Judge Bush's order, and directed Patterson to take Martin back to Hopkinsville on the next available train. Although it was a command of questionable legality, the relieved sheriff gladly saluted.

Thinking it would be good to have some local color with him when he went to Murray, Governor Stanley turned to Deputy Bailey and asked him if he would be willing to go with him on the final leg.

Deputy Bailey replied with words that would remain down through the years as a testimony of his own personal loyalty and valor: "Governor, I'll go with you anywhere."

Another crisis then confronted Stanley on that Paducah lay-over: west Kentucky was on the verge of a civil war. More specifically, two towns were about to take up arms against each other. The two cities, Hopkinsville and Murray, were on the verge of all-out war against each other.

Needless to say, when word got back to Hopkinsville on Wednesday night, January 10, that a mob in Murray was holding their own Judge Bush and Commonwealth Attorney Denny Smith hostage, it didn't set very well with the home folks.

The town instantly became abuzz with anger–simmering at first, and then erupting into outward displays of resentment. By late Wednesday night an army of three hundred men, armed to the teeth, had gathered under the command of Sheriff Jewel Smith. By the time the governor of Kentucky arrived in Paducah on Thursday morning, the troops from Christian County were mobilized, arranging for a special train out of Hopkinsville, ready to invade the Jackson Purchase and rescue their two public servants.

There was Governor Stanley's army if he wanted it.

But the wise leader quickly dismissed such a possibility as a blue print for disaster. He was too good a student of history to fall into that trap. A train load of armed men from Hopkinsville rolling into Murray to meet head on with the armed and angry mob awaiting there would be worse than the violent clash at the stone wall at Gettysburg.

Stanley quickly sent word to Hopkinsville ordering Sheriff Smith and his men to stand down. He was in Paducah on his way to Murray. He would take care of things himself.

Like all good soldiers, the Christian County lawman and his troops dutifully obeyed, and the men were all dismissed. It is to the credit of these rural lawmen involved in this crisis that they did not let their egos get in the way. Although elected officials themselves, charged with the responsibility of keeping order, both Patterson and Smith respected the age-old military principle of the chain of command. People might quibble over the legal niceties of the process. But in the fearful confusion of rattling musketry, in the uncertain moments of the predawn darkness, they unquestionably followed the command of the state's chief executive.

Like in Louisville, there were friends of Stanley in Paducah who were deeply concerned about his going to Murray alone.

J.W. Morris of Benton, Kentucky was one such friend. There in the Union Station lunch room, he frightfully brought the governor up to date on the dangerous state of affairs in the Calloway County seat. He reminded him of the awful consequences in ordering Martin back to Hopkinsville, especially for the

Present day Murray depot where Governor A.O. Stanley disembarked on his dramatic arrival in Murray. It is no longer used as a train station.

safety and welfare of the two hostages–Bush and Smith.

"Do you think they would go so far as to kill a judge?" Stanley exclaimed once again in wonderment. "Don't those people respect the honor of a judge?"

Morris somberly replied, "I'm afraid not."

Then his Marshall County friend gave the governor other ominous news.

The mob in Murray, hearing of the governor's coming, had declared that they might just have to hang Stanley along with the judge and commonwealth attorney.

Those heavy words fell upon the ears of A. O. Stanley as he finished his breakfast there in the Paducah depot.

"Well," he spoke at last in a tone of resignation, "they will just have to do it."

Others in the sizable gathering there requested to travel along with the governor to Murray. He declined their gracious offer.

"I don't want them to think that I'm bringing a force of men with me. I want to calm them by showing them what it would

108

mean for them to bring harm upon a circuit judge."

So, at 5 a.m., Kentucky's head man walked across the platform of Union Station to the N.C. & St. L. railroad tracks where the giant engine waited, steam up and ready to sprint out into the disappearing night. He and his handful of associates climbed up onto the coach and the door slammed shut.

The big iron horse began to pull out of the station, into the tailing darkness of a restless night, carrying its passengers toward the uncertain fate of the new day.

The trip from Paducah to Murray that morning took about one hour.

Benton. Glade. Dexter.

The train whistled by the empty platform at Almo—the same spot from which Sheriff Patterson and his deputies had departed with their prisoners 24 hours earlier.

Then the locomotive began to reduce speed as it lumbered into the city limits of Murray on the eastern edge of town.

There in the straightaway running due south, the first hovels of the Negro section of town came into view. Threading through the tar shacks and shanties on both sides of the track, the churning rods and massive wheels slackened their pace. As Stanley peered out the window, he saw the settlement of ex-slaves and their heirs, waking to the winter morn. Wood smoke from new fires poured from narrow stove pipes and crooked chimneys, up, up, up, into the cold gray streaks of dawn. Coal oil lamps, freshly lit, cast dim glows against cardboard walls and blinds. A few, beating away the cold with their arms, and breathing frosty puffs into the air, fed hogs and milked cows.

The governor of Kentucky majestically glided past the humble abode of Lube Martin, and for a few seconds he was only a few feet away from the sleeping black face of Lube's child and the weary and worried face of his wife.

This colony of a troubled people, burdened by their miserable past, clinging to the edge of town, to the edge of existence, to the jagged edges of an ancient era; waking to this morning darkness like all days of labor, not knowing–not even dreaming–that some of them would live to see epoch and glorious changes in their dismal world.

One glowing ember of that future cause was stirring in his mother's shanty on that frosty morn just a short distance from the governor of Kentucky. Mary Chandler Howard, a black cook at the Mason Hospital in Murray, was coaxing her 9-year-old son Ted out of bed, and onto his daily chores and school. Ted Howard would grow up to be a doctor himself, a close friend and ally of the martyred civil rights leader, Medgar Evers, and one of the leading Negro leaders in the nation.

And the first small stirring of the young lad's new world yet to be–infinitesimally minute as the early March quiver of a hibernated root–was announced by the lonesome whistle of Governor A.O. Stanley's train.

In the early light of dawn, the Murray depot came into view. As predicted, a large crowd gathered there to await the governor's train.

At long last, after a long night of travel–a long night of alarming reports, rumors, and frightening stories and sleepless anticipation–A.O. Stanley and his friends had arrived.

Crowds had never bothered Stanley, the consummate politician. They had been nectar to his rise to power, fuel for his grand oratory skills. They had meant votes; lots of them, in huge chunks at a time. But the middle-aged governor had never confronted a mob, bent on vigilante justice.

As faces began to slide slowly pass the windows of the ebbing train, he could see familiar people and names.

After a night full of demons and doubts; miles of lonely brooding on dreadful possibilities, a shaft of warm sunlight must have suddenly fallen across the soul of this bold and fearless governor.

In the midst of uncertainty, one reassuring thought surely lifted him.

He was among friends.

In no other county in the grand breadth of the Commonwealth was Governor A.O. Stanley more respected and revered, than in Calloway County, Kentucky.

In his razor-thin margin statewide victory over Republican Edwin Morrow some 14 months before, he had trounced his opponent by almost three to one in Calloway County.

To this community which rode upon the backs of tobacco farmers, Congressman A.O. Stanley had been their hero in the bitter and violent struggle against the suffocating trust of the American Tobacco Company only a few short years before. The current state of agrarian prosperity, to their mind at least, was due in part to this man now riding into Murray on the early morning train.

His great strength, in this town now embroiled in passions gone amuck, was about to be tested.

CHAPTER 6

THE SPEECH

Governor Stanley started pumping hands as soon as he bounced off the train.

His apprehensive little knot of friends tagged along, close upon his heels, not knowing what to expect in the murmuring crowd.

The presence of Deputy Felix Bailey, moving by Stanley's side, made them feel better, if slightly.

Moving along the platform away from the train, the popular governor recognized old friends, and familiar faces, one after another.

It soon became evident that this was not a hostile, angry crowd. The visitors took courage when they began to hear friendly voices from the gathering.

"We're glad you came, governor," came one voice from the throng.

"Thanks for coming," came another.

A sizable segment of the welcoming mass at the depot, at least, were apparently relieved that the governor of Kentucky had come to save them from disgrace.

Shops and stores were just opening along Main

Street as the governor made his way toward the Murray House Hotel. Waving and smiling, Stanley ducked into some of the stores, shook hands with the surprised proprietors–many of which he knew by name.

New smoke billowed out from rooftop chimneys and the pungent scent of coal soot hovered in the frigid air. Stooped old black men, or strapping young boys of the same hue, stoked the hungry coal furnaces at the larger buildings in town, including the Murray Bank building on the corner of the courthouse square where the Diuguid name reigned. The metallic clang of empty scuttles signaled the refueling of lesser establishments. It was cold, below freezing, the temperature having dropped from a high of near 60 degrees just two days before.

En masse they moved, the governor with his associates and faithful entourage, up the steep grade of Main Street toward the Murray House Hotel. Then, like the fresh cool waters of a spring becoming absorbed and lost in the larger, murky stream, the mood of the crowd began to change. The supportive cast gathered at the depot was quickly dissolved into the widening river of discord. There were few smiling faces milling in front of the hotel. It was an assemblage of grim-faced and sullen men. This mass did not give way easily to the buoyant Stanley's brisk walk.

Governor A.O. Stanley parted no waters here.

He was descending into the belly of the beast.

It was the mob. Worn down and quieted by the long night of vigilance, it still teemed with subdued rancor and persistence. Undaunted, Stanley nudged his way along, forcing his way into the entrance.

A murmur went through the crowd as some recognized the distinguished-looking visitor and his friends.

Others were not so informed or impressed.

"Who is that?" called out one of the angry men.

He was told quickly that it was the governor of the Commonwealth of Kentucky.

"He doesn't look any bigger than Judge Bush to me," was

113

the chilling reply.

Stanley, along with his small band of loyalists, literally cold shouldered their way through the lobby past hostile stares and defiant faces.

Finally he reached the room of Judge Charles Bush and Commonwealth Attorney Denny Smith.

What he found there was a pitiful sight.

Bush was in bed, trying to cope physically and emotionally with his terrifying plight.

Smith was hovered over a coal-burning stove, worn and sleepless, trying to keep warm.

Two beleaguered public servants, alone and embattled without aiders and abettors, caught up in a maelstrom of mass hysteria and lawlessness.

Seeing Governor A. O. Stanley, however, immediately enlivened their spirits, resurrected both of them, physically and emotionally.

Sitting on the side of the bed, Bush's first anxious inquiry was, "Governor, did you bring the Negro back?"

Stanley not only firmly informed him that he had not brought Martin back with him, but furthermore, Martin would not be coming back to Murray—at least not on that January day.

"Then they are going to hang me," the old circuit judge muttered pitifully.

"Probably," the governor matter-of-factly affirmed.

"Do you think public opinion is going to stand for you allowing a white man being hanged to let a Negro go free?" Bush pushed on, knowing that he was talking to a man whose livelihood rode on the fickle tide of the popular whim.

Neither the long and hard midnight ride over hundreds of miles, nor the belligerent throng just outside the doors, dented the governor's ardor.

"I'd say that if they hang you, then they will probably hang me. Don't you agree?" Stanley replied.

Judge Bush nodded.

"Well, I don't have to worry much about public opinion after I'm hanged, do I?"

No one in that drab and melancholy hotel room ever reported whether there was a smile on the face of the governor when he made that remark. But the gallows humor was not lost upon the group.

The levity, however slight, served as a jolt to the morale of this small knot of Kentuckians. Stanley began to steer their thoughts away from the problem, to the solution.

For a long while, serious and studied discussions took place on how to rescue the hostages from their plight.

Rainy T. Wells, friend and ally to the governor, had joined the group. He suggested a daring escape. A car would be pulled up to the front of the hotel. With the aid of local friends, the governor and hostages would make a run to the waiting automobile, which in turn would whisk them to the waiting train.

This idea, charged with excitement, was also pregnant with great danger.

The room had become crowded. Bush, Smith, Governor Stanley, Hines, LaRue, and Parnell, had been joined by a small knot of local friends including Wells.

Out of bed and dressed, Bush now became energized by the governor's presence and leadership.

Stanley listened mostly as the group kicked around the various possibilities, most all of which were fraught with grave risks. The greeting at the depot earlier indicated he had many friends ready to come to his aid. In fact, on the way to the hotel he had gone about the dubious legal business of "deputizing" some of them who followed along.

So, the state's number one decision maker went into decision making mode. The chief executive pondered the grave and desperate conversation around him.

A.O. Stanley was a student of history, steeped from formal education in the classics. But he was also a student of his times, his people, their varying hues of influences and cultural backgrounds.

The west Kentucky governor of Henderson, born and raised in the Bluegrass, was keenly aware of the peculiar history of each region of his beloved and diverse Kentucky.

The men outside their doors were tough farmers and rustics of the west, heirs of the rugged and tempestuous Andy Jackson, not of the genteel compromiser Henry Clay. Stanley had seen their fathers, stooped and gray, gathered in shaded courtyards and encamped at ancient springs at Cerulean and Kuttawa, some missing arms, others missing legs, speaking in hallowed tones of Shiloh, Missionary Ridge, and Vicksburg. He had seen their gaunt faces at Guthrie, the smoldering ruins of the tobacco warehouses at Hopkinsville.

They were not men with whom to trifle.

Try to make them look foolish; try to dishonor them–even if their own pursuit was far less than honorable–and there would be hell to pay. Ropes would stretch, blood would flow; buildings would burn.

But he also knew something else about these men and their fathers.

At an early age, Stanley had been called to the arena of public service. He possessed a deep-seated belief that running through the core of every human being–within deeper ravines and crevices for some more than others–was a river of basic goodness. He believed that, sure enough, this stream flowed to influences of outer forces, but the thread of good will was always there. It was his conviction that if one wished to lead, they must not lose sight of this basic truth. Otherwise a would be leader would be just another follower of the base and temporal whims of passion. If one wants to be a great leader, Stanley's life proclaims, he must by word or deep tap deep into this inner stream of nobility, truth and justice. Then stagnant lives will respond, and they can be bent, around curves and shoals of circumstance, out into the sunlit plains of reason.

The desperate men at their doors were victims of mindless passions, led by prejudice and the vengeful manipulation of a bereaved brother.

116

But they were men of great moral strength; good husbands and fathers, protectors and defenders of the family hearth; willing hands for their neighbors stress; aiders and abettors to the widows and orphans; dedicated and loyal servants to the ways of nature, wrestling from her sometimes fickle ways their very existence. They respected men of courage and they respected truth—even when seen through the error of their ways.

Stanley had come to town without troops, armed only with his courage, and the power of truth.

And his eloquence.

He would talk his way out of town.

The governor interrupted the wild and disconnected discourses of the frantic group and announced the plan.

Court would be adjourned at 8 a.m. at the Calloway County Courthouse. He would speak to the mob.

And the devil take the hind part.

There are no reports as to how the close group of friends in that Murray hotel room responded to the governor's simple and daring plan.

But he was the governor. And they followed his lead.

Shortly before 8 a.m. they made their way out of the hotel toward the courthouse. Word quickly spread that court would convene.

Many thought the actual trial was going to begin. Some on the fringes of the morning happenings may have even thought that the Negro had been brought back to Murray and his fate was soon to be told.

Most probably did not know what was about to transpire. Only that there was going to be a meeting in the courtroom. Judge Bush, the governor, and others would be there.

In that short time the crowd, depleted from the long night of waiting, was replenished, and swelled to over five hundred. They moved en masse, like a river of mercury, to the courthouse.

There, the giant edifice-which still stands today, defiant of all history including this which was enveloping it on this January morn-absorbed the tribe into its wings, up to the top floor, up still for many into the balcony of the courtroom. Slowly, though orderly, the large room filled to the brim. People stood in the back, in the aisles, in the hall and in the stairway.

August Owsley Stanley never recorded what raced through his mind as he made that short sprint from the Murray House Hotel to the courthouse on that gray day. As far as is known, he never shared those critical moments with anyone. It was not part of his nature. He was a man of action. He recognized reflection as the prudent prologue of decision. But once committed, it served little purpose.

To act, to act in the present moment, that was the mission of this happy warrior.

According to the newspaper reports of the happening it was not a particularly rowdy or boisterous crowd waiting for him there. But one surmises from available sources, it was more curious than demanding at this point. They were there to see what the governor, and to a lesser extent their circuit judge, had to offer upon the pyre of their burning passions.

Judge Bush, looking like a used bar of soap, climbed up behind the bench and stared uncomfortably out over the group. Smith, one can only guess, took his familiar chair at the counsel table. Before he did so he made one cryptic comment to the crowd. It was either a gallant piece of humor, or a monstrous lie.

"Good to see all of you people out here this morning."

Stanley moved in front of the jury box which fronted the judge's bench. He turned, his back to the judge, and faced his large audience.

The courtroom grew quiet.

"Gentlemen, a little more than one year ago," that sonorous, clear and familiar voice began, "in the presence of a vast multitude, I laid this good right hand upon a Bible, and called upon my God, whom shortly I must face, to witness that as the chief magistrate of Kentucky, its highest exemplar and enforcer of the law, that I would maintain it in its integrity and majesty."

After a pause, he continued.

"The drops of blood which course through my tired heart are not so dear to me as my honor as a man and I will enforce the law."

It was immediately clear there would be no trial today.

Turning and peering into one face and then another, "What would you think of a governor who would countenance lawlessness; who would sanction a lie? The least that can be said of law is that her voice is the harmony of the spheres. I came here in the wee, small hours of the night, and I thought on this solemn occasion, as I looked forth into the eternal firmament at the twinkling stars, many of them a thousand times larger than the globe upon which I stand, of the perfect obedience which those stars render to the supreme law.

Dethrone the law of the heavens and all would be a dark chaos. Upon the law rest the life of every man, the honor of every woman, and safety of every community. Tear down this edifice, the temple of justice–and there is but one more sacred place than this, the Temple of God–and what is left?"

Now there was a tomb-like silence which had fallen over the attentive throng. From the crowded rows of wooden benches up next to the rail, to the far flung corners of the hovering balcony, men of all rank and file of rural life were locked into the magnetic pull of the master orator's sway.

Stanley let the soundless pause take hold, for quick reflection upon the question.

Then he continued.

"In obedience to that command which was thundered down from the heights of Sinai–that whatever the provocation, except self-defense, the killing of man is murder. If I should go forth and arm myself and slay the murderer of my brother I would be a murderer.

Yet I could do worse. I could gather a mob of a thousand men, arm them and take a man's life–and then go before my God with his blood upon my head, only to hear Him say, 'Get thee away from me, thou murderer!' "

Incredibly, there were preachers in that audience. One can only wonder as to what twisted logic brought them to this lynching party. Now they must have felt the tables turned upon them.

"There are ministers in this audience and I will say to them that the maintenance of law and order is dearer to me than life itself.

For twelve long years I represented the Second Congressional District, your neighboring district, in the Federal Congress. It was a great honor and I feel grateful to my countrymen. And oh, how often have I been called upon to defend this great state. How I blushed with shame as men spoke of Kentucky as a 'mob country,' where human life is not safe; where one hundred men may defy the law, invade the temples of justice, and with the wild, unthinking decree of a mob, condemn a prisoner to an awful death.

And how could I defend it?"

Here undoubtedly many a veteran from the Night Rider wars of just a few years back must have felt a warm rush of affection for this man, as they remembered the speaker's strong and gallant stand on behalf of the western Kentucky tobacco farmers in the U.S. Congress. They could not, even near ten years distant, forget that this man before them had been there for them when it counted, working toward the repeal of the onerous tobacco tax which in turn increased consumption, and eventually a restoration of decent prices in the Black Patch. And Stanley, most adeptly and almost imperceptibly had not only reminded them of this, but also wove it into the fabric of their current predicament.

"The bravest men in the world live in Kentucky," Stanley continued.

"You may start at the blue lakes of the Aurora Borealis, where the midnight sun glitters on the mountain of ice, and you may travel on until you stand by the soft, warm limpid waters of the Gulf of Mexico where balmy breezes blow–from the pole to the equator, there's not a battle where Kentuckians have not shed blood, where Kentucky bones do not lie bleaching in the sun, the sand stained with their own life blood."

At that very hour during which he spoke, on that January morning of 1917, the deadly boom of big guns, bloody battles and clashing arms were enveloping Europe, casting a dark ominous cloud upon the American horizon. Before that very year was over, the bloody altar for the sacrifice of American lives, to include those of Kentucky boys, would be enlarged from the western hemisphere Stanley described to the world at large.

But on that morning, in the Calloway County courtroom, these men were most likely thinking of kinsmen lost at Missionary Ridge, Shiloh or Vicksburg.

Stanley then beckoned to the grand and courageous icons of Kentucky history including Henry Clay, former Vice President Richard Johnson, Confederate hero, John Cabell Breckinridge –even the noted sculptor and poet, Joel T. Hart. The governor's reference to this varied crowd of noted and some lesser-known Kentuckians reflected Stanley's broad and exhaustive knowledge of his state's history and culture.

"God in His infinite goodness had made of Kentucky a garden of the Lord, and especially is that true of Calloway County. He has blessed you abundantly. You have bountiful crops, peace and order and law here, while a dreadful, devastating war goes on in Europe. This courthouse is evidence of your culture."

The Greek Revival edifice of brick and stone was–and indeed still is–a stout and impressive structure of dignity and strength. At the time of Stanley's remarks it was less than four years old, having been constructed at a cost of slightly less than $50,000–still a considerable chunk of public money in those times.

"Where is the man who would raise his hand against the sanctity of a judge upon a bench? In some countries the judges are clothed in robes to indicate the very sacredness of their positions."

This passing allusion to judicial dress is rather quaint and typical of rural courtroom decorum of that era. It would be over fifty years before judges would be robed in west Kentucky.

"God forbid that there should be a man in Calloway County who would lay hands upon this man," Stanley nodded toward beleaguered Judge Bush sitting behind him at the elevated bench.

"I cannot believe it," Stanley intoned in a lowered voice, not unlike a lecturing parent responding to the embarrassing misdeeds of a child. Surely among some of his listeners at least, the first faint, dull stirring of shame began to seep into their beings.

The eloquent lawyer, now the state's highest office holder, paced slowly in front of the empty jury box, and the brimming courtroom.

Collecting his thoughts, he went on.

"Last night I sat in the lobby of the Seelbach Hotel in Louisville. There came a long-distance call from Paris, Tennessee. A man named Barrard told me that men here had notified the judge upon the bench that his life would pay the penalty if that Negro was not brought back here for trial."

Here for the first time the issue of race surfaced. Stanley had spoken to this point of grand design and principles of law and justice for all. He had not abased the life of Lube Martin in any appeal to this Southern audience for patronizing sympathy or compassion. In the grand scheme of things, on the wide wind-swept battlefield of morality, color became irrelevant.

"If he had been a federal judge, the penalty for touching him would have been death.

Death!

I said I did not believe it.

There is not a county in Kentucky where there are so many churches, or where there are so many church members. I said, 'You are insane. Crazy! It is a lie!' The intelligence of Calloway County, the law and the culture of that district is too great and noble for such a thing to happen."

One wonders if Stanley began to notice that the mood of these angry men was slowly beginning to change. The red-hot irons, searing with smoke only minutes before, were now fading into a cooling gray.

Pressing on, "I'm glad so many of you are here this morning. Since I arrived here this morning more than 500 good Calloway County men have shook my hand and said they were glad I was here; that they were ready and willing to stand with me in this question.

The relatives of the slain man have said they want to see the law carried out."

This is a significant piece of news reported by Stanley.

Guthrie Diuguid's lawyer brother, George, from Paducah had been the trouble-making fire brand in the mob movement. When reading of the account of that dramatic event, the name of his more accomplished brother Edwin Diuguid, president of the Murray Bank and community stalwart, is conspicuously missing.

One can assume that the more respected banker, Edwin Diuguid, had moved behind the scenes, most likely at the behest of the politically powerful Rainy T. Wells to help corral and diffuse the rage of his brother. It is a reasonable guess that all three may have been present in that early morning gathering at the hotel room of Judge Bush. Calmer nerves and cooler heads had come from somewhere to arrest the mad crusade of the vengeful family. No doubt the astute politician, A.O. Stanley, had utilized his long standing skills of working upon the reason of men behind the scenes, in cloak rooms and hallways and hotel rooms. This is only a guess, albeit one based upon the history of the players and the game.

"If a judge had been torn down from the bench here, and so much as a hair of his head harmed, the newspapers of this country would print such a stigma of wrath upon your good county that you could never escape.

Back there in Paducah this morning I told that sheriff to hold that prisoner in safety. I told him that I would go to Murray, alone, unarmed and unaided. I come not as a soldier, for I have that which is more powerful–I have the dignity and the majesty of the law."

Live a thousand years, give a million speeches, Augustus

Owsley Stanley would never be better than he was at that moment.

The battle now belonged to him. All he had to do now was to drive it home.

"I am the governor of the Commonwealth of Kentucky. I'd rather you would tear me limb from limb now than to live to an age of felicity by my failure to do my duty. I'll see that the laws are enforced and enforced with vigor. I'll protect that Negro from mob violence. And I believe in the death penalty, too. If cold-blooded murder is committed, then the murderer should pay with his life."

Here the courtroom erupted into cheers. He now had them; he had given them the assurance of justice, provided them with an honorable way out of their ignominious impasse, a chance to save face.

Calm and quiet once again, they listened as their governor led them home.

"What is the difference in this community and one that is insecure? Will you let the law avenge the crime, or will you let the man with a bludgeon, battle axe or spear, avenge it? That is the difference between savagery and civilization.

We had civilization, then peace and then law and order.

So, gentlemen, I call upon you as good citizens–am I right or am I wrong–to try me upon the highest tribunal, a place more sacred than this courtroom or the temples that lift their slender spires heavenward.

Men of Calloway County, go back to the good women who love you and look into the gentle faces of your wives and say the governor of Kentucky has said he would preserve the law with respect, even if it cost him his own life."

Once again applause. This time a softer, prolonged, almost reverent approval.

With his mission accomplished, he declared the benediction.

"Now, I appeal to you in the names of your mothers, your wives and children......and the dignity of the Commonwealth of Kentucky and Most High God to assist the governor and this circuit judge in the maintenance of law and order."

A low buzz of normal conversation took place and some of those standing in the fringes and corners eased out the back doors.

Judge Bush arose, and in almost inaudible words announced that the court would go into conference with the lawyers. With that, a pack of lawyers, including prosecutors and defense attorneys, as well as the governor and Rainey T. Wells, retired from the courtroom.

It was over.

Slowly, and with some reluctance, the crowd began to disperse. Some gathered in small groups in the courthouse yard. Others made their way back to their shops, wagons, motor cars. Like air easing slowly out of a huge balloon, the combustible tension of the town began to dissipate into the cold, gray January sky.

To the relief of most, and the suppressed joy of many, the crisis of the past two days was over.

Around 10:30 that morning, Judge Charles Bush and Commonwealth Attorney Denny Smith announced to a sparse gathering in the hotel lobby that the trial of Lube Martin had been set for February 5. This date would be later moved to February 19, when it was discovered that it conflicted with the first day of circuit court in Trigg County.

The winter day warmed up.

Just before 11 a.m., Governor Stanley and a group of men left the Murray House Hotel on foot, heading down Main Street toward the depot. In the group were his friends of the long night train ride, and some local friends and supporters, including Rainey T. Wells.

Also in the club of noteworthy pedestrians were a tired and weary Circuit Judge Charles H. Bush and a much-relieved Commonwealth Attorney Denny Smith.

Storekeepers still waved at the delegation passing their doors, and the ebullient Stanley was still pumping hands and slapping backs.

But the town had been transformed from what it had been

just hours before.

It now went about its midweek business as usual. Farmers loaded feed and new tools onto wagons, mules snorted into the frosty air. Motor cars, sharing streets with horse drawn carriages coughed and cackled their way through the downtown.

No one just arriving in town would have ever known that just a short time before the bustling little country town had been held hostage by a lynch mob.

At the train station, the locomotive had been turned around heading north. The engineer had built up a full head of steam, getting ready for what had been expected to be a hurried getaway. Hissing and spewing, the giant iron beast sat waiting.

On the platform, warm hand shakes were exchanged. Gratitude, no doubt, expressed. One has to believe that by that time some pressing issues, other than the crisis which had brought the governor there were discussed. After all, it wasn't everyday that the governor of the Commonwealth of Kentucky came to town. Rainey T. Wells might have even hit upon the subject of a future college for their little city.

Stanley's tested friends who had made the trip with him boarded the train. Old Judge Bush made his way up the steps and into the coach. He was followed by Smith. Deputy Sheriff Felix Bailey, local attorney Joe Lancaster and State Representative T.R. Jones also boarded for the ride as far as Paducah. Finally, as the train began to make its move, Stanley hopped onto the steps, waved, and disappeared inside.

A shrill scream of the whistle cleared the throat of the awakening beast, and the huge wheels, rods and pistons began to rumble and move. Slowly, the engine and its coach of passengers pulled out of the station. Picking up speed, it threaded the Negro section of town where life went on, seemingly unaffected by the visit of these out of town big shots.

By the time the train whistled its way through the small terminal at Almo, she was hitting her stride.

Northward she flew toward Paducah, fires burning, white

smoke pouring from the stack, sparks flying, kicking up cinders.

Governor Stanley and friends were leaving town, with Circuit Judge Charles Bush and the state's prosecutor, Denny Smith, safely tucked aboard.

CHAPTER 7

ACCOLADES AND ASHES

News of the dramatic events in Murray, Kentucky soon reverberated throughout the nation.

A Southern governor giving lip service against a lynch mob attempting to hang a black man would be news. For one to actually put himself in harm's way to protect an intended victim was big news.

Governor A. O. Stanley of Kentucky became an overnight hero, proclaimed coast to coast for his heroics.

First, from close to home, *The Paducah Sun* seized upon the dramatic rescue with these words:

The Sun has on occasion differed with the governor of Kentucky on many things. It does not share his views on various matters of public interest, and possibly never will. It feels, therefore, that he will know, and so will all others, that in applauding his action of today, as vigorous and courageous, it means everything those words imply. It was a splendid thing, splendidly done, and A.O. Stanley has lived a day to which he may look back with pride in years to come.

Affairs are bad enough as they stand, but it would have

been unbearable had Kentucky suffered again this day under the spur of violence, and had the reported threats of the mob in Murray been carried out against the officials of the court there, no penitential hours in time to come would have served as atonement for the crime.

Paducah has not the right to sit in judgment on Murray, and The Sun does not presume to that office, but merely wishes to congratulate the people of Murray, to whom it is applicable from the bottom of its heart, that they were willing and able to see the grievous wrong in the going that some had counseled, and ready to withdraw from a morally untenable position.

To Governor Stanley is due the highest praise that can be accorded a courageous man. He has done more than his duty with the deliberate invitation to danger, when it would have been infinitely easier to avoid it as others have done under the circumstances.

It is altogether probable that the good people of Murray would have eventually suppressed any attempts to do violence to Judge Bush or Mr. Smith, but the necessity for his interference was a fact in Governor Stanley's eyes, and whether a final analysis would have proven him wrong or not, he is entitled to the utmost credit for possessing the courage of his convictions and undertaking an unpleasant task in a manly way.

The prestigious Louisville *Courier Journal* which was hardly ever in Governor Stanley's corner, and which only hours before had issued a scathing indictment of him for paroling the Jackson County murderer, Tom White, was quick to applaud Stanley's brave stand.

Perhaps most significantly, the governor's instant fame exploded upon the editorial pages of the large city newspapers of the north, even if they got some of the details a little skewed.

Stated *The New York Times*:

Governor Stanley of Kentucky, who took a special train Wednesday from the state capital to the town where a mob thirsted to lynch a Negro accused of killing a white man, and threatened to lynch the judge and prosecuting attorney in the case because the trial of the Negro was postponed, did a good day's work for the reputation of his state. He at once appointed seventy-five deputies. He told the mob that he was going to protect the law and the court with his own body, if necessary.

Kentuckians admire courage. The hotheads who had vapored that they would kill the governor if he resisted their tumultuous motions against a continuance cooled down. The Negro is safe in jail in another town.

Doubtless he will be protected against violence at his trial in a less excited community. Apparently the judge and district attorney are to be permitted to live. The governor has maintained the law, even if most of the Kentucky guardsmen were on the Mexican border."

The writer for the Boston newspaper showed special awareness and insight into the cultural and historical setting of the drama, including the writing of Paducah writer Irvin S. Cobb, when he wrote:

Probably nowhere in the country is the appeal of personality so strong as in the South. Human nature is elemental, hearts are warm, and men are swayed more by their emotions than by their reason than is the case in our Northern states where oratory for the good old picturesque flowery kind that prevailed in Civil War times has gone out of style. It hasn't gone out of style in Dixie where the people are tremendously moved by the theatrical.

This is why Governor Stanley, a type of Kentuckian that we in New England rarely see, held back the mob and prevented a lynching. It would be difficult to picture a governor of Massachusetts, in frock coat and silk hat, going into the crowded courtroom and telling a frantic mob from the judge's bench that if they were bent on lynching somebody they could start on him first.

He would stop the lynching, but he would probably find some other way to do it. Probably no other way would have been effective in Kentucky. It was Stanley's drama that caught the crowd, and won them over, and saved the state from the disgrace of a flagrant disregard of the law and courts.

The meager newspaper reports do not give us the speech that Governor Stanley made to the hostile crowd in the courthouse. More's the pity, for we suspect that it was a gem.

It was as dramatic as anything a Southern governor had done in years and set a splendid example for those states where lawlessness too often was permitted to have its way and the militia commonly arrives in time to cut down the body from the bridge...

Governor Stanley's prompt and courageous handling of a difficult situation may yet put him in the United States Senate.

The Pittsburgh Courier and other northern papers followed suit.

From "Bloody Kansas," a state which had in the past endured its own time of racial discord and violence, came these words from Governor Arthur Capper to his Kentucky counterpart:

Let me send you my warm personal commendation and hearty congratulations upon your fine and courageous action in the face of the threatened mob at Murray. The people of your state, indeed, the people of all the states should, and I am sure will, applaud the fine service you have rendered in the name of justice and higher citizenship.

From the pastor of the Bushwick Avenue Congregational Church way up in Brooklyn, "We need presidents like you, and I hope to have privilege of voting for you someday."

On and on came the rising applause of public acclaim. Hundreds of letters and telegrams poured into the capital congratulating and praising Governor Stanley.

Even in Kentucky, ordinary citizens and public officials rallied to their chief executive's side.

The circuit clerk in Springfield, Kentucky boldly announced, "If you need 100,000 unarmed Kentuckians to go with you to Murray to insure this Negro a fair trial, call upon me and Washington County will furnish her full quota."

From Rev. John H. Riley, pastor of the Church of the Annunciation in his boyhood home of Shelbyville, came these grand plaudits:

I have just read your appeal to the people of Murray against mob law and in behalf of justice, and must say it enunciates with dignity, clearness and force of majesty of the law, both of God and man.

It is nothing short of a classic and I dare say it will be read with much profit by thousands and show forth in unmistakable language the true worth of Kentucky's sterling governor. You are in a position to use the gifts God gave you with telling effect against the humbuggery, charlatanry and what-not of the present day, and I hope and pray you will not be slow to grasp the opportunity.

Stanley seemed to take the avalanche of public praise in stride. "All these communications came as a surprise," he commented, "Naturally I didn't take time to think how my course would be looked at from the outside. There wasn't anything else to be done, so far as I could see."

No doubt the most heartening commendation for Governor Stanley came from Murray, from those who were on the ground and saw first hand the feats of their governor.

Calloway County Circuit Court Clerk L.C. Trevathan wrote to the governor:

In the stir and bustle you got away from Murray before I had an opportunity to tell you how much I appreciated your coming here, the effort you put forth and your success in quelling the disturbance. But I want you to know I do appreciate it and regard it as an act of providence.

Murray barrister Joe Lancaster, friend and ally of A.O. Stanley, had shown his own loyalty and support by boarding the train with the governor on that historic getaway and riding with him to Paducah. He most likely spoke for the vast majority of Calloway countians when he followed up his bold stance with this written message to the governor:

People in Murray and Calloway County today have been loud in their praises of your action here, and every person of influence has expressed himself as believing that you were the right man at the right time. It seems that your visit here was almost a visit of holy powers, from the influence you had over a frenzied crowd.

When all was said and done, after the captains and kings had departed, Stanley must have realized once again–he had been among friends.

When Governor Stanley met the awaiting crowd at the Paducah train station on his victorious journey back from Murray around noon on January 11, he gleefully assured them that "Everything's lovely."

It may have been "lovely" for Governor Stanley. But the unfolding events of those past few hours would not conclude that favorably for the Circuit Judge Charles Bush. If A. O. Stanley received nothing but accolades for his effort, poor old Judge Bush was showered with ashes.

The leading newspapers of the country were merciless in their attacks upon the embattled jurist, perceiving him to have weakly given in to the mob to save his own skin.

No newspaper was more scathing in their attack than Kentucky's leading publication, The *Courier Journal*. Under the headlines "The State's Cap Sheaf of Shame" its editorialist expounded at length and with venom:

A Negro charged with murder is brought to Murray for trial, having been imprisoned elsewhere for fear of violence. A lawyer is appointed to defend him and after consultation asks for time to prepare his case. This reasonable request is granted by the judge, who names a future date for the trial and orders that the prisoner be sent to Paducah for safekeeping. He is hurried away and the hangers-on gather around the judge on the bench and demand that the Negro be immediately returned to Murray. 'I issued an order for the return of the Negro to Murray', confesses the judge. 'I was compelled to do so to save my own life, the mob having threatened to blow me up with a bomb if I did not comply with its request.'

When asked whether he did not think it would be unsafe for the Negro at Murray, the judge replied: 'It would have been unsafe for me if I had refused to issue the order for his return.' The governor, as soon as he hears of it, countermanding the judge's order for the return of the prisoner to Murray, hastens to that place, which he reaches the next morning: In the courthouse he faces the people–the mob–he finds there, appealing, demanding that the law be allowed to take its course; then going over to a hotel where the judge is temporarily retiring and securing from him still another order setting the trial for the Negro the first week in February, he leaves the town, accompanied by the judge.

Has the case a parallel? All extremes of crimes have been perpetrated by American mobs, but where has there been another judge who this openly, avowedly took orders from the mob and turned his court over to the lawbreakers as an instrument for outraging the law instead of upholding it?

The name of Circuit Judge C.H. Bush today is a byword in all the land wherever an American newspaper penetrates; the name of a Kentuckian who, confessing that he knew his duty, yet confesses that he refused to do it because he was afraid to do it; confesses that being the only man who, because of his office, could perform that duty, used his office not as it was intended for the maintenance of law and order, but as an instrument to serve the ends of those who spat upon law and order.

Could the contrast between the course of the governor in this emergency and that of the circuit judge be more impressive? Judge Bush must today look upon Governor Stanley's decision and action in the case with envious admiration rendered all the more acute because he must realize that but for his own infirmity he could have won even greater admiration for himself instead of the pity–and worse–now universally linked with his name.

Assuming he is a man of intelligence; the Courier Journal does not deem it necessary to tell him in just what light the people of Kentucky look upon his conduct. The most charitable attitude toward him for the present is to take it for granted that having discovered his weakness which unfits him for the performance of the office he holds, he will have the manliness to resign the office he holds without having to be removed from it by process of law. He knows as well as others know, that there are certain qualities essential in the man who would perform the duties of a peace officer–that even the humblest constable or policeman must be willing at any time to risk his life in the perform-ance of those duties–and he knows that there is no higher peace officer than the man who sits on the bench. Will he have greater courage now to quit his office than he had to fill it?

Other papers across the country jumped all over Judge Bush. From way upriver on the same Tennessee River which slid through Calloway County, *The Chattanooga Times* sounded this blast:

Are judges and officers of the court afraid of the mob, and does that fact account for the frequency of lynchings and the failure of courts to punish lynchers? This question gains force from an incident that has just occurred in Kentucky. It seems that a Negro was arrested at Murray, the county seat of Calloway County, on a charge of murder. The judge, Bush by name, appointed an attorney to defend the accused, as the law provides. After a conference with his client the attorney asked for a postponement until he could summons witnesses and prepare his case, which the court granted. Then the trouble began. The fiery citi-zenry, thirsting for Negro gore, appeared to have risen in its wrath. A mob was formed and rushed to the courtroom, as soon as the dastard-ly face became known that the Negro was to get justice according to the law, and the judge was told that unless he proceeded with the trial he and the attorney general stood a good chance of being themselves lynched. And right then was given the suggestion that, perhaps, after all, judges on the bench and officers of the law are in large measure accountable for the prevalence of the mob spirit.

Instead of ordering the sheriff or his deputies to arrest the leaders of the mob and calling on all law abiding people of the town to support him, Judge Bush, in cowardly fear of his own life, rescinded his ruling for a postponement and ordered the Negro back for immediate trial!

This Tennessee newspaper writer must have had a double dose of gall for breakfast the morning he wrote this. For just ten years previously the picturesque Lookout Mountain city of Chattanooga had been shamed by the racial perfidy of its own public officials, making the Murray incident look like a high school prom. On a March evening in 1906, after a black man named Ed Johnson had been convicted of rape of a white woman in a trial which by all accounts was a travesty, he was dragged out of his jail cell, hanged and shot. This was done with the tacit approval of the sheriff and other law enforcement officials, and in violation of a stay of execution which had been entered by the U.S. Supreme Court. For the one and only time in the history of the United States, an enraged U.S. Supreme Court tried and convicted the local sheriff, his deputies, and members of the lynch mob for contempt. Several of them were sent to prison for their deadly misfeasance, casting a dark shadow across this lovely Southern city.

Judge Charles H. Bush staggered under the blows to his character.

It was most unfortunate that this elderly public servant who had served his profession so well up until the Murray standoff would, in this late stage of his career, have to fight to salvage his own reputation.

The editorial by *The Courier Journal* was particularly stinging because it was the leading newspaper in the state, still widely read even in the far reaches of west Kentucky.

Judge Bush recovered physically and emotionally from his

ordeal at Murray and began to fight back.

He rallied the local bar in Hopkinsville, including Denny Smith, to come to his defense.

The Hopkinsville New Era ran a front page story on January 19 in defense of Bush:

> *At a meeting of the Hopkinsville Bar Association which was held Monday afternoon, strong resolutions were adopted denouncing all adverse newspaper criticism which has been made of Judge Bush since the excitement at Murray last week and commending him for his bravery at that time.*

The story went on to recite the long resolution wherein the lawyers reaffirmed their confidence in Judge Bush, asserted that contrary to the reports of most of the newspapers, the judge actually resisted the mob and placed his life on the line in doing so.

Two days later, *The Louisville Herald*, a bitter rival of *The Courier Journal*, printed a long statement from Commonwealth Attorney Denny P. Smith which placed "the judge in a much more favorable light before the public, and belies the alleged interview with the judge published in a Louisville newspaper."

Continued that article: "Prosecutor Smith vigorously defends the court officials and asserts that both he and Judge Bush would have sacrificed their own lives before they would have permitted the mob to have lynched the Negro prisoner."

Even in Murray, a group of citizens, including defense attorney Pat Holt, lawyer Joe Lancaster, and the local stalwart, Rainey T. Wells, went on the offensive for Judge Bush against the news coverage of his role in the affair. Said in part the petition:

> *We, the undersigned citizens of Murray, Ky. do hereby denounce and brand as false, malicious and cruel the attack made on Circuit Judge Charles H. Bush in the editorial which appeared in the Louisville Courier Journal of January 13, 1917.*
>
> *We know that Judge Bush did not order the return of the pris-*

*oner Lube Martin to save his own life, or on account of personal vio-
lence to himself, or even death. We know that he did not order the prisoner returned, in obedience to the demand of the mob."*

The group went on to make the case for the besmirched
jurist. The petition also provides some insight into what pressures
were being brought to bear upon Bush before Governor Stanley
arrived to save the day. According to the delegation of mostly
lawyers and court officials, Bush did resist the demands of the mob.
    For awhile.
    Then he was approached by what appeared to be a commit-
tee of "good guys" offering him a way out with his life and his
honor.

*.....finally a committee speaking for the family of the dead
man, including all of his brothers, one of the spokesmen being George
Diuguid, again appealed to the judge to save bloodshed and human life
and order Martin back, and that if he would do that and let the proper orders be made in open court in the prisoner's presence, they would
guarantee absolute protection to Martin, and that George Diuguid
and the other brothers and friends would help protect him and march
to the train with him. It was only after all this that Judge Bush agreed
to the order, and he said that if his own life was involved, he would not
agree to it under any circumstances and would die first.*

The local *Murray Ledger and Times*, through the bold and
sometimes brash pen of its editor, O. J. Jennings, rushed to not
only defend Bush, but to downplay the heroics of Governor
Stanley, claiming there was never an "armed mob" or "a thousand
or more men."
    It was a weak and rambling attempt by Murray's loudest
cheerleader to rationalize and redeem not only Judge Bush's behavior, but also the besmirched view of his community in the nation's
eye.
    Lastly, Judge Bush turned to the main man of the day him-

self to help resurrect his sagging public image. He appealed to Governor Stanley to step in and defend the media assault upon him.

In a four-page letter dated January 24, a rather frustrated and irritated governor responds to Bush's plea. It is obvious that Stanley, who appointed his friend Bush to the bench just the previous summer, is pained by the jurist's current predicament. But, he finds very little in the action of Bush on that fateful January 11 which he can either defend or explain.

Stanley recites for history his recollection of the events leading up to his trip to Murray and what he found when he arrived at the hotel room of the beleaguered judge and commonwealth attorney. His written account is given more credence by Stanley's reference to having it confirmed by his traveling companions on that trip, Commissioner Henry Hines, State Fire Marshall Tom Pannell and Dr. Fred LaRue.

In an empathizing tone the governor assured Bush:

I have said time and time again to those who were inclined to judge harshly, that they must remember that for many hours you refused to obey the demands of these people, and that you acceded only upon the advice of others in whose judgment you had implicit confidence. I can not say, of course, that I think you were well advised, approving an order I instantly countermanded—a proposition too ridiculous for serious consideration.

.......I made the trip to Murray because I could not consent to having the Negro returned to what I believed then and believe now would have been his certain death. Realizing that by this refusal, I exposed you to imminent peril—the direct result of my action—it was my plain duty to share your danger and to exert myself to the utmost to protect you, to do anything except surrender to the demands of a bloodthirsty mob. This I would not have, to have saved your life or to have saved my own.

From the letter it is clear that Stanley could offer his old friend little help or consolation. Perhaps painfully, he concluded:

> *I regret that I can not unqualifiedly approve of all you did at Murray. I should more regret to be forced to publicly express condemnation of any act or deed of my appointee. It has been my pleasure to bestow signal honors upon you. My personal regard has been demonstrated by a more supreme and crucial test. I can not however, and I will not, stultify myself to save you from censure or humiliation.*

Then, as late as March, one last volley was fired in the defense of Charles Bush's honor. This time it was by the Christian County grand jury which on March 13 took the most unusual step indicting both *The Courier Journal* and reporter Claude W. Perry for "criminal libel" against their own favorite judge. Also, included in its report was a ringing endorsement whereby they expressed their "fullest confidence in Judge Bush and their firm belief upon that occasion he conducted himself as a fearless, upright and honorable judge and that any reports to the contrary were false, malicious and libelous."

Of course facts are powerful things. And all the scathing newspaper accounts aside, there was one irrefutable truth conveniently forgotten by the Bush supporters. He had directed that Lube Martin be taken to Hopkinsville for safe keeping from the mob. And Charles H. Bush had changed his mind and ordered him returned to Murray.

In the long view of history, the heroics of A.O. Stanley remain undiminished.

But our perspective on the actions of Judge Bush are somewhat altered. He deserves better treatment than was given to him by the far-away journalists of his day.

True enough, as Stanley points out in his letter, the old judge did not act wisely, or courageously.

In short, he was duped–duped by that small cadre of friends who came to him in sheep's clothing.

The chameleonic George Diuguid was the big bad old wolf wearing grandma's cap and gown. Well-intended and principled Charles Bush had held up against the mob for awhile. But after being physically pushed around in the courthouse yard, threatened and buttressed about by the rising tide of anarchy, Bush broke, both physically and emotionally. He could not have been in his right mind to give in to the preposterous terms proposed for the bringing of Lube Martin back to Murray. If he had been, he would have seen if for what it was.

A ruse.

It should have been evident with George Diuguid himself bearing the white flag of truce. And to have him to assure safe passport of the prisoner would be like the fox assuring the chicken safe passage through the darken woods.

And for what? What kind of orderly and sensible proceedings of due process could have possibly been carried on in the Calloway County Courthouse in the midst of such a cauldron of public chaos and rancor?

It is hard to believe that the respectable Rainey Wells signed on to such a proposal. Most likely, he protested in vain.

It was ridiculous.

But in Bush's enfeebled mind, and under the frightful and paralyzing terror of the time, he most likely believed that it was the proper way out. He ostensibly acquiesced to "avoid bloodshed." But whose life and limb was primarily in jeopardy but his own?

Commonwealth Attorney Denny Smith must shoulder some of the blame for the debacle. He was much younger than the aging judge, physically stronger and presumably with much more vim and vitality. As commonwealth attorney, he was not only charged with the responsibility of prosecuting felony cases, but had the much more arduous responsibility to see that justice was done.

Kentucky's highest court has eloquently defined this duty:

One of the finest offices the public can give to a member of the legal profession in this state is that of commonwealth's attorney. Its very

141

status becomes a mantle of power and respect to the wearer. Though few are apt to wear it lightly, some forget, or apparently never learn, to wear it humbly. No one except for the judge himself is under a stricter obligation to see that every defendant receives a fair trial, a trial in accordance with the law, which means the law as laid down by the duly constituted authorities, and not as the prosecuting attorney may think it ought to be.

Smith admirably recognized this role when he agreed to the continuance the night before the mob scene. But it is doubtful that Judge Bush would have given in to the outlandish proposal of George Diuguid and company had his commonwealth attorney objected. And objected he should have, strenuously. The older judge's lapse of good judgment under the strain, while not condoned, is understandable to a degree. But the judge's role is to be neutral. It's the commonwealth attorney's duty to be an advocate for the people of the community in accordance to law, justice, and those things which are right and decent. Although popularly elected, he is not to be a pawn of a lynch mob. And that, from all indications, is exactly what Smith was when the chips were down.

It should have been him—cloaked in the mantle of law and order—making the speech to the mob instead of Stanley.

But, "feet for men, wings for angels." Alas, he, like Bush and perhaps others, lacked the intellectual strength, moral fiber, and personality to resist the temper of the fractious citizens.

Two good men who, in this critical crisis of their careers, faltered.

When the dust had settled, Governor Stanley had returned to his duties in Frankfort, primarily preparing for the special session of the legislature.

Judge Charles Bush and Denny Smith were safely back in Hopkinsville.

Murray had returned to normal, the people going about their business as usual.

Fixed upon the calendar was February 19, 1917 when the

Commonwealth of Kentucky would prosecute Lube Martin for the murder of Guthrie Diuguid.

CHAPTER 8

OPENING SKIRMISH

Between January 11 and February 19 the world turned 39 times.

The war in Europe became bloodier, especially in the Verdun region of France. German submarines escalated their deadly onslaught upon the open seas.

The United States moved ever closer to entering the affray by severing diplomatic relations with Germany.

Mexico announced the signing of a new constitution.

Closer to home, Admiral George Dewey, the famed "hero of Manila" in the Spanish American War died at age 79.

In sports the legendary major league pitcher Grover Alexander was wrangling over his contract with the Philadelphia Phillies, demanding $15,000 for the upcoming season–an $8,000 raise from the year before.

Out of Durham, North Carolina came an announcement which would affect western Kentucky. Confederate General Julian S. Carr, millionaire manufacturer, George W. Lifflefield of Austin, Texas and Bennett

H. Young of Louisville, outlined plans for the erection of a $150,000 memorial to Jefferson Davis. The planned obelisk would be 350 feet high and built at Fairview, Kentucky, the birthplace of the president of the Confederate states, and only a few miles east of Hopkinsville.

Renowned west Kentucky writer and humorist Irvin S. Cobb of Paducah, paid a visit to Eddyville, Kentucky and the home of his ancestors.

People in Paducah were excited about the growing prospects of landing a government armor plate plant there. Also their county fiscal court was asked to expend sufficient funds for the construction of a bridge across Clarks River north of the city, to connect the new road built in Livingston County to Paducah.

Pursuant to the call of Governor Stanley, a special session of the Kentucky General Assembly opened in Frankfort for the sole purpose of considering tax reform.

Tobacco prices, after an exciting start, had dropped to a more normal range of between 9 to 10 1/2 cents per pound.

Significantly, and at the behest of Governor Stanley, three Kentucky infantry companies were designated to return from the Mexican border. On January 25, the National Guard units passed through Paducah on their way home from El Paso.

The governor was no doubt thinking of the upcoming Lube Martin trial when he made the request.

Winter weather in west Kentucky was typically unpredictable. There is a saying in this region of the country, "If you don't like the weather, wait till tomorrow. It will change."

As it is today, so it was in 1917. Temperatures ranged all the way from zero to seventy during this period of time. An extreme cold spell hit the entire South and blanketed west Kentucky with 8 inches of snow on January 15. It didn't last, however, as balmy temperatures soon returned, hovering in the fifties and sixties, peaking out as high as over seventy.

But on February 2 the mercury took another nose dive, down to almost zero–a 72 degree drop in less than 48 hours.

It is not certain as to what Circuit Judge Charles Bush and Commonwealth Attorney Denny Smith were doing during this time. Most likely their thoughts and pursuits followed along three different channels.

First, they undoubtedly were giving a great deal of reflection upon the upcoming trial of Lube Martin, and the serious security problems which they would likely encounter.

Second was contemplation as to what should be done about the anarchists who had led the uprising in Murray which had held them hostage and placed both their lives and the integrity of the judicial system in jeopardy.

And lastly, the demanding docket of the other three counties of the 3rd Judicial District of Kentucky.

Servicing the circuit court needs of four rural counties was not an easy task, especially in that day of bad roads, and slow and sometimes unreliable means of transportation. The unpredictable nature of winter weather in west Kentucky also added another hardship of getting about and holding court in this wide area of real estate, split down the middle by two major rivers prone to flooding.

There were other cases to be tried, the plight of other litigants to be resolved, other people waiting in Christian, Lyon and Trigg counties for their circuit court.

The O.J. Simpson trial would have been shortened considerably if Judge Ito would have had to be in Eddyville on Monday.

Although it is not certain, undoubtedly Judge Bush and Kentucky's governor conferred at some time on the upcoming trial in Murray.

For on February 13, Stanley announced that Company D of the National Guard out of Hopkinsville and Company A out of Louisville would be deployed to the Calloway County capital for the Lube Martin trial.

"I'm not taking any chances," Stanley stated. It was also apparent that Judge Bush would be riding the train with them.

No doubt this was comforting news to Bush, as well as most Calloway Countians.

It was not particularly good news to all, however.

Forty-three-year-old O.J. Jennings was the editor and publisher of the *Murray Ledger*.

Energetic, capable, and devoted to his community, Jennings would be at the helm of this lively little paper for 28 years, until at his death, in 1944, he passed it off to his son Kirby.

Fiercely proud of Murray and Calloway County, he was very sensitive to the image the rest of the world held of his hometown.

The Night Riders had, in his opinion, been an embarrassment to all of Kentucky, expanding upon the reputation of violence and lawlessness the state already had.

But most importantly he had resented the state militia which beat the Night Riders to town, and kept them from causing havoc in Murray. They outstayed their welcome. Garrison duty for these young bucks proved to be tedious and uneventful. So, like all young single men away from home, they began looking for ways to entertain themselves, including the local damsels. They were not a serious problem, but more like relatives who had stayed past their welcome.

But the notion of his town being occupied by troops was irritating to Jennings to say the least. It may have been a slight hangover from the days of the Civil War. If the troops came for the trial, it would give Murray the dubious distinction of being the only Kentucky town occupied by "foreign troops" for the third time.

If there was one thing Jennings did not savor, it was his beloved Murray once again becoming an armed camp of occupation forces.

On February 2, 1917, O.J. Jennings petitioned Judge Bush to request Governor Stanley to rescind his decision to send the troops to Murray for the Lube Martin trial. He even brought Sheriff Patterson into the picture by inferring it was, in fact, the chief county lawman's belief that he and his deputies were sufficient to maintain order.

Said Jennings in his letter to Judge Bush:

"I am confident that troops are not needed. Murray has had much undesirable notoriety for the past several weeks and we feel keenly the humiliation, and to order state troops here for the special term of court will again offer excuse for slanderers and libelers to pour forth their vituperation upon this community."

Judge Bush would have none of it. He had stared into the green eyes of the monster. He wanted no more of it.

In a gingerly-worded response to the irresponsible Jennings request, the jurist stated in part, "You say that Calloway County has had enough unpleasant notoriety. In this you're eminently correct, and therefore it is my judgment that such apparently necessary precautionary measure should be adopted as will prevent a recurrence of such conditions as existed on the 10th of last month."

So on a warm and pleasant Sunday, February 18, for the third time in sixty years, occupation forces began to arrive in Murray. On the late afternoon train they whistled their way into town, disembarking at the depot in full combat gear. Two highly-disciplined and war-tested companies from Hopkinsville and Louisville smartly made formations and, to the barking cadence of platoon sergeants, began to make their impressive way through the streets. The nice, almost spring like, weather brought out the curious citizens of the town who were no doubt in awe of this impressive gathering of doughboys. And, unquestionably, though the welcome was not particularly rousing, the law-abiding majority felt reassured and comforted with their arrival.

In a recent serialized version of the dramatic Lube Martin story in *Montage* magazine, writer Chuck Shuffett describes the rather relaxed presence in Murray of the National Guard during their second visit in eight years:

The smartly uniformed young men were warmly welcomed as they mingled in the community. The young ladies of the town were conspicuous among the admirers, scandalously, according to some of the more pious. One newspaper reporter, explaining the fact that the guardsmen appeared so well groomed at all times had this assessment, 'There's a reason for the spruce, candified appearance of the troops here. And that reason is Murray's bevy of beautiful and charming girls. The soldiers are not missing any opportunities, either, to meet the young ladies.'

Guard duty in Murray was a pleasant affair compared to being on the border. Company D went to the border with 52 men and all returned to Hopkinsville. It was the only company in 40,000 troops not to have a man drop from the ranks on a 200 mile hike they had just completed.

On the border the young soldiers were charged 20 cents for egg sandwiches. The same treat was available in Murray for a nickel.

And they brought with them important people–the defendants.

Lube Martin, and his co-defendants, brothers Sylvester and Ann, as well as Ed Jordon, were being brought into Murray from the Hopkinsville jail. Deputy Sheriff William Langston, along with a bevy of troops, marched them to the jail on Third Street just a short walk from the courthouse. There they were locked up and four soldiers were posted to guard them.

The rest of the Guard marched along Walnut Street to the armory where they "fell out" to set up camp.

Though he intended to be on the same transport with the National Guard, Judge Charles H. Bush arrived on the 7:20 train from his home in Hopkinsville. Unescorted, and unnoticed, he made his way to the Murray House Hotel. His arrival had attracted little attention and he settled in at the same hotel in which he had been held hostage just a few weeks before.

All was quiet in the county seat. But as if fate wished to make sure that all would remain that way, the town's electric plant went on the blink and a blanket of darkness covered the city.

At 11 p.m., the last calming touch was placed upon the town with the melancholy playing of taps by a National Guard bugler.

Bank of Murray at Fourth and Main, circa 1917-1920 T-Model.
Photo compliments of John E. Scott and Sid Easley

The town came alive with a buzz the next morning. It was a full courtroom at 9 a.m. on Monday, February 19, when Judge Bush called the special term to order and announced the case of the Commonwealth of Kentucky vs. Lube Martin, Sylvester, Ann Martin and Ed Jordon. Soldiers were stationed in the court-room, and roamed the hallways of the courthouse.

The mood of the crowd was one of great interest but little emotion.

Judge Bush had ordered that everyone who entered must be searched, a directive certain to guarantee a late start as the process no doubt took time, creating a line down the narrow steps leading up to the courtroom.

Members of the National Guard were also conspicuously scattered throughout the courtroom.

Old jail at Fourth and Walnut Streets where Lube Martin was held during the trial.   *Photo compliments John E. Scott and Sid Easley*

There was no excitement shown even when the prisoners were ordered from the jail to the courtroom.

To no one's surprise it was ordered that the indictment of Lube Martin for murder would be tried first. The others were ushered back to jail.

Local attorney A.D. Thompson was assigned to assist Pat Holt in Martin's defense.

Reported the newspaper the next day:

...Judge Bush then made a statement in which he said he would insist upon a legal and orderly trial and asked that when the seating capacity of the courtroom was exhausted that the doors be locked. He accorded the newspaper men the privilege of seats inside the bar, but voiced his disapproval of any unpleasant notoriety.

151

Site of the old jail as it is today.

Many people were surprised to find Judge Charles Bush on the bench that winter morning.

It had been assumed that because of his harrowing experience the previous month and all of the publicity surrounding his being held hostage by the mob, he would recuse himself from hearing the case. In fact, newspapers had even conjectured as much.

Neither is there any evidence whatsoever that the defense lawyers requested him to step down.

It is reasonable to speculate that Charles Bush did not give way on the case to another judge because he was seeking vindication and redemption of a sort for the shellacking he had received from the national media over his role in the lynch mob events in January. Most likely he wanted to stay in the ball game, come back to Murray and face up to the local crowd once again, if for no other reason than to prove that he had not been intimidated into placing the black defendant's life in jeopardy.

Steeped within this reasoning may have been the same motivation for the defense lawyers not challenging Bush off the case. Lawyer Pat Holt and his associate A. D. Thompson may have perceived Bush's beating at the hands of the press as reason for him to now bend over backwards to give their client a fair trial. Plus they knew Judge Bush, practiced before him regularly. Better the known and familiar, than the unknown–perhaps assigned from some other part of the state.

All of this teems with sound logic.

What the packed courtroom of waiting jurors and spectators watched that morning, were lawyers wrangling and the judge scratching his head.

Once again, attorney Pat Holt pleaded for another continuance. He filed affidavits with the court of what he believed four missing witnesses would say on behalf of the defense.

Holt had done his work well. Four witnesses–Andy Chance, Burt Hardin, Avey Rose Williamson, and Lube's brother Clarence–had all been duly subpoenaed by Sheriff Will Patterson.

According to the affidavit signed by the defendant with his mark and entered of record, their testimony would be critical.

Clarence Martin would testify that during the county fair in Murray the previous October he had run into the victim Guthrie Diuguid. Diuguid had told Martin to inform his brother that he would kill him when he "laid eyes on him." Clarence communicated this to Lube, who was still hiding out most of the time in Tennessee.

The expected testimony of Neal Williams was even more powerful. It was believed that Williams would tell about a meeting he had seen the previous September on the streets of Murray between Diuguid and Lube Martin. At that encounter, Diuguid, who was then the deputy town marshal, had pulled his pistol on Martin and threatened him. "Come on with me to the council," he said, "and change that affidavit you made, you damn black son of a bitch. Or I will shoot the top of your head off. I've been looking for you all the year and you damn son of a bitch, you have been dodging."

It was not reported in the writing what transpired after that.

If present at trial, the affidavit went on, Avey Rose would

153

tell of seeing Diuguid in the black section of town near Lube's home on a night that past September. He looked for Lube and asked her if she had seen Martin. The lawman was armed with a long gun–either a rifle or shotgun.

It was not recorded what Burt Hardin would say.

Holt must have known that the last thing that Judge Bush was going to grant him on that morning with a courtroom of Calloway Countians staring at him was another continuance. Not even with the National Guard there to protect him. Not for all the armed troops in the world or for all the tea in China.

Here Commonwealth Attorney Denny Smith finally stepped to the plate and took the judge off the spot. As part of his tactic, Smith agreed to the reading of the affidavit to the jury in lieu of a continuance. The reading to the jury of what a defendant says certain witnesses would say, if present and testified, normally carries little weight with the jury.

The alternatives were not attractive. Most certainly Judge Bush would in his "sound discretion" deny the request for a continuance, perhaps planting a seed for reversal on appeal. And, if for some incredible quirk of fate, Bush granted the continuance, their lives would undoubtedly be once again placed in jeopardy. Besides, in such a scenario if they survived, and the attendance of the witnesses secured, their "live" testimony might be devastating.

Smith wisely conceded to the reading of the affidavits. The continuance issue quickly went away.

Not before, however, Judge Bush ordered the "attachment" or arrest of the missing witnesses for not complying with their subpoenas.

Lube Martin, faced with the reality of going to trial for his life, was not faring very well. He was suffering from what was called "nervous hysteria" and appeared weak and frightened out of his wits. After hearing that there would be no continuance, and the trial would go forward, he fainted.

A recess was called, and local physician Dr. Ben Keys was summoned to the courtroom. Martin soon revived, and apparently with new ardor, took up the challenge of standing trial for his life.

Needless to say, the morning was moving along at a rocky pace.

Surprisingly, although there was a large crowd packing the courtroom, the gathering was low-keyed, the humor of it "good to the extreme" as one newspaper writer reported it.

It was in the presence of this attentive, but orderly audience that the proceedings continued after the break for Martin's recovery.

Judge Bush then broached a matter with the lawyers that was of monumental importance, but seemed to have caused neither surprise nor controversy.

He announced that he did not believe an unbiased jury could be secured from Calloway County. Lawyer George Diuguid, brother of the victim who was assisting the commonwealth attorney, parted ways with the prosecutor and objected to Bush's decision. The fractious lawyer argued that at least an attempt should be made to seat a Calloway County jury.

But Bush stuck to his guns.

As if to reassure the throng which was hovering over his every word, Bush stated that the case would remain in Murray, but that he would send to an adjoining county for fresh jury venire.

Charles H. Bush almost got it right. There on that sunny winter morning, at the crossroads of a black man's life, the state's most critical gate keeper of justice came close.

But not close enough.

Standing in the vortex of swirling currents of public sentiment, passions and prejudices, the circuit judge of the 3rd Judicial District boldly took a step for equal justice under the law. He would place the life of Lube Martin in the hands of a jury not chosen from the venue in which his fate had already been decided. But the tired old jurist was not up to the task of moving the venue of the case itself.

There under the protection of armed soldiers, and fresh off re-election to a spanking new six year term, it would have been a relatively small matter to announce to the softening crowd that he was moving the trial of the matter to another county.

But he didn't.

Of course there were at that time, as there is today, appropriate times to cart a jury in from outside. The criminal rules state:

> *If the judge of the court is satisfied......that it will be impracticable to obtain a jury free of bias in the county wherein the prosecution is pending, he shall be authorized to order the sheriff to summon a sufficient number of qualified jurors from some adjoining county in which the judge shall believe there is the greatest probability of obtaining impartial jurors.*

The bringing in of jurors from another county avoids shifting the entire logistical burden and expense of administering the trial to another county. But such a procedure is usually reserved to situations where an impartial jury cannot be obtained because of the popularity or notoriety of one of the parties; or in some instances, where pretrial publicity has been so evasive, but not necessarily inflammatory, to make it improbable of obtaining an untainted jury. A sensational trial with high visibility of one of the public officials would be such a case. The prospective venire may be already opinionated, but not hostile.

Undoubtedly, a total change of venue, to include the location of the trial site would have been the right choice by Judge Bush in regard to the Lube Martin case.

The law provides that:

> *...whenever any circuit judge is satisfied from his own knowledge.....that such a state of lawlessness exists in the county of his judicial circuit or that such a high state of excitement or feeling of prejudice exists therein against the defendant that there is apparent danger of mob violence in which loss off life or destruction of property may occur unlawfully, and that a trial in the county cannot be fairly and impartially had, or that the officers of the court may be prevented from*

discharging their duties or the jurors intimidated or deterred from fairly and impartially rendering a verdict in the case, he may order the action removed to some other county in which a fair trial can be had.

It was a textbook case for moving the trial out of the county—not simply bringing fresh jurors into the stew.

But Charles Bush—for whatever reason, be it political or personal—was determined to give the Murray people their trial.

It should have been obvious to all then, just like it is to all today, that it was the wrong call. "Once to every man and nation," wrote James Russell Lowell, "comes the moment to decide, in the strife of truth with falsehood, for the good or evil side....and the choice goes by forever 'twist that darkness and that light.' "

That distant light.

Seamlessly, the judge and lawyer moved into a discussion of the appropriate county from which to draw the new jury.

Bush suggested McCracken, most likely because of the easy and direct rail link with that populous city.

Pat Holt wisely objected. He didn't want citizens coming to try his black, hapless client from a county where just a few months before they had lynched, burned and mutilated not one, but two men of color.

For an assortment of reasons he also objected to calling in jurors from Trigg, Marshall and Graves counties.

Finally a deal was struck. It would be Christian County—hometown of the judge. The law required that in any change of venue case, preference be given to a county within the same judicial district.

Most likely in the back of Holt's mind was the ill will which had erupted for a short time between these two cities when the Calloway County lynch mob held two of their elected officials hostage back in January. Maybe a Christian County jury would consider it pay back time for the irresponsible citizenry of Murray and vicinity.

So, Judge Bush slowly and methodically dictated the decision to his court reporter, who wrote the order out in long hand for his signature.

Whereas, the defendant, Lube Martin was indicted at the special January term of the Calloway Circuit Court for the alleged willful murder of Guthrie Diuguid, and whereas, there were certain proceedings had at that term resulting in the continuance of said prosecution and which were attended and witnessed by large crowds of people from all over Calloway County; and whereas it was and is apparent to the court that there is such excitement and feeling in the case and that it has been given such widespread publicity and notoriety that it is impracticable to obtain a jury free of bias in Calloway County, Kentucky, and whereas, the commonwealth attorney engaged in the prosecution of said case and the attorneys for the said defendant agree with the court in his conclusion in this matter. It is therefore ordered by the court that W.A. Patterson, sheriff of Calloway County, or one of his deputies proceed to summon a jury from another county and the attorneys for the defense, namely A.D. Thompson and J.P. Holt having moved the court to summon a jury from Christian County, Kentucky, which is in the same judicial district with Calloway County and counsel for the Commonwealth having agreed to said motion. It is therefore ordered by the court that the said sheriff or one of his deputies summon a special venire of sixty sober, discreet, disinterested housekeepers of Christian County, Kentucky and over twenty one years of age for jury service at the special February term of the Calloway County Circuit Court from which is to be selected a panel to try the said Lube Martin; And they are hereby ordered and directed to at once communicate with the sheriff of Christian County and obtain his assistance in selecting the said jurors and is ordered to have them report to this court as speedily as possible and by one o'clock, P.M. Feb. 20, 1917.

Sheriff Will Patterson was once again called upon to lend his office to the mighty forces of the law. Surely, as he proceeded to phone his counterpart in Christian County to give him the news,

Sheriff Will must have wondered if the case would ever go away.

With the entry of the order, Sheriff Patterson's work began, and the court's business came to a close for that day. Near noon, the trial was recessed until 1 p.m. the following day.

CHAPTER 9

THE PROSECUTION

At 12:30 on Tuesday afternoon, February 20, two to three hundred Calloway County citizens were gathered at the Murray train station. They watched, mainly in silence, as 52 men fresh from Hopkinsville got off the train.

Deputy Sheriff Dick Langston, who had been sent by Patterson to fill the judge's order in Christian County for a new jury, escorted them toward the Murray House Hotel.

Clutching their meager necessities in a variety of shapes including small valises, suitcases, and even paper bags, they were led to their lodging for quick registration.

Many, if not most, had never been to Murray, this west Kentucky neighbor with which they held so much in common. Undoubtedly these simple and honest men held an assortment of emotions as the local eyes peered upon them. Most likely they all knew about the case for which they had been summoned, and held certain apprehensions accordingly. Undoubtedly they left wives, children, mothers, and sisters who were not at all comfortable with the notion that their loved ones had been sucked into the maelstrom.

At 1p.m. Calloway County Circuit Clerk L.A. Trevathan began to call their names in the packed Calloway County Circuit Courtroom, as the roll call opened up the Lube Martin trial.

To the right of the bench was a table full of prosecutors.

There was a practice in Kentucky at that time, which remained in place until very recent times, that the family of a murder victim could hire their own private lawyer to either prosecute or assist in the prosecution of the case.

The family of Guthrie Diuguid had not hired a special prosecutor. They had simply sent his own brother George, the Paducah lawyer, to assist Commonwealth Attorney Denny Smith and County Attorney N.B. Barnett. George had of course been one of the leading firebrands in the near insurrection in January. It would have taken all the horses in Kentucky to pull him away from the prosecution's counsel table.

Ever the agitator, the 67-year-old elder brother of the victim had kicked up a flurry of controversy in January when he reported to the newspapers that the prosecution was weaving a chain of evidence that would implicate white men in the murder of his brother.

For some unexplained reason, these three lawyers were joined by attorney Robert Shemwell of Benton.

Across the room was the lonely table of Lube Martin. The black defendant was joined by his lawyers, Pat Holt and Holt's partner, J.D. Thompson.

Martin's deeply apprehensive family knotted together behind him at the defense table. For a short while, his two-year-old daughter, Queen, sat in his lap.

After the men from Christian County answered the roll, both sides announced ready and the serious business of picking a jury began.

Many think the debate over capital punishment is one of recent vintage.

Not so.

A curious crowd gathers around the National Guard on duty in Murray,
looking south at the corner of Curd (now Fourth St.) and Main,
during the Lube Martin trial.   *Photo compliments of Chuck Shuffett*

In fact, this very issue used by the lawyers in questioning prospective jurors as they were called took up a great deal of the time .

The maximum punishment Lube Martin could receive if he was convicted for the murder of Guthrie Diuguid was death.

So, the commonwealth attorney and his entourage wanted to make sure that the twelve jurors finally selected to hear the case were "death qualified." That is, they were not against the death penalty as a matter of principle or religious conviction, and would be able to impose it under the right circumstances.

If not, they then could be struck for cause.

Both sides thusly began their tedious questioning of the jury–the voir dire, as it has been known for centuries. The packed courtroom of spectators looked upon the rather monotonous process quietly and patiently.

After two hours, at about three o'clock, the case had a jury of men selected. Fifteen had been struck as having conscientious scruples against the death penalty. Eight had been struck because they had formed opinions about the case.

The twelve jurors seated directly in front of the bench were Harry Edwards, a farmer; Lewis Starling, a machinist; Tandy McGee, a tobacco buyer; E. H. Reynolds, a farmer; George McChord, a farmer; L. A. Shepherd, a livery man; J. C. White, a carpenter; W. R. Smithson, a farmer and livery man; Mat Winfree, a farmer; Ed Drake, a restaurant owner; Jesse Eglin, a farmer; and J.D. McGowan, a merchant.

All male. All white.

Sitting to the right of the bench, busily taking down all of the happenings, was the court stenographer, John C. King, of Trigg County. He would later become a fiery commonwealth attorney for many years, and his daughter would one day transcribe the court business of a subsequent circuit judge.

In today's courts, with a case of this magnitude, and a jury finally in place in the late afternoon, the court would no doubt heave a sigh of relief and recess for the day, ready to get down to

Same location, recent picture.

business the next morning.

Not then. Judge Bush was away from home trying cases. The sooner he got them all tried, the sooner he'd get back to Hopkinsville. He had announced before the trial that night sessions would be used if necessary to complete the case that week.

So, with the jury sworn in and the sun sinking low in the late winter sky, the old judge pushed on.

Commonwealth Attorney Smith made his opening statement, laying out the evidence he said would easily show that on December 9, the defendant Lube Martin had, with the help of his confederates, brutally and in cold blood shot and killed Guthrie Diuguid.

In a criminal trial in Kentucky, the defense lawyer has the option of either making his opening statement immediately after the prosecutor states his case, or may "waive" it to the conclusion of the state's evidence and before the defendant puts on his case. It's a tactical decision. Most lawyers in that day waited. There was no need to get up in front of a jury and lock in one's defense before the Commonwealth had put on its proof. Sometimes the unexpected happened, causing defense strategy to change.

True to form, Pat Holt reserved his opening statement.

Seated in the courtroom through the afternoon's tedious proceeding had been the mourning widow of Guthrie Diuguid, Carrie. Her two stepdaughters had been at her side.

Such is the doleful scene in most murder trials. The bereaved and grief-stricken members of the victim's family, sadly huddled together on one side of the large room, usually behind the table of the prosecution. The fearful and forlorn family of the accused knotted together on the other side. In many cases such as this one, a matter of black and white; those adorned in the finer habiliments of mourning and those in the tattered and worn uniforms of the impoverished accused.

Carrie Diuguid was called as the Commonwealth's first witness. Carrie had been Guthrie Diuguid's second wife. His first wife, Eudora, had died in 1898 after bearing two daughters, Ethel and

Edna. Carrie and Guthrie had one son, Rex, who was then eight years old. There is no record of the young boy being present at the trial. Most likely, he was in school.

The crowd leaned forward, somberly straining to hear the soft voice of the one most affected by the terrible events of December 9.

They heard the poignant story of a wife losing her husband, the call to the doctor's office, and then her vigil by her dying husband at the hospital. Eyes watered to hear of the departing father asking to see his children before he died. Inexplicably, they did not make it in time.

There was more to Carrie Diuguid's testimony than just arousing sympathy for a heartbroken widow, however. Prosecutor Denny Smith was attempting to get into evidence the last remarks Guthrie Diuguid made as to how the shooting occurred. This is hearsay testimony however, and not admitted unless it can come under one of the exceptions to the hearsay rule. One exception is the "dying declaration." For such a statement to be allowed to be heard by the jury under this exception, it must be shown that the declared victim was dying, knew he was dying, with no hope of recovery.

The sound reasoning of the law concludes that there is an irrefutable ring of truth and authenticity in statements made by people who know that they are only moments away from going to meet their Maker.

Q. At any time after you got to him on Saturday did he express any hope to you that he would get well?

A. No, sir; he did not.

Q. After he told you that this shot would get him, and just before he called the children, you say he said he wanted to see them before he went, did he make any statement to you?

A. Yes, along about that time. When he was awake he seemed to realize all the time that he was seriously ill.

165

Smith then asked her what her dying husband had said about the shooting.

Holt objected. Eyes turned toward Bush. The judge vacillated, mumbling almost to himself, doubtful and uncertain. Finally he stated that he would defer his ruling until later, and Denny Smith withdrew the question.

Only the lawyers in the courtroom would have caught the clear signal which had been inadvertently sent by Judge Bush's momentary ineptness. The statement of Guthrie Diuguid, attempted to be repeated by his widow, was a classic textbook example of a "dying declaration." It was obviously admissible as very incriminating evidence against the defendant. The judge's misplaced reluctance to let it in was a true indication that the beleaguered, sometimes limited, old jurist was going to try his best.

Try his best to give Lube Martin a fair trial.

After Mrs. Diuguid left the stand, Smith jumped right into the events of December 9, 1916. He called as his next witness Mrs. William Owen.

At noon on that day, Mrs. Owen was standing in the doorway of her house on the west side of Curd Street only about 150 feet from where the shooting took place. She saw Guthrie Diuguid pass by her house walking toward town on the opposite side of the street.

She also saw a group of Negroes–two or three–including some of the "Martin Negroes" walking north away from town on the same side of the street as Diuguid.

When the group met up with Diuguid, a scuffle immediately ensued as the black men grabbed him. He jerked loose, and then she saw one of the Negroes shoot him four or five times. Diuguid then walked on toward town. Immediately after the shooting the three or four blacks ran north on Curd Street, past her house and out toward Rowlett Tobacco Factory.

All of this highly-damaging evidence she reported on direct examination.

Defense lawyer A.D. Thompson took her on cross and in

the process of his questioning stumbled into some significant evidence.

It came about in a weird sort of way. It was as if neither the lawyers for the prosecution or defense had fully interrogated this witness before trial. Thompson and Smith ended up bumping heads on an evidentiary question that had a peculiar twist to it.

During the questioning by Thompson, Mrs. Owen began to volunteer information which Thompson thought might be highly prejudicial to his client.

".........Mr. Diuguid walked on towards town and the Negroes came by running......." she related, "........a man in my yard asked, 'what's the matter with you niggers down there, and they says....' "

At this juncture Thompson objected, stating that what the other blacks said was hearsay and not admissible.

Smith countered with the argument that it was admissible because it was part of the *res gestae*–a Latin term which literally means "things happen." The *res gestae* rule declares that where a remark is made spontaneously and concurrently with an affray, it carries with it an inherent degree of credibility and will be admissible because of its spontaneous nature. It is another legal exception to the hearsay rule.

Of course Smith was right, and Bush let her continue.

One of them had responded to the question of the man in the yard by saying, "Guthrie Diuguid is shooting at us!"

There was a slight stir in the courtroom.

Of course this was a gift to the defense, evidence which greatly boasted their claim of self-defense. But neither lawyer apparently knew what she was going to say, and ironically it helped the side which was objecting to it, and cut into the case of the commonwealth attorney who was instrumental in getting the evidence admitted.

Thirteen-year-old Orvis Purdue moved down the aisle of the courtroom, up to the bench, and was sworn as the Commonwealth's third witness.

The shooting took place right in front of the youngster's house and he viewed it through his window only a few feet away. He turned out to be the witness closest to the scene, other than the participants, and gave the most detailed information about what happened.

He knew Guthrie Diuguid. He knew Lube Martin. Yes, he saw Lube Martin shoot Diuguid several times. But he also gave something to the defense by testifying that the victim himself did indeed have a pistol and had it drawn.

The testimony of the young boy was substantially repeated by his neighbor George Hepner. He also saw Lube shoot Diuguid. He also saw a gun in Diuguid's hand. Hepner saw the mortally-wounded former town marshal walk a block toward town without giving any signs he had been shot. In fact, Hepner testified that he "didn't think he was shot at all."

Other eyewitnesses were called who for the most part painted the same picture of the actual shooting.

Guthrie Diuguid was walking south on the east side of Curd Street toward town around noon, close to the home of Dr. Grogan–near the current site of the Calloway County Judicial Center. As fate would have it, Lube Martin and his three friends were at that same time heading north away from town on the same side of the street. Across the street from the Purdue home they literally ran into each other. Words were exchanged. A scuffle broke out and both Lube Martin and Diuguid pulled pistols. Martin did all the shooting, firing four to six times–depending on the witness. Ed Jordan, Sylvester and Ann Martin all three "lit out" running north on the west side of the street right by the Owen and Purdue houses. Lube headed in the same direction but on the east side of the street, down to the Rowlett Tobacco Factory where he turned right and disappeared.

Incredibly, the mortally-wounded Diuguid, showed no signs of his distress and started walking back toward town. He met Curt Owen who was driving a delivery wagon north on Curd. He flagged down Owen, had him turn around and take him to the office of Drs. Will and Rob Mason uptown.

That was the upshot of the stories given by the seven eye-witnesses that afternoon–nothing particularly shocking or earth-shaking there.

But the testimony of the next-to-last witness, Negro Felix Skinner, brought the crowd to the edge of their seats.

On direct examination Skinner reported that back in the fall he had been in Lube Martin's house. He was shown a pump shotgun which Martin kept hidden under his bed.

"I asked him what he was going to do with it," the witness stated, "and he told me he was going to kill Guthrie Diuguid."

With that last question, Smith sat down.

Pat Holt, on cross, quickly ignited the most dramatic revelation of the day.

Q. Was that all he said?

A. Said some more parties told him to do it.

Q. Who was it? What did he say?

The commonwealth attorney objected, and one could feel the electricity in the air as the crowd awaited Judge Bush's ruling, every soul in the gathering begging silently that the old jurist would let Skinner answer.

"Overruled," Judge Bush pronounced to the joy of all but the prosecution.

Skinner continued, "He told me that was Mr. Harold Schroader's pump gun."

Holt pressed on.

Q. What was it you said a while ago about somebody telling him to do it?

A. Some parties told him to do it.

Q. Did he tell you who it was?

A. Yes, sir.

Q. Who was it?

A. Told me it was Harold Schroader and Judge Schroader and Mr. Waterfield.

Q. Who else?
A. That's all.
Q. Told him to shoot him?
A. Yes, sir.

So there it was–the breathtaking hint of a broader conspiracy involving leading white men in the community, an idea which had been first revealed by prosecutor George Diuguid in January. Now, it had been unveiled by the defense lawyer Pat Holt's questioning. And as intriguing as this evidence was, Holt did not find it compatible to their theory of self-defense. It gave direct proof to premeditation on behalf of his client to kill Guthrie Diuguid.

But the newspapers covering the day's proceeding picked up on the explosive nature of the testimony. Reported the *Paducah News Democrat*:

A sensation was sprung here yesterday afternoon after the case went to trial when the names of Police Judge J.R. Schroader, his son Hal Schroader and Chief of Police P.F. Waterfield were mentioned in connection with the killing of former town marshal Guthrie Diuguid. Felix Skinner, a Negro witness for the State, swore that last fall Lube Martin took him to his home, showed him a shotgun and told him that he was going to kill Diuguid. According to Skinner, Martin told them that the police judge, his son and the chief of police had told him to do it.

What the newspaper account did not say was that Felix Skinner was one of the more respected blacks in town. He was light skinned and aristocratic–even regal–in his bearing and the father of eight children. Felix's wife, with the exotic name of Canary, worked as a maid for one of the respectable white families in town.

J.R. Schroader had been city police judge since 1914. There was undoubtedly bad blood between him and Guthrie Diuguid which contributed to the latter's demise as an employee of the city.

Police judges in those days would hear minor criminal cases

brought to them by the city police. No doubt Schroader was privy to the shenanigans of Diuguid in "Pooltown," through his alleged co-conspirator Chief P. F. Watterfield. Why he would want Diuguid killed, even after his firing from the city, would never be explained.

A modern-day trial attorney would be aghast at the pace of trials in the days of Judge Bush. If one were to be told that in a death penalty case, jury selection would begin at 1 p.m. and by 5:30, a jury would be seated, the prosecution would have stated its case and called nine witnesses before 5:30, the contemporary lawyer would think the bearer of such a report was smoking crack.

But that was exactly the situation on February 20, 1917 in the case of the Commonwealth of Kentucky vs. Lube Martin.

There were several reasons for this.

Judges and lawyers were in town to try cases. When they finished and the term was over, they could go home. Therefore, their questioning of witnesses went straight to the point. No extensive introductions of their family background, names of wife and children or other personal data. "Your name, and what did you see?" was the thrust of direct examination.

Also it was long before television came along, to create the unrealistic melodrama of quivering witnesses breaking into devastating admissions under the searing snare of Perry Mason's cross-examination. Lawyers of yore labored under no such illusions, and did not wander endlessly on cross in search of the dramatic knockout punch. They got in, got what they wanted, and got out.

And the all male juries did not need coddling with time-consuming breaks. These were hardened men accustomed to back-breaking labor. Sitting for three or four hours at a stretch with their wagon train bladders was a piece of cake.

Finally, at 5:30, after the prosecution's ninth witness, John Grogan, had testified, and just after the lonely winter sunset cast shadows across the courtroom, Judge Bush adjourned the proceedings until the next morning.

The spectators were required to remain seated until the

guardsmen and sheriff deputies had escorted the prisoners out of the courthouse back to jail, followed by the jury and court officials under guard. Members of the jury were ordered back to the Murray House Hotel, where they would remain sequestered and under heavy guard. At long last, the huge crowd drained out of the balcony and main floor of the courtroom, down the steps to the first floor and out into the twilight–all in an orderly manner and under the watchful eyes of the soldiers.

There had been no problems during the day with the respectful gathering. Judge Bush had been nervous, however. At one time he pointed out a suspicious looking spectator to one of the guardsmen. Soldiers were interspersed throughout the citizens in attendance. In addition, there had been a reserve squad of 20 men lingering throughout the day in the jury room just behind the bench. The balance of the company was armed and standing by at the armory, just two blocks away.

The veterans of the Mexican border expedition had things well under control.

No doubt much of the town must have been buzzing with the information given by witness Felix Skinner which implicated Murray Police Judge Schroader, his son Harold, and Chief of Police P.F. Waterfield. One had to wonder what more would come of that during the rest of the trial, and to which side it would advantage.

Later that Tuesday night, Avery Rose, the absent Negro witness for the defense, was apprehended in Paris, Tennessee on a witness attachment. She was brought under guard to Murray and lodged in the jail to await the needs of the trial.

One has to wonder if Sheriff Will Patterson and his deputies ever slept.

Ash Wednesday, February 21, the beginning of Lent broke bright and clear. This forty-day religious observance was commemorated mainly by Catholics, Episcopalians, and Lutherans. That meant most all Calloway Countians gave it absolutely no heed as they awoke on that delightfully mild morning.

Most had their minds on other things. And it wasn't the Lube Martin trial.

Thoughts began to turn to the upcoming planting season.

Routinely spring comes to west Kentucky in February—for a while.

It slips into town for a week or ten days, looks around, drops its bags, and then meanders off for a while.

During this small window of respite from winter's otherwise unpredictable path, the farmers knew exactly what custom required them to do.

Burn off tobacco beds.

So, fate was smiling on the town of Murray on the mild and sunlit second day of Lube Martin's trial. Most all of the farmers in the county were too busy piling brush, torching and searing plant beds, to come to town and cause trouble.

For the first time since the criminal prosecution of Lube Martin began there were empty seats in the courtroom when the trial continued on that day. Tension was noticeably relaxed.

A reporter from a Paducah newspaper set the scene:

The day dawned bright and clear, with Murray absolutely quiet, there being much less trial talk since Lube Martin, the alleged Negro murderer of Guthrie Diuguid, former city marshal, was placed on trial Monday.

Absence of the usual packed crowd that has been in the court troop was noticeable this morning. Many vacant seats were in view but this probably was due to the beautiful weather which afforded the farmers an opportunity to toil at home.

The first few witnesses called that morning centered primarily on the victim Guthrie Diuguid, and his acts and condition immediately after the shooting.

He must have known he was shot, and shot bad, immediately after the shooting. Diuguid had continued toward town and flagged down Curt Owen for assistance. Owen testified that the victim had his pistol in his scabbard when he climbed aboard his wagon. He hurriedly turned his rig around and transported Guthrie to the office of Will and Rob Mason which was located above Sexton Hardware Store on the court square.

Owen testified that when three or four of them took Diuguid out of the wagon and up the stairs, they took the pistol–a revolver–and found that the gun was loaded, with no spent cartridges.

With this evidence Denny Smith had pretty much discounted any possibilities that the victim had actually fired at the defendant.

There was not a whole lot of trial strategy or chess piece maneuvering by the prosecution in those days. Trying cases one right after another while sleeping in strange beds did not afford them that luxury. They pretty much herded their witnesses to the courthouse, had a general idea what each would say, and maybe interviewed a few themselves. In routine cases it was not unusual for the commonwealth attorney to be talking to his witnesses for the first time while the county attorney was selecting a jury. So, they put on their witnesses, asked the questions, and let the chips fall where they may.

In the process, much of the prosecution evidence continued to offer the accused much grist for his self-defense mill. While showing bad blood between the two men, Smith was at the same time shoveling in proof that Martin was genuinely afraid of the former lawman.

On the morning of the 21st, the Commonwealth recalled Tine Swope. Said Swope:

Lube was very familiar with me anyway, he generally did work for me, and he said, 'Mr. Tine, I am in a whole lot of trouble and I want to ask you what to do.' I asked him what it was about, and he said him and Mr. Diuguid had some words, and I believe he said Mr. Diuguid had threatened to kill him, and he said 'I want some protection. What must I do?'

I said, 'well, if I was afraid I would have him put under a peace bond,' and he said he didn't want to do that, that he thought as much of his wife and children as anybody, and he wanted to stay at home, and he said 'Me and Diuguid, some time or another, will have some trouble.'

It was fast becoming clear that the victim and the shooter had a bad relationship before the killing. And it was also becoming apparent that there had been threats from both sides. It was not yet evident as to exactly the cause of the bad blood, but there was already a sense of foreboding in the courtroom, among the spectators if not the jury, that the victim Guthrie Diuguid had reduced himself to the level of a common vendetta with this murder defendant. And that this bitter and acrimonious relationship had cost him his life.

In the Wednesday morning session, co-defendant Ed Jordon was called by the Commonwealth to testify. All spectators leaned forward with anticipation as the Negro was brought forward by the jailer to testify.

Prosecutor Denny Smith had already jumped into his questioning, and only after Jordon was asked about being jointly indicted with Martin did Judge Bush awaken to the situation.

Belatedly, he interrupted the questioning.

"Does anybody represent this boy?" the old jurist inquired surveying the courtroom.

"Yes sir," replied Pat Holt from counsel table. "I do."

Bush bore in on him, "Do you object to this testimony?"

"No sir," was the defense lawyer's answer.

Bush paused to ponder the situation. Trial judges are in the dark most of the time as to the trial strategy of the defense lawyer. Obviously there was potential conflict here. If Holt represented the interest of both Martin and Jordon, he could not throw the latter to the wolves in an attempt to save his client then on trial. But there is not always a conflict. Co-defendants may sometimes actually help each other in their testimony. Only their lawyer knows.

Being the capable and competent judge that he was, Bush did not let it rest.

"Ed," he turned to the young man, whose father lived in a day when a black man would not have even been allowed to testify in that courtroom, "you are indicted, and it is my duty to tell you that in giving your testimony you don't have to make any statement that might incriminate yourself in any way. If any questions are asked you that are liable to incriminate you in this affair, you are not required to answer it. Of course, you may make any statement you choose on this trial, and answer anything that does not incriminate you, but any questions asked tending to incriminate you, you don't have to answer that."

Wisely and fairly, the commonwealth attorney chimed in, "Do you know what 'incriminate' means?"

Judge Bush explained it to him.

Jordon nodded that he understood and the questioning by Smith continued.

It soon became apparent why Holt had no fear of his client on the stand incriminating himself. As it turned out, Jordon was simply a bystander in the whole incident. He was originally from Marion, Arkansas and had met up with Lube's brother, Ann, in Cairo a few days before. He was on his way back to Arkansas via Memphis and had only stopped off in Murray, with Ann, for a short visit. Jordon had only known Lube Martin for less than thirty minutes when the shooting took place. He, and the three Martin brothers–Lube, Sylvester, and Ann–were walking up Curd Street when the foursome confronted Guthrie Diuguid, a man who the witness had never seen before in his life.

It was a black man's worst nightmare in the South in those days. Being in the wrong place at the wrong time and either a white woman being offended, or a white man being killed.

That was basically what had happened to ill-fated, drunken Luther Durrett in Paducah a few months before. By sheer devilish luck he had come upon a rumbling lynch mob, when he took some foolish and booze induced actions, and paid for it with a terrible death.

Jordon had simply been walking down the street with some newly found acquaintances. Now he was in jail charged with accessory to commit murder.

According to Jordon, it was Diuguid who first spoke. He and Ann were walking about ten feet behind Lube and Sylvester.

"When they passed," the witness related, "Mr. Diuguid asked Lube, 'I thought I told you to come around to the office,' and Lube told him, 'I went off, but I will go with you now' and from that the shooting occurred."

The next thing he knew, Lube pulled his gun and started shooting. At that point, according to Jordon, they ran.

In his testimony, it was related for the first time that Diuguid had a walking stick. But it had not been used in a menacing manner. More importantly, according to Jordan, both hands had remained on the handle through the affray, strong indication that he had not made a grab for his own pistol.

Ed Jordon had made a good witness for the Commonwealth, discrediting any self-defense claims of the defendant.

One wonders why the prosecution called the next witness. County Judge L.A.L. Langston offered very little for the Commonwealth. On direct examination he only related that when Guthrie Diuguid was shot he was in the employment of the county, as a crew manager for prisoners being worked out of the jail.

On cross-examination the clever Irishman Pat Holt asked only one question. But it was a bombshell:

I want to ask, Judge Langston, if you recall the defendant Lube Martin coming to you some time in March or April last year, probably the last day of the fair here in Murray, it was October last year, and asking you to protect him from Mr. Diuguid?

The prosecution's table exploded in a chorus of objections.

Judge Bush sustained the objection.

Both sides approached the bench, and Pat Holt entered into the record, outside the hearing of the jury, that the witness would say, if allowed to answer, that Lube Martin had approached Langston in October and complained that Diuguid had threatened his life. The hapless Negro had then requested some protection from the judge.

The ruling stood, and the jury was left to wonder about the answer. Of course one cannot unring the bell, and the adroit defense lawyer had loaded his question with enough information that they could draw their own conclusion.

In those days the county judge was, without question, the most powerful man in the county. Not only did he control the government of the county through its fiscal court, including public expenditures and jobs but at that time, and even until the mid 1970s, he possessed judicial power over misdemeanor crimes and low-grade civil cases. He was in most instances also the most popular politician in the county, through which many state jobs were funneled.

So, from the Commonwealth's perspective, he may have been intended to be used as just window dressing for their case. But Holt had used him to drive home further the point that Diuguid was carrying a vendetta against his client.

Bush's ruling was technically correct: before self-serving statements of the defendants as to fear of the deceased could be introduced, the claim of self-defense must first be raised by the defendant. At that point of the trial, the defendant had not yet testified, nor was there any guarantee that he ever would. But it is doubtful that Bush was that keen of an evidentiary technician. Significantly, Holt did not ask for leave to recall Langston after his man took the stand.

If the stern, regimented militiamen began to look more relaxed in their posture in the courtroom, there was a reason. Almost imperceptibly, with the revelation of possible aggression on behalf of the victim, Guthrie Diuguid, toward the defendant, the seething anger of the local populace began to slowly drain out of the crowd. The whole case was beginning to change–as far as the onlookers were concerned–from one of a vengeful crusade, to a criminal case of great interest.

As the Commonwealth began to wind down its case, it produced what was by far, the most damning evidence against the defendant–the testimony of the victim's widow.

Carrie Diuguid was recalled to finish up what had been attempted at the beginning of the state's case.

Judge Bush had deferred his ruling whether to allow the remarks of her dying husband to be repeated for the jury.

Now the competent and adroit Denny Smith once again, as if the witness had never been on the stand, began to lay the foundation for the dying declaration.

Defense attorney Holt, knowing the dire straits of her testimony, objected all along the way to all of Smith's questioning.

She had seen her husband on Saturday just after the shooting and even at that time he stated that he thought he was going to die.

And then as he worsened and continued to fade on Sunday, he called for his daughters. It was a painful and poignant recollection for the pitiful widow as she stated to a sympathetic courtroom, "He asked where his children were, said he would like to see them before he went."

Fading in and out of consciousness, Diuguid saw his daughters for the last time about 2:30 in the afternoon.

He died two hours later, spending most of his final hours heavily medicated with opiates.

Then the critical questions and answers came from Smith and his witness:

Q. When was it you heard the statement of the way the difficulty occurred, if you heard him make any statement about it at all?
A. It was about twelve, I think.

179

Q. Sunday.
A. Yes, sir.
Q. State to the jury, please, what he said about it?

Of course Holt continued to object, but Bush ruled against him.

A. What he said, how it was done?
Q. Yes
A. Well, he just said, he called his two brothers' names, and said, 'they had hold of me and was beating me, and Lube shot me.'"

The pronouncement fell heavy upon the gathering–testimony from the grave, from the dead man's own lips.

And, of course Bush had been correct in his ruling to let it in. It was a textbook case of the "dying declaration" exception to the hearsay rule–a prosecutor's dream.

As the state pushed toward the end of their case, it called one of the most respected citizens of the county.

Dr. Will Mason, Jr.

The Mason family was one that contributed greatly to the healing profession of Calloway County and western Kentucky. Dr. Mason's father, William M. Mason, Sr. was born in North Carolina in 1844, and served in the Confederate Army. He established his practice in Hazel after graduating from the University of Louisville Medical School. All three of his sons, including Will, graduated from Vanderbilt University and became physicians.

Mason was a political novelty in Calloway County.

He was a Republican. In fact, just the spring before he had been elected a delegate to the Republican National Convention in Chicago.

In reporting his selection of Mason over Thomas Hazelip of Paducah, to the convention, the local *Murray Ledger and Times* proudly proclaimed:

Every Calloway citizen, regardless of party affiliation, will rejoice to know that decency prevailed and that Hazelip, who owes his political prominence to Negro domination, was defeated and that a respectable gentleman from Calloway administered the rebuke.

There was irony in this news story which apparently belittled Mason's opponent for nomination for his support of the Negro. Mason himself befriended and mentored a young Negro boy who was the son of a worker at Mason's hospital. This namesake, Theodore Roosevelt Mason Howard, who was small child at the time of the trial, would go on to become one of the country's leading civil rights leaders in the 1960s.

It had been Mason who had treated Diuguid on that fateful December afternoon when the mortally wounded man was brought to his office.

In that time, every country doctor who had spent any time practicing medicine in the rural South, had plenty of experience treating gunshot wounds.

Dr. Mason calmly related to the jury the gory details of the victim's condition.

Diuguid was shot twice. One of the .38-caliber bullets entered in the right chest area, and then ranged downward and almost exited the back. Significantly, the fatal bullet actually entered "the very top portion" of the left shoulder, and was deflected by bone and hard tissue into the base of the heart. To the jurors and spectators at that time, the trajectory of the bullet seemed of little importance. But this small piece of evidence would later loom monumental in Smith's closing argument.

His patient died on Sunday afternoon, over 24 hours after the shooting, "from shock, from the proximity or closeness of this bullet to the heart."

On cross-examination, Pat Holt gave indication of the thoroughness of his preparation by quickly passing through what amounted to the uncontroversial medical evidence, to one of greater import.

Q. I will ask you whether or not in the fall last year, before the killing took place, if you did not see the defendant in Paris, Tennessee?

A. I did.

Q. Did you have a conversation with him there as to why he was away from Murray?

A. I did.

Q. Will you please state the substance of the conversation?

He never got to answer that question—at least not in front of the jury.

Commonwealth Attorney Denny Smith was out of his seat objecting. Judge Bush sustained the objection.

If the good doctor had been allowed to talk about it, he would have given helpful evidence to the defense.

He would have told about surprisingly meeting Lube Martin on the street in Paris. "Hello Lube," he had greeted the black man in exile, "What are you doing here in Paris?" Martin had answered him forlornly, "Well, Dr. Mason, I have been here for several months. You know I can't live in Murray. I am afraid to live there on account of Mr. Guthrie Diuguid's threats on my life." The jury never heard it.

So, there it was: the State's case against Lube Martin.

There is always a collective sigh in the courtroom, even if subtle and indiscernible, when the pronouncement comes from the prosecutor, loud and clear.

The Commonwealth rests.

The state, with all of its resources and might, has done its best—or if you are a criminal defendant—its worst.

CHAPTER 10

THE DEFENSE

To the onlookers in the courtroom, and readers of the press, the case against Lube Martin had been convincing and conclusive. Yet, at the same time, there had been some problems. There was both good and bad, if one was looking for a conviction of murder one. This was the highest crime of the state, which carried death by electrocution for the guilty. Lube Martin had shot and killed Guthrie Diuguid, a white man, at high noon on the streets of Murray, a white man from a prominent family, a white man serving a public office. There was little evidence in the state's case that Martin had actually acted in self-defense. There had been four in Martin's party, only one of Diuguid. Martin was armed. So was Diuguid. But only 13-year-old Orville Purdue stated that Diuguid pulled his gun in the affray. There was evidence of bad blood between the two. There was a strong hint that Guthrie Diuguid was not "lily white" in a more meaningful sense than the color of his skin. The defense had raised questions about Diuguid's prior behavior, and the reasons for the shooting were murky. It made the crowd want to know more.

As for the jury–who knows about jurors? These stoic, tough and weather-worn men of the soil were inscrutable. They listened impassively and without expression. But no doubt they, as well as the rest of the gathering, were looking at the counsel table of the defendant, after the Commonwealth had closed out its work.

Pat Holt arose and gave his opening statement.

Then, he called his first witness.

Lube Martin.

In those days, in a criminal case, if the defense did not call the defendant first to testify, then he was barred from testifying. So, Lube did not have the option of sitting back and listening to his other witnesses, before he committed himself to his version of the incident.

After affording the jury a little glimpse at Martin's personal life–32, married, one child–Holt went to the most pressing question at hand.

Lube Martin and Guthrie Diuguid.

There was trouble between them. What was it?

The courtroom grew tense and every head bent forward to hear. There was a general suspicion in the community and among the spectators of what gave rise to the antipathy between these two men.

It was Bettie, Lube Martin's wife.

This very attractive Negro woman had been the object of Guthrie Diuguid's attention, and he had used his powerful positions of authority in law enforcement to advance his amorous designs.

How far the endeavor went was not quite clear. But it was evident that his romantic and illicit intrusions into the marriage of Lube and Bettie Martin had been sufficient to bring on complaints from Martin to the town fathers. The complaint had cost Diuguid the job as deputy town marshal for Murray. After that, Martin became dogged and threatened by the angry lawman.

Miscegenation in 1917 was illegal in Kentucky as throughout all of the South. Even the mention of it raised emotions to a fervor pitch, and provoked harsh, many time violent reprisals. History is replete with terrible atrocities committed against black men for the slightest–sometimes imagined–indiscretions involving white women.

While there was definitely a double standard–they usually did not string white men up for messing around with black women–amorous mixing between the races was not only illegal but socially unacceptable no matter who instigated the affair.

But it was not uncommon for white men of authority, whether a plantation owner or a local cop, to abuse their power by pushing themselves upon good looking, light skinned, Negro women.

Decent people living by the social mores of the day not only abhorred such practice as improper, but also as morally wrong. That is why prosecutor Denny Smith immediately went to war with a barrage of objections as Pat Holt tried to weave a story through his client of the bitter feud between the two men. Not

Two young boys leaning against the door to Pat Holt's Law Office beside First National Bank, then Peoples Bank, at Fifth and Main Streets. Photo compliments of John E. Scott and Sid Easley

only was the reputation of his victim at stake, with the bereaved widow and daughters just a few feet away, but the moral force of his whole case would be diminished. And of course the victim's brother, George, was seated next to Smith at the counsel table and was part of the prosecution team.

Objections rained down from the Commonwealth every time the explosive topic was broached by Holt's questioning.

Bush was like a traffic cop at rush hour.

He knew that prior threats by Diuguid and his constant badgering of Martin were relevant and admissible as to the claim of self-defense. But he did not think the source of that problem was admissible, and did not want to see a character assassination of a prominent member in the community take place in this crowded courtroom. So as the objections came hurtling to him in droves, he attempted to surgically satisfy both ends with his rulings.

The defendant's testimony of one encounter between him and Diuguid, as far back as the previous September, was one example of the intense battle unfolding before the packed courtroom.

Holt: In September did Mr. Diuguid threaten you personally?
Martin: Yes, sir.
Holt: State what he said to you.
Martin: I started to run from him and he said, "Stop, I will kill you, you black son of a bitch. I have been looking for you all this year and you have been gone. Where have you been?" I told him I had been to Paris working, and he said, "Come on and go to the office with me," and I said, "Mr. Diuguid, wait till morning and I will go up there with you," and he said, "No, you black son of a bitch, you will go now or I will take off the top of your head," and he drawed his pistol on me........
Holt: Did he give any reason for wanting to kill you then?

An objection was made by Smith, which was sustained by Bush.

If Martin had been allowed to answer he would have related the rest of the conversation in which Diuguid stated, "You have made affidavit against me about being intimate with your wife, and if you don't go up and take it back before the council I am going to kill you."

The jury never heard the rest of the story.

The cause of the threats was vitally important for the Christian County jury to know. They would remain in the dark as to why the lawman was stalking Martin and making threats. The men who would decide the fate of this young black man would never hear the complete truth: that Martin, fed up with Diuguid's advances on his wife, had complained to the town fathers; that his petition had fallen on sympathetic ears; and after he reduced it to writing, the victim had been disciplined by being denied the job as town marshal and had in fact been relieved from the force altogether.

For all this jury knew, Diuguid may have had some understandable reason for his deep resentment of Martin. They could surmise that Martin himself may have done something unacceptable which would justify Diuguid's endangered reaction.

Many, if not most of the natives in the courtroom looking on, knew the scoop.

As far back as the early part of 1916 trouble was brewing. In January of that year, Guthrie Diuguid was the deputy police chief for the city of Murray. The chief, P.F. Waterfield, had received a complaint from Lube about Diuguid's improper harassment and advancements against his wife. Chief Waterfield had Martin sign an affidavit, which Diuguid denied. Nevertheless, Waterfield believed Martin, as did many others. An intense feud developed between the chief and his deputy. Finally, on March 28, Mayor W.E. Walton called a special meeting of the council in an attempt to ease the friction between the city's two lawmen.

It was a heated meeting, with both officers giving their views, and with no resolution. The controversy was made even more intense by the fact that Guthrie's brother, Billy, was on the council.

Two days later the council met again. By a 4-2 vote Diuguid was asked to resign. A week later, at their regular meeting of April 7, 1916, Diuguid's resignation was submitted.

He was out of a job. And of course he blamed Lube Martin for all of his woes.

After hacking through the bramble of objections and bench conferences over Diuguid's inclinations, Pat Holt finally got down to the shooting itself.

Of course Lube's version differed somewhat from the other witnesses.

After arriving in Murray from Tennessee on Friday night, December 8, he went to his father's home to spend the night. He did not go to his home because he was afraid of Diuguid. The next morning, he visited a relative at the "colored grocery" before going to the post office to see if his check had arrived from Paris. Close to noon he ran into his brothers Sylvester and Ann, as well as Ed Jordon, a friend of Ann's but a complete stranger to him.

All four started north on Curd Street toward his father's house to eat dinner. They were moving along the east side of the street when they met Guthrie Diuguid walking on the same side heading into town.

Then Lube explained what happened next:

When I seen Mr. Diuguid I was in about fifteen or maybe twenty feet of him, and I reached up and pulled my cap down. I thought maybe he wouldn't recognize me and I might pass on by him. But I got even with him and he called me, and I made another step, and he called again. I turned around and said, "Sir?", and he said, "Lube, I thought I told you to come up yonder: I said "Mr. Diuguid, I had to go away and couldn't come, but I will go with you now or any other time, if you want me to." And he said, "No, you black son of a bitch, you don't have to go nowhere." He reached and got his pistol and throwed it on me, and I reached under my overall bib and got my pistol and shot."

Lube told of how Diuguid wielded his walking stick in his left hand as he brandished the pistol in his right. Martin could not relate how many shots were fired by either man.

I thought that was the last chance of my life....Lube insisted. He told me he was going to kill me if it was the last thing he done...

His story of what happened after the shooting dovetailed with all of the other witnesses. They all scattered to the four winds. All except the mortally wounded Guthrie Diuguid.

That was it, a simple case of self-defense.

Of course Lube's version of the shooting consisted of a huge gaping hole. None of the witnesses attested that Guthrie shot first. And those men examining Diuguid's pistol afterwards found no spent cartridges.

Prosecutor Smith inexplicably failed to hone in on that obvious flaw. Instead he engaged in a rather rambling line of questioning dealing more with Martin's conduct immediately before and after the shooting.

Finally Denny Smith sat down. Judge Bush examined the clock, dinner time. Court was adjourned until 1:30 p.m.

Almost a complete transformation had taken place in the courtroom and upon the streets of Murray as far as trial sentiment was concerned. It now was even being bantered about without rancor that Lube might even "come clear." The newspaper reported that it was believed by most citizens now that it was more likely that a lesser verdict such as manslaughter would be returned. The possibility of both a murder conviction and a death sentence seemed to be remote.

The proven trouble between Lube and Diuguid in the courtroom had been fleshed out in detail in the gathering places around town. Rumors, gossip, and street talk had made the small town circuit. Now Lube was not all black, and Diuguid was not all white. Many of the villagers knew the truth, and the whole truth. But the inscrutable faces of the twelve Christian County men in the jury box gave no clue as to what they suspected or surmised.

In the Jim Crow South of 1917, all the way up through the mid-'60s, the cultural principle regarding the races, "separate but equal," was only half true.

The Negro man and woman definitely lived in a separate but inferior world. These social mores, steeped in the ages, passed generation after generation without question, even without notice. So entrenched was the apartheid that it was deemed appropriate, even necessary, to properly identify the skin color when names were placed in print. Public water fountains and rest rooms were not the only place for the inscription "colored."

In obituaries, news reporting, even advertisements, people had to be reminded that there was a difference.

"Molly Brown (colored) of Donnivan Street passed away Tuesday morning at ...."

"Jake Long (colored) was arrested on public drunk in front of his home late Friday..."

Sometimes in show bills for the local movie, the paper would advertise, "Admission 15 cents, Colored 10 cents."

Separate, separate, always separate. But not equal.

Even the transcriber of court proceeding did not want the reader to be misled by the indiscriminate simplicity of the printed word. Seven of the nine witnesses called by the defense in the Lube Martin trial were labeled in the official transcript as "colored."

For what purpose was the reader informed of the color of a person's skin, when the substance of the story had nothing whatsoever to do with pigmentation?

Was it meant to be taken less seriously? The death of a colored baby? Was it meant to be sad, but not as bad as a white? The drunken colored man—no surprise there, what do you expect?

Different price of admission for the colored? A recognition of harsh economic reality. They could not afford the same price as the white man.

So it was within the social cauldron of skewed notions of justice and basic humanity that Lube Martin strove against the odds to put forth a defense with mostly "colored" witnesses.

One's admiration and respect for defense lawyer Pat Holt grew as he gallantly struggled through the witnesses for Lube Martin. These mostly black faces looked out over a sea of white, punctuated with armed soldiers, knowing that whatever they said would be remembered. That when they left the stand, they would be back upon the streets of Murray, living in the same seedbed of racial prejudice which only weeks before had erupted. Needless to say they were intimidated. They hedged. In trial lawyer parlance, they "waffled."

From time to time Holt had to "refresh" their memory of things they had reported to him about Diuguid's dogging Lube Martin with threats and deeds.

Everyone eagerly awaited the testimony of Avey Rose, a defense witness who was so reluctant to come and testify that she had to be arrested and kept in custody.

She totally evaporated on the witness stand:

Holt: Tell the jury whether or not one night last summer or late one afternoon or night you saw Guthrie Diuguid in the neighborhood of Lube Martin's house, near a bridge or trestle down there?

Rose: No, sir; I didn't see him.

Holt: Did you see him any other time down there?

Rose: No, sir.

Holt: To refresh your recollection, didn't you see him down there one night on that bridge or trestle with a gun, and he asked you where Lube Martin was?

Rose: No, sir.

Holt: You did not?

Rose: No, sir.

Undoubtedly growing exasperated, Holt pressed on.

Holt: Do you recall being in my office about ten days ago with Bettie and Alex Martin?

Rose: Yes, sir.

Holt: Do you recall saying you were afraid to come to court to tell what you knew, that you were scared to death to tell what you knew about this case. Do you recollect saying that?

Rose: No, sir.

Holt: Didn't you go off to Paris, and have to get an attachment for you here three days ago?

Rose: No, sir; I was in bed sick ever since last week.

Holt: Didn't they come down and arrest you, an attachment?

The quaking black witness gave no answer to the last question, and Holt finally gave up.

But the fierce loyalty of bloodlines held boldly. Martin's family members were unflinching in their defense of their loved one.

Co-defendants Sylvester Martin and Ann Martin both waived their rights against self-incrimination and took the stand in defense of their brother. According to their testimony Lube tried to avoid Diuguid on that morning and the former lawman pulled his gun first. They both denied holding the victim while Lube shot him.

Prosecutor Smith did very little with them on cross. He did raise the prospects of some drinking going on that morning between the brothers. Both brothers denied it. To Ann, whose real name was Chesley, the Commonwealth concluded his cross-examination:

Smith: What did you do with that whisky you had?

Ann: What whisky?

Smith: That you drank down there before you started up the street?

Ann: I don't know, sir. I didn't have none.

Smith: Are you the one that had the whisky glass and put it up

to Ed Jordon's nose.
   Ann: No, sir, I didn't. The last whisky I seen was in Cairo.

This was in sharp contradiction with the testimony of Ed Jordon who told of whisky drinking that morning. Although a small matter in and of itself, it served to undermine the credibility of both of the Martin brothers.

Brother Chester was called and he told of Diuguid coming to his house one night in October with a gun looking for Lube.

The most poignant and powerful evidence from Lube Martin's family never got to the jury. And it came from the grave.

Lube's mother, Lue, had died while he was in Paris running from Guthrie Diuguid. Before she died, Lube had considered slipping into Murray to see her and also to attend the county fair in October. She had Chester's wife, Duma, to write her hounded son this letter dated September 9:

Dear Son: I wrote you on the 7th not to come home, and I was afraid that you'd didn't get the letter, and don't come home for they have a trap set for you when you come, and don't you come here to no fair. That old fellow says the next time you come that you or him one will have to go down, and for gods sakes stay away and don't you let no one persuade you to come home. Your life is better than all the fairs in the world. Chester said tell you howdy, and stay up there. That old man has been talking about you to him.

On the back of the letter Chester had scribbled a note, "Lubbie, I would stay up there for it will be dengious(sic) for you to come home and your mamma is down here this morning having her letter wrote. Will be safe for you to stay up there where you are."

Denny Smith objected to the introduction of the letter and Judge Bush sustained the objection. It was an egregious error on the judge's part–keeping out persuasive and eloquent evidence of a worried old mother's care and concern for her son, who subsequently shot and killed the man complained of.

For the letter to be admissible to show the state of Lube Martin at the time of the shooting, it had to be shown that Lube received the letter. When Holt had attempted to lay the foundation with Lube on his direct questioning, he had asked him if he had received the letter. Smith had objected and Judge Bush had sustained the objection.

Apparently Smith did not believe the letter constituted a direct threat from the victim, and therefore rank hearsay. But justification to use deadly force in defending one's self is determined by looking through the eyes of the defendant. The law of self-defense provides for a subjective test and if the defendant actually believes at the time of the shooting that his life is in danger, then he is entitled to use deadly force in his defense. Such a letter as that received from his mother would have definitely given Lube reason to believe that Diuguid would carry through on his deadly threats.

In summary, the haunted plea of the departed mother was hushed and shoved back into the grave.

One of the few white witnesses for the defense was Dr. B.B. Keys, who apparently was a director at the Bank of Murray in charge of hiring at the bank. Lube had worked at the bank at one time firing the furnace during the winter. He had quit in March of 1916 and had told Dr. Keys the reason. His answer was pregnant with intrigue and never got to the jury. Smith objected before Keys could answer. Judge Bush, once again, sustained the objection.

At the bench Holt put the testimony into the record by avowal, so as to preserve it for appeal.

Martin had told Keys that he had to quit the job and leave town because Diuguid had threatened to kill him. Lube reported that Diuguid wanted him to make a false affidavit which would say other parties had procured Martin to kill him. Since it was not true, Martin had assured him, he could not make the affidavit. Therefore Lube was afraid that he would kill him if he did not either swear a false statement or leave town and move to Tennessee.

Finally Pat Holt concluded the case for the defense by reading Lube Martin's affidavit of what two missing witnesses would say. These witnesses further attested to threats by Diuguid against the life of the defendant and which were communicated to Martin.

It was a tired and weary Pat Holt who stood by his counsel table as the Wednesday evening gloaming began to darken the windows. "The defense rests, your Honor."

He had called fourteen witnesses, including the defendant and the affidavits. It had not been an easy go. Battling through the bramble of continuous objections from the gnarly prosecutor, wrestling with recalcitrant and evasive witnesses, absorbing adverse rulings from the bench and protecting the record for appeal, had all coalesced with the desperate and emotionally draining testimony of the defendant and four of his family members including two brothers and his father.

An equally exhausted Judge Bush rapped the proceedings into recess until 8:30 a.m. the following morning.

Less than a courtroom full of spectators who had stayed the course of the day slowly made their way out of the chamber. Little interest was shown along the street as the faithful soldiers marched Lube Martin back to jail.

Deputy Sheriff J.R. Langston escorted the jury out the back, narrow stairway to the street. Pursuant to Judge Bush's directive and based on a request made earlier by the jury, Langston led the jury down Curd Street to the scene of the shooting. It was a short walk, down the hill north of the court square. They crossed a small stream near the intersection of Olive Street. Then they proceeded up the hill to the location of the shooting

In keeping with the oath administered to him by Judge Bush, Deputy Langston said not a word. There they stopped and the twelve taciturn men silently surveyed the scene, the street, the houses from which witnesses had attested to have seen and heard the altercation on that fateful December day. What went through the minds of these rough hewn men is unknown. But surely they tried to relive in their own minds what exactly transpired that day between Lube Martin and the controversial Guthrie Diuguid. Finally, after a nod from the jurors, the deputy sheriff led them back to the hotel for supper and their last night in Murray.

It was prayer meeting night in Murray. The sensational trial had lost its steam and had drained into only an interesting trial. At churches that night and around the town the talk was now that Lube Martin might even be acquitted.

Reporter Arthur E. Bailey would write for his next day's Paducah paper:

The State built up a strong case, but on the other hand, the defense presented a good case, saying that Martin killed Diuguid in defense of his own life. It is the general impression among those familiar with the evidence that the jury will not render a verdict for either a death penalty or a life sentence. Some say Martin's acquittal would not be wholly unexpected.

The thought of it rankled but a few.

In the history of mankind how many men have been killed over a beautiful woman?

And that, after all was said and done, was the enduring theme of the Lube Martin case.

Lube Martin did not fire the pistol at Guthrie Diuguid because he, Martin, was black. And Diuguid was not on the receiving end because he was white.

He died because he was having an affair with Lube Martin's wife.

Surely some of the twelve men making up the jury were worldly enough to read between the lines and, in spite of Denny Smith's efforts, figure it out.

Yet, very little is known about the object of this bloody affair.

None of the newspaper accounts of the trial mention Bettie Martin nor any of his family other than those who testified.

So what we know about Bettie is what has passed by word of mouth down through the years in the black community. And that is not much.

She was good-looking, according to the reports, and light skinned. Negro women of this hue were the ones who normally attracted the sexual pursuit of white men.

And it is quite possible that the romantic connection between her and Diuguid was consensual on her part.

But what was "consensual" in that time and place with affairs of miscegenation is very much open to debate. The black woman–be she maid, wash woman, or simply a house wife in the "colored" part of town–was, by her lot in life, placed at a disadvantage if a white man took a liking to her. Local justice provided her with little protection. This was especially true if the aggressive male was one of rank, power, or wealth.

And of course Diguid was not only of a family of wealth, but of the powerful position of a policeman.

Diuguid, like many other unscrupulous and predatory white men of the South, was attracted to the chocolate-colored females of his town. Edward Ball, author of the memoir Slaves in the Family, has captured the underlying motivation of Diguid's kind, "There was the uncontrollable, unconscious attraction to the otherness of black people."

And of course in 1916, the lure of Bettie Martin was made more exciting, no doubt, by the societal taboo acknowledged by the Southern community. Not only was interracial marriage forbidden by Kentucky law, but also was adultery and fornication.

Section 1320 of Carroll's Kentucky Statues stated, "Every person who shall commit fornication or adultery shall for every offense be fined not less than twenty and not more than fifty dollars."

By 8:30 a.m. on Thursday, February 22, school kids across Calloway County settled in their seats to hear stories of the American icon George Washington, as the country celebrated his birthday. Undoubtedly Lube Martin gave it no thought, as he was once again escorted by soldiers from the jail and up the street to the courthouse.

Once again the courtroom filled up for what was expected to be the last day of the trial. That meant closing arguments, and no matter how the interest might wane in a criminal trial in the country, the old fashioned oratory in the trial lawyers' summations always attracted a crowd.

In a surprise move, however, Denny Smith requested the right to call one more witness.

He called Ethel Diuguid, the 22-year-old daughter of the deceased.

The courtroom grew deathly quiet as the crafty prosecutor gently and reverently pulled from a bag, the coat and shirt which her father had been wearing when he was shot.

Showing the items to the woman, he asked her if they were the same clothes he was wearing on the day he was shot.

Fighting back tears, she solemnly nodded in the affirmative.

With that all the evidence was concluded.

In the parlance of modern trial lawyers, Smith's closing move would be termed a "cheap shot." It could not by any stretch of the imagination be considered rebuttal. It was done solely for the purpose of raising the passions and prejudice of the jury by displaying the bloody clothes of the victim in the pitiful hands of his orphan.

In 1917, however, murder trials were all about passion and emotions.

At some point, probably the night before, after the jury had returned to the hotel, the lawyers and Judge Bush had argued instructions to the jury.

In lesser trials of that day, the trial judge might script out the written instructions longhand on the bench as the evidence evolved. In this case however, Bush had his instructions typed by the court reporter, and ready to present to the jury.

Judge Bush would give the jury three options. Not guilty by

reason of self-defense, or guilty of either murder or manslaughter.

If you believe....the self-defense instruction read in part, ...he was acting in his own necessary self-defense, or apparently necessary self-defense, or that he had reasonable grounds to believe, and did in good faith believe that he was in danger of losing his life, or suffering great bodily harm at the hands of the said Diuguid, which danger was either real or to the accused apparent, then accused had the right to use such force as was necessary, or apparently necessary to save his life or to protect his person from bodily harm..........you should excuse him on grounds of self-defense, and acquit him.

Holt tendered and argued strongly for a supplemental self-defense instruction which read:

....the law does not require that in order to save himself from death or great boldly harm, a man must fly for safety when he casually meets his enemy; nor does it require that he should stay away from his home, family or place of business to avoid an encounter with him; nor does the law require that, after one has been threatened and upon casually meeting his adversary, he must wait to be actually attacked before defending himself if he believed and had reasonable grounds to believe that he was then and there in danger of death or the infliction of some great boldly harm at the hands of Guthrie Diuguid.

The proposed instruction was an interesting and telling piece of legal work by Holt. It would have served as a subtle reminder to this Southern jury that slavery was over–that a black man no longer had to scrape and cower to a white man by giving up his own right to move about the community as he pleased. Nor did the submissive role of the Negro in this community require him to forfeit the blessings of liberty of home and family.

Bush refused to give this instruction, but in general, his treatment of the defense on the law was fair and reasonable.

On that winter morning, as guns blasted and men died by

the droves in distant Europe, Pat Holt stood before the jury to give his closing argument on behalf of Lube Martin. He most likely did not realize, and most likely was never told, that he was at the mountain top as a lawyer and as a human being. Somewhere in future years, he must have retreated to the noble and sunlit plains of his soul, and basked in the warm remembrance of this dramatic setting. Live a thousand years, this would be his finest moment.

Deep in their hearts, every lawyer worth his or her salt desires to be, at sometime in their life, an Atticus Finch. It was years before Harper Lee penned her classic *To Kill a Mockingbird*. And this was not make believe but within the terrifying realm of reality. What Pat Holt said to that jury of 12 white, stone-faced men was not scripted by Hollywood, but came from the heart and mind of a country lawyer, with still a bite of the Irish in his blood. It came from the real God-given notion of what lawyering was all about, what it had always been about.

Justice.

And only those now living, who lived in the Jim Crow South, can fully understand and recognize the moral magnitude of this lawyer's seismic effort.

The son of a Confederate soldier pleading for the life of the son of a former slave. The embryonic stirring of America coming into its own.

To a hushed audience bent forward to hear, Holt spoke.

"Duty is higher than life itself," he began, stressing at the very beginning a most important virtue of these men who had come of age and lived when "duty" had carried heroic, even bloody obligations.

"It is higher than the life of one man, for it represents all that mankind can do in this world. It has been man's right to a trial by jury ever since the adoption of the famous Bill of Rights in our national Constitution, and the right of trial by jury is no more important that the duty of every jury man to give every defendant a fair and impartial trial."

And that included Lube Martin, even though his skin was black.

Holt then proceeded to give his own rendition of the A.O. Stanley masterpiece on the majesty of the law. It too was moving.

"This courthouse is holy ground, in a sense of the word. Gentlemen, I ask that you do not let prejudice or sympathy govern your decision in this case."

He clearly meant racial prejudice against his client, and sympathy for the victim's family.

Holt then spent a great deal of time on the evidence. Of how the poor Martin had been hounded and threatened by Diuguid. How that even on the day of the killing the defendant had tried, without success, to skirt by Diuguid on Curd Street on that fateful December day.

In closing out his passionate plea, Pat Holt once again returned to the powerful draw of the transcending virtue of duty.

"Life is full of stern duties, gentlemen: duty to our homes, our state, our country and our God."

Then in a subtle and ingenious manner, he urged them to follow him in buffeting the social currents of that time and place. "I feel I have discharged my duty to this defendant, and I'm going to leave it to you, to do your duty to yourself and your state."

With his conclusion, the silence of the courtroom was relaxed slightly as the audience shuffled their sedentary positions, exhaled and dared to whisper to each other. Quickly however, all eyes turned to the other side of the arena where Denny Smith arose and approached the jury rail.

It was the state's advantage and the defendant's misfortune that by all accounts this veteran prosecutor would turn in his most powerful and magnificent orations in this case of the Commonwealth of Kentucky versus Lube Martin.

He did it with a masterful mix of subtle racism (subtle for that time and place), hard evidence, and sympathy for the fallen victim and his family.

Smith too alluded to duty, that of a different sort. "Crime, like a landscape had its mountains and its cliffs, and sometimes its volcanoes. I know of no greater duty or responsibility than that of a jury sitting in judgment on a citizen in this land. I shall not shrink from my duty, even if it be unpleasant. If this man is convicted it will be but retribution for the awful crime which he has committed."

Whether to remind his jurors of the realities of the times, or simply a natural manner of talk at that time, the commonwealth attorney frequently referred to Smith as "the Negro" and his friends "the Negroes."

But perhaps Smith's most powerful thrust legitimately went to the hard evidence.

Displaying the powder burns on the clothes and recounting the testimony of Dr. Mason, he sized up the attack and shooting of Diuguid as a brutal ambush. According to his argument "the Negroes" made the victim think that they would simply pass him on the street, and then took him from behind, wrestled him to the ground and held him while Martin inflicted the fatal shots. The lethal bullet hole going straight down into his shoulder was, according to the state's attorney, irrefutable proof that he was down on the ground when he was shot.

As to the bad blood between the two? With some dubious disregard to much of the evidence Smith adroitly turned the evidence to his liking:

If is shown in the testimony here that there was some grudge between the men—doubtless incurred by some false charge which Martin made against Diuguid and which the latter desired corrected. If Guthrie Diuguid had the grudge against Martin he had every opportunity in the world to harm him if he wanted to. The testimony about Diuguid's wanting Martin to come up to his office indicates that Diuguid wanted Martin to come up and correct that charge which he had made about him and to straighten the matter out.

With his emotions rising to a fever pitch and tears stream-
ing down his cheeks he pointed to Diuguid's widow and recounted
the dying man's last request to see his children:

*Even that privilege was denied him. The most precious thing
next to the salvation of his own soul. Then realizing that he was
approaching death, and that the great curtain of the future was about
to be rolled back, Guthrie Diuguid–almost in the presence of his
God–told his wife that those Negroes held him while Lube Martin shot
him.*

Then, in an obvious response to Holt's noble plea he
implored:

*We do want a verdict by the law and the evidence, and we
want it registered in the archives of this court that a disinterested jury
had determined that this crime shall be punished to the fullest extent,
and that a judgment commensurate with the crime has been entered.*

By this time in Smith's argument, Lube Martin, obviously
distraught with the devastating barrage of words, simply buried his
head in his elbows on the counsel table.

Smith's last words reverberated like thunder around the
courtroom, packed to the upper reaches of the balcony with mes-
merized listeners. The momentary pause of the seasoned orator was
met with deafening quiet, as if the entire congregation was not even
breathing.

Then he took a white handkerchief from his breast pocket,
and slowly wiped the tears from his face. Lowering his voice with
the expected effect of his listeners bending closer, he calmly concluded. He finished on a note which combined a little from the
play book of Pat Holt, and a little which vaguely called to the faint
fears of race embedded in the minds of the jurors:

If ever a man under oath had tried to do his duty, I have, and

I call upon you in the name of your God and all that you hold dear—your loved ones at home, whom the strong arm of the law protects even now—to render a verdict that will stop such crimes.

Keep them in their place, or they will take over the streets, and pillage your homes.

Letting his final words settle into the ears of all listeners, Smith slowly walked to the counsel table and sat down.

It was 12:30 in the afternoon.

Judge Bush brought everyone back to life by recessing court until 2 p.m.

In Kentucky, then as now, the jury determines guilt or innocence and also sets the penalty. At that time they did it within the same deliberations.

So when court reconvened at 2 p.m. Judge Bush instructed the court that if they found Martin guilty of murder they could sentence him to life imprisonment or death. If found guilty of the lesser crime of manslaughter, he could receive a prison sentence of 2 to 21 years.

At 2:20 p.m. the jury got the case. The twelve filed out of the jury box and into the back room behind the bench. The door was shut, the bailiff, Deputy Sheriff F. A. Bailey sat down at the door. Judge Bush recessed court.

The courtroom relaxed. Some got up and left. Others chatted among themselves. The soldiers stretched, yawned and visited with their fellows. Everyone waited.

For lawyers and judges the time that a jury is out deliberating is time suspended. The battle has been fought, for better or ill. There is nothing left to do but wait. The results lie solely in the hands of twelve people behind a closed door.

And no one ever knows how long a jury will be out.

In a murder case of this type, with the evidence as close as it had been, most people were guessing hours—maybe even overnight.

So the whole courtroom, loitering around in disarray, was jolted to attention at precisely 3:30 p.m. when a loud knock came upon the jury room door.

The jury had a verdict, only a little over one hour into deliberations.

It was not a good sign for Lube Martin.

Quickly the National Guardsmen on the scene scurried to various locations, pulling together at full force in the courtroom in anticipation of the verdict.

When the courtroom was sufficiently secure to Judge Bush's liking and the spectators returned to their seats, Judge Bush nodded to the bailiff.

The door opened and the twelve men filed out and into the jury box. Their expressions were inscrutable, serious. They did not look at either counsel table.

Matt Winfree, a farmer by trade, was carrying the paperwork. He was the foreman.

Once they were all standing in the jury box, Judge Bush inquired, "Gentlemen, have you reached a verdict?"

"Yes sir," Winfree replied.

"Pass it to the clerk," Bush directed.

The written instructions with the verdict were passed to Bailey who, in turn, handed it to the Circuit Clerk L. C. Trevathan seated next to Judge Bush.

Breathlessly everyone waited as Trevathan scanned the paper.

Then he pronounced in a voice loud enough to be heard in the far reaches of the balcony, "We, the jury find the defendant guilty as charged in the indictment and fix his punishment at death."

Lube Martin had buried his head in his folded arms on the table for the entire time the jury was out. Undoubtedly suffering from severe and debilitating depression, he did not even raise his head from the table when the verdict was read.

The crowd seemed to have exhaled a collective sigh of relief.

Pat Holt appeared shaken by the verdict. The prosecution team–especially troublemaker George Diuguid–was openly elated.

Considering the magnitude of the moment however, the courtroom scene was relatively subdued and without commotion.

A newspaper reporter would write, "As the verdict was read a sigh of relief was heaved from the breast of all present, for all knew that if the verdict had been other than it was that trouble would have been imminent."

The jury was then led out of the courtroom by the bailiff.

A special train was standing by just in case a hurried getaway might be needed. Now it prepared to leave town at a leisurely pace. The men moved down the street and met up with their meager luggage at the station. Very few people even noticed them as they strolled the three blocks to the depot. Under the watchful eyes of the soldiers and deputies they boarded the special car.

Hissing steam and the barking call of a porter were soon answered by the thunderous sound of pistons nudging the giant iron wheels into motion. As winter twilight began to fall over Murray the train picked up speed and headed out of town, through the pitiful hovels and tar-papered shanties of the people of color.

CHAPTER 11

AFTERMATH

By the time the jury was out of the courtroom Pat Holt had recovered.

Few people were listening when he told Judge Bush that he would be moving for a new trial.

Judge Bush nodded. "We'll hear it in the morning," he replied. "And we'll set sentencing for in the morning at 9:00."

It didn't look hopeful for Holt's motion for a new trial.

Court was adjourned, and the courthouse emptied peacefully. Once more the soldiers took their prisoner and led him back to jail.

Judge Bush and Denny Smith made their way back to the Murray Hotel unmolested.

Word of the verdict spread quickly throughout Murray and the surrounding community. To most there was a sense of much-welcomed closure and relief. While the outcome came as a surprise to some, it was standard fare to most.

Reported a newsman, "There is no excitement in Murray tonight. The jury's verdict appeased any wrath against the Negro."

Normally, motions for new trials are made and perfunctorily denied.

So, Pat Holt did not have much steam in his argument on that Friday morning as he and Lube Martin stood before the judge for sentencing. The usual crowd was not in the courtroom. No wonder. The temperature would reach 70 degrees on this balmy day; time for folks to look to farm chores and preparations for spring planting.

For all intents and purposes the whole matter was over.

Over for all, of course, except for the defendant, Lube Martin.

It did not take Bush long to overrule the motion for a new trial. As far as the judge was concerned, Martin had received a fair trial. With that piece of business taken care of, the judge turned to the most immediate task at hand.

"Does the defendant have anything to say, before sentence is imposed?" Bush sternly asked, as the courtroom grew deathly still.

The black man, who had once collapsed during the trial and had shown signs of utter despair the day before, was now somehow fully composed.

Perhaps he was somewhat relieved that it was over–even if the worst possible verdict had been rendered. It is not an uncommon reaction. For most criminal defendants, and for even parties in a civil dispute, the greatest agony in a trial is the unknown and the waiting. Once the question is decided, good or bad, people seem to grow calm with resigned acceptance.

Martin appeared relaxed, and spoke boldly for all the courtroom to hear.

"I do not think I received a fair trial," he began. "I shot Mr. Diuguid in self-defense. I have never been guilty of bothering any white people."

And then after a pause, he seemed to have risen a bit higher in his shoes and in a clear and convincing voice he finished, "I will go before God with a clear conscience."

A fleeting but profound feeling of both sympathy and respect for this defendant swept across the courtroom, and was reflected in the solemn face of old Judge Bush.

Recovering, Bush quickly pronounced:

It is adjudged by the court that the defendant be taken to the jail of Calloway County, there to be safely kept to await the convenience of the sheriff of said county, who shall safely convey and deliver it to the warden of the state penitentiary at Eddyville, Kentucky, there to be safely kept until Friday, the 18th day of May 1917, on which day and before sunrise, the warden or his deputy within the walls of said penitentiary shall cause to pass through his body a current of electricity of sufficient intensity to cause death as quickly as possible, and the application of such current shall continue until death ensues.

On request from Holt, the court suspended the sentence for sixty days "in order to give the defendant time to prepare and perfect his appeal to the Court of Appeals."

Almost as an afterthought the trials of Lube's two brothers and Jordon were set for April. The latter, whose involvement was now recognized by all to be marginal at best, was released on bond posted by his employer out of Tennessee.

With that final piece of judicial housekeeping, Judge Bush adjourned court.

It was a strange and assorted group of people who boarded the train on that sunny Friday afternoon.

Judge Charles Bush and Commonwealth Attorney Denny Smith, relieved with the ordeal being over, climbed aboard and settled into their car. The entire company of soldiers, relaxed to the point now of joviality–knowing they were heading home, loaded on for the ride. In one car, guarded closely by the doughboys were the condemned defendant Lube Martin, and his two brothers, Ann and Sylvester. They were being transported to Paducah where they would be lodged, safely away from residue of ill will which might still be lingering against them in the Calloway County capital.

No one knows what thoughts and regrets bored down upon Lube Martin's mind as the train pulled out and passed the homes of his neighbors and loved ones, the home of his father, the house of his wife and the mixed chorus of memories which had to be wedded to that spot. One must wonder whether he thought of this as the last time he would see these familiar landmarks of his young life.

They had sad and heavy hearts, vacant eyes staring across the coach, brothers still in chains and shackles–three of the same blood and bondage, trying to place their minds in a traveling mode for the dark and uncertain road ahead. One on the way to death row, the other two on the way to uncertain handling at the hands of a system foreign and strange as if still chattel of the strict and ever changing white overseer.

Other hearts in this train of mixed purpose and emotions were happy soldiers heading for home, to the rejoicing and enfolding arms of loved ones. Judge and lawyers were sighing with relief and fatigue as they retreat from the battle scene, wishing for a stiff drink.

All of them of varying missions were thrown together by fate and circumstance on a train heading north through the naked woods of winter and meadows brown and sear. On the cold rail they rode through the lonesome landscape of west Kentucky made strangely bright and spring-like by the unusually warm weather.

In Paducah, the soldiers made their final deposit of the prisoners in the county jail for safekeeping. After happily checking over their responsibility to the local authorities they boarded the train to Hopkinsville, light hearted and gay. Many, if not most, however, would soon be summoned to do much bloodier battle, in a far-away land across the sea.

Judge Bush and Denny Smith were no doubt delighted to be rid of the whole Lube Martin affair. On the following Monday, they would be opening court in Trigg County and dealing with less volatile, but just as essential matters. There in Cadiz–the pretty little city on a hill–they would make their way into the elegant, old brick courthouse with the lofty clock turret and once again do battle against the surging sea of troubles. In a different temple, among clans of different plaid, they would continue the same battle of circuit riders upon a different shore.

> *With records of the things they lived by, if not for.*
> *Debris of the local courts, circuit and county,*
> *In the fusty vaults, blind:*
> *Land transfers, grants, indictments, inquests, plaints,*
> *Stompings and stabbings, public blasphemy,*
> *Lawings and mayhem, the slap dash*
> *Confusions of life flung*
> *In a heap like the kitchen-midden*
> *Of a lost clan feasting while their single fire*
> *Flared red and green with sea-salt, and night fell–*
> *Shellfish and artifact, blacked bone and shard,*
> *Left on the sea-tongued shore.*
> *And the sea was time.*

In Murray things returned to the normal routine. Most wanted to forget the whole unsavory mess which had engulfed their town and cast their bucolic community of well-meaning people into the national headlines as violent hooligans and rabid vigilantes.

With most, concerns were turning more and more to the growing war in Europe and talk of the freshly re-elected president.

On March 13, the Murray contingent of the State Militia returned to a thunderous welcome of bands and speeches after nine months on the Mexican border. As world developments would unfold, they were destined not remain at home for long.

Scant reports began to filter into far west Kentucky about tremendous rumblings of political and social upheaval taking place in Russia. Slowly, the picture unfolded of a deposed Czar, the murder of him and his family, and the bloody establishment of a new communist government. Few at that time knew what monumental changes that far-away revolution would have upon America's future.

After weeks and months of gathering war clouds, President Woodrow Wilson asked Congress for a declaration of war. On April 6, his request was granted.

Anti-German and frenzied patriotic fervor swept the country. A stern-looking Uncle Sam suddenly appeared everywhere on posters pointing his bony finger and demanding, "I want you!"

The Selective Service Act was passed and young men throughout Kentucky and the rest of the nation were drafted into the military. Many volunteered.

Feelings against Germany were so strong that it was considered treasonous for anyone to even mention a different viewpoint.

The picture of Paducah Police Chief Luther Graham appeared on the front page of the *Paducah Evening Sun*. He had given orders to his men to arrest anyone making un-American remarks. The city police judge said he would back him to the hilt by "throwing the book" at anyone so charged.

On June 26 the American boys began to arrive in France under General John J. Pershing.

"Lafayette, we are here!" was their proud pronouncement, showing our respect and appreciation to the French for the aid given us during our war for independence.

But in Murray, time still went forward through the daily routine, given cadence by the more mundane things of life.

On June 19, the Confederate monument was completed on the northeast corner of the courthouse lawn. The edifice, sculptured in Italy, was unveiled at a cost of $2,500 raised by the United Daughters of the Confederacy.

The County's first group of the American Red Cross was formed, and memberships sold for one dollar. Famed Confederate veteran Captain A.M. Ayers was one of the first to join.

Tobacco plant beds flourished, the delicate seedlings drawn and set out in the muddy fields by the leathered bondsmen of the soil. The president had to fight a war, but a farmer had to feed his family.

In Murray, Kentucky, however, there was one person neither preoccupied with the Great War or other matters closer to hand. He had not been able to put the Lube Martin murder case behind him.

That was defense attorney Pat Holt. Lube Martin's life depended upon this country lawyer staying the course through the appellate process. Holt did not waiver or desist from that responsibility.

He filed his notice of appeal and began the tortuous road of petitioning and briefing the Kentucky Court of Appeals, which at that time was the state's highest tribunal.

With the hindsight of over eighty years, it's not hard to find fault with much of the murder trial of Lube Martin. But when cast in a comparison with other trials of rural Kentucky during that time, even those devoid of racial issues, Judge Bush did as well as to be expected. Most of his rulings were correct, and generally the proceedings were orderly and fair.

There are some glaring lapses, however, which even to this day beg for reasonable explanation.

First and foremost was his failure to move the trial out of Calloway County. Perhaps more puzzling is the absence of any evidence that Pat Holt attempted to have the trial moved. It would seem ludicrous to think that even fresh jurors from two counties away could have been brought into Murray and sit there among its citizens and not be intimidated. These jurymen were no doubt affected by the memory of Calloway Countians, just weeks before, kidnapping the judge and prosecutor at ransom for the lynching of the accused. One must wonder how a judge could expect strangers, knowing the history of the case, to coolly and rationally listen to the evidence and return a fair and just verdict while all the time wondering if they were going to get out of town in one piece if they came down with the wrong decision.

Both Holt and Bush agreed that 12 impartial Calloway

Countians could not be found to try the case. But that was only half –maybe the least important–part of the problem. The teeming and vengeful mood of the community, this cauldron of prejudice against the defendant wherein the case was to be tried was at least equally worthy of consideration.

In Kentucky then, as now, a change of venue is a drastic procedural matter to be taken only under the most urgent circumstances. When it is granted, there is a strong preference to be given to moving the trial to an adjoining county within the same judicial circuit. In the Martin case that would have been Trigg, just across the river. Many times this is not far enough. So Christian was not a bad choice, although that community had also been embroiled for a time in the January drama when it became inflamed by their own Judge Bush and Denny Smith being imperiled by the Murray citizenry.

Therefore it is puzzling as to why Bush didn't move the case to Hopkinsville, instead of having Hopkinsville come to Murray. This importation of jurors is not an unusual method. It keeps the administrative burden of the trial in the county where the crime was committed. But to bring in jurors from another county to try a case is normally when the parties are so well known in that community that it would be difficult to get jurors who did not know one or more of the parties. But where public passion and prejudice is involved, bringing in a jury from another county is only a band-aid approach to the problem.

Why did Holt himself not push hard to move the trial out of the county?

The question remains a mystery.

Hidden under the debris and ashes of almost a century, never to be recovered, is the mental process of this country lawyer. And sometimes trial strategy, so fine and subjective, comes into play to explain what the cold, written record leaves unanswered.

Pat Holt knew his friends and neighbors. Comments at the restaurant, at church, collective impressions of the community may have led him to believe that his client was better off in staying home. There the soiled reputation of the victim, Guthrie Diuguid, might find its way into the jury room. It is remarkable to note that it was Bush, not Holt, who initiated the summoning of jurors from another county.

If the ghost of Patrick Holt could be summoned back to the land of the living, he no doubt would have a logical explanation for his acquiescence to the trial remaining in Murray. But alas, we mortals are left wondering.

Also, in retrospect, most of Bush's rulings from the bench appear evenhanded and thoughtful.

There is at least one notable exception.

It would seem the exclusion of the letter of Lube Martin's mother, made more poignant and pitiful by her being dead at the time of the trial, was an unjustifiable blow to the defendant's case. All people, even toughened and calloused men of 1917, are moved by the pleas of a mother. It seems that it would have been a moving, perhaps even pivotal, piece of evidence for the jury to have. "Don't come home son, I'm afeared for your life," was the essence of her desperate plea. Who could not have been moved by such a voice from the dead?

The letter was definitely not inadmissible hearsay, because it was not being introduced for the truthfulness, or even the legitimacy of the mother's statement. But it was the message itself, a call for care, which was the gist of the matter as it might have affected Lube Martin's fearful attitude toward his deadly adversary. It went to the issue of whether he had reason, in his mind, to think he would have to act in self-defense. A person who shoots into a bush after being told that it hides a bear is proven no less reasonable when afterwards it is learned that the report was false.

It is true that the letter does not refer to the victim Guthrie Diuguid by name. But when considering all the evidence it is obvious that the "old man" referred to in the letter as a threat to Martin's life was Diuguid. Also, it made little if any difference who the menace in the letter actually was, if Martin reasonably believed it was Diuguid.

This egregious ruling by the old judge was undoubtedly the unkindest cut of all against the defendant.

When spring comes to stay in west Kentucky, she is a sight to behold. All dressed up in white dogwoods, redbuds and an explosion of green, the goddess of hope and revival takes over the lush landscape. Winter woes and cares evaporate into the warm, balmy air.

On May 17, 1917 John F. Kennedy, who would one day as president take serious aim at the segregationist practices of the South, was born in Brookline, Mass.

Three days later, on May 20, over at Fulton, a scant 35 miles west from Murray, a mob quietly lynched a 45-year-old Negro by the name of Lawrence Dempsey. The victim was being held in jail there for seriously knifing a white, Illinois Central Railroad worker. The vigilantes worked so quietly on this early Sunday morning in forcing open the jail and hanging Dempsey from a telephone cable, that the hanging did not become known until later in the morning when his lifeless body was found dangling from the end of a rope about 200 feet behind the jail. Coroner H.C. Barrett made the perfunctory finding which closed the book on the crime, "Dempsey came to his death by being hanged by the neck until he was dead by unknown persons."

As the weather warmed up, so did the violent storms of spring. One week after the death of Lawrence Dempsey, the good Lord unleashed His wrath upon the countryside. A deadly tornado tore through far west Kentucky, killing over 50 people, injuring scores more, and causing extensive damage.

Through this tumultuous spring, lawyer Pat Holt continued to work on the appeal for Lube Martin.

He recognized his own limitation and knew that appealing a death penalty was much more than writing a persuasive brief.

It also meant arguing the case before the big boys in Frankfort, the Court of Appeals. He also recognized that as a country lawyer practicing in far-flung west Kentucky, he needed help.

And he got it–big time.

The Confederate Army was stronger in Kentucky after the Civil War than it was during the bloody conflict.

As if to assuage its political conscience for not officially withdrawing from the Union with its sister Southern states, the state house and local courthouses were invaded by Confederate veterans who were immensely popular with the voters. These returning warriors- some of them relegated for a time as fugitives to Canada and Mexico, until pardons were secured from the federal government- moved about under a romantic halo of the lost cause. The state, especially the western part, was solidly Democratic. From the Civil War 'till almost the end of the century, it was one long, interrupted parade of Democratic governors to Frankfort, including former Confederate heroes James B. McCreary, Luke Blackburn and Simon Bolivar Buckner.

The newly formed Democratic *Courier Journal*, led by its young editor, Henry Watterson, a former Confederate soldier, began its meteoric rise to not only the state's most influential newspaper, but one of the most respected in the country.

By 1917, the secessionist soldiers had turned into old gray men, no longer spending their time in high offices, but gathering instead at poignant reunions. There, in dwindling numbers as the years went by, aging old men, some missing a leg, some an arm, stared into the cameras for one last photograph, their flowing white beards unable to hide the persistent pride and defiance in their faces.

But a few of them, even then, still toiled in the public trenches, wielding powerful influence over the minds of Kentucky citizens.

One such Confederate veteran was Bennett Henderson Young of Jessamine County.

Born in 1843, and a graduate of Centre College, he enlisted with John Hunt Morgan's calvary in 1863. He was best known for leading the Confederacy's most northern action–a raid across the Canadian border on St. Albany, Vermont in October of 1864.

The Canadian government charged him with being a renegade but he was cleared of the charge. He went into exile in Scotland after the war and was educated at the University of Edinburgh.

In 1868, he was pardoned and he returned to Louisville where he became an outstanding trial lawyer. He also succeeded in various business enterprises. Young expended his efforts in the railroad industry, developing the Monon Railroad, the Kentucky and Indiana Bridge, and the Louisville Southern Railway.

A strong Democrat–as were all Confederate veterans–he became highly respected in his party as one of those nonelected public men of influence and persuasion. He contributed greatly to the 1890-91 revision of the state's Constitution.

But he was most respected as a man of high character. He was an eloquent speaker and possessed of a gracious and charitable heart. A devout Presbyterian, he gave much of his time in helping numerous educational and charitable institutions, including the financially stressed Louisville Free Public Library.

The old soldier's most ardent passion was for his fellow veterans of the "lost cause" and memorialization of the old Confederacy. He was the primary promoter of the Kentucky Confederate Home in Jefferson County and the Jefferson Davis Monument in Fairview. Because of his tireless efforts on behalf of the United Confederate Veterans Association, Young received the honorary title of "Commander in Chief for Life."

He was a prolific writer of various published works of history.

By the spring of 1917, seventy-four-year-old Bennett Henderson Young was one of the most respected and revered gray beards of the grand ole Commonwealth.

On May 31, the morning newspapers boldly declared a new and dramatic development in the Lube Martin appeal.

Bennett H. Young would assist Pat Holt in the cause of Lube Martin and would argue the case for the convicted murderer before the state's highest court.

Everyone agreed it was good news for Lube Martin. Each of

the 7 jurists who sat on the state's highest court–then named simply as the Court of Appeals–were elected to that high bench. A person with the political stature of Young would have to be given great deference by the jurists.

It is not known for sure how Young became interested in the case of Lube Martin.

But one can make a highly educated guess.

Most likely, the much younger Pat Holt knew the Confederate hero. Both were lawyers, but most importantly, they probably knew each other through the networking of the Confederate veterans. Holt's father and Young undoubtedly had known each other. And Holt was wise enough to seize upon the connection.

And what has been lost to all but the most serious historians is that many of the leaders of the Confederacy, including its military, did not share the same views when it came to slavery and the Negro. For most it was a war of state's rights, slavery being the most emotional and aberrant sticking point of the larger political issue. Many who fought and died for the right of states to maintain slavery, were personally and morally opposed to it. Foremost amongst these was Robert E. Lee. Kentucky's own John C. Breckinridge, who rose to vice president of the United States only to join the Confederacy and eventually become its secretary of war, was suspected by many of his Southern brethren as being at least ambivalent to slavery. He was an ardent opponent of the Ku Klux Klan after the war.

Even Jefferson Davis himself, with the war turning against the South in late 1864, sent a secret emissary to Europe offering emancipation of the slaves in return for recognition and aid from the European powers. He advanced legislation at the bitter end to enlist slaves into the Confederate Army in exchange for their freedom.

Many of the ex-Confederates who did not see the black man as their equal at least felt paternalistic toward them, and saw their responsibility as former slave owners to work as the protectors in the turbulent wake of emancipation, reconstruction, and resettlement of the Negro race. In short, the former slaves and their heirs had many friends from the former ranks of the gray. Unfortunately, through the first five decades after the Civil War, the Southern political leadership did not build upon that dwindling cadre of powerful ex-Confederates to give true equality to the Negro.

And sadly, rabid racists, bigoted ruffians, criminals, and hate mongers rushed in to fill that leadership void with a violence from which the South has yet to fully recover.

But to the matter at hand, in the first quivering of spring in 1917 the familiar tobacco plant beds began to make their annual appearance around the Calloway County countryside and the days became longer. Pat Holt proceeded to prepare the appeal for Lube Martin. The addition of Bennett Young to the defense team came with the breath of spring.

The trial of Lube Martin's co-defendants, Ed Jordon, Ann Martin, and Sylvester Martin was scheduled for the April term of court. The co-defendants were not foremost on the mind of Judge Charles Bush when he arrived in town on April 9, the day after Easter.

The countryside may have been alive with the beauty of spring—snow white cottonwoods and redbuds in bloom, lush emerald pastures, and canvas tobacco beds dotting the rolling hills of far west Kentucky. But when the old jurist addressed the new grand jury he was still thinking of the humiliations he had suffered in the thick of winter.

He wanted the leaders of the mob who had taken him and his commonwealth attorney hostage brought to justice.

In his stern charge to the 12 member panel, Bush most eloquently summed up the whole harrowing experience from his perspective:

I consider it my duty as a man and officer to speak to you about a most unfortunate affair. I profoundly regret to feel called upon to mention it. In fact, I would prefer that it be buried in the sea of ever-lasting forgetfulness. Of course, I refer to that inexcusable exhibition of lawlessness that took place in this town on January 10.

This is the first grand jury that has been impaneled in Calloway County since that occasion and hence I present this matter to you, and will tell you plainly what is your duty in the premises. This court had performed a judicial act prompted only by an earnest desire to do his duty and to save human life as he conscientiously believed by ordering a prisoner to be transferred to the jail of another county. This was the head and front of his offending, provoking a storm of indignation which found expression in an organized band of men composed of at least 1,000 noisy and boisterous persons who with their leaders packed the courthouse and thronged the streets interfering with and temporarily suspending the business of the court denouncing the court, threatening to hang the judge crying out in the most angry manner, 'Shoot him! Hang him!'

The judge and the commonwealth attorney tried to appeal to the mob to keep quiet while they could explain why Lube Martin was sent away, but their appeals were in vain. The infuriated crowd only grew worse. The judge and the commonwealth attorney, having no protection, and seeing that it was useless to try to remain in the courthouse at that time, left for their hotel. The judge was followed by the mob, and the unlawful, riotous assembly surrounded the hotel and collected in large number in front of the hotel and threatening the life of the judge and sending their leaders to him, making certain demands, accompanied with threats of death if he did not yield.

It is proper that I should say to you that the judge never yielded to a mob leader nor made any concessions to one in spite of statements that have been made to the contrary by some who were not present during the most trying ordeal. Good men and women know that the judge said to the last that he would die before he would surrender the prisoner to a mob. The news was then brought to the court that they were preparing to enter the hotel and were threatening to blow it up, and it was urged by good people that there was probability of much bloodshed.

Gentlemen, this was the appalling condition that existed in your midst on January 10. I have not exaggerated it. It is impossible for me to overdraw the picture. It was a scene that beggared description. What was the occasion for it? A most harmless act upon my part. When I found the poor Negro could not be tried I thought it best to send him away, not only for the black but best for Calloway County and her good people, and gentlemen, when I beheld that vast throng of people swept off their feet by prejudice and passion I was confirmed in the belief that I had saved Calloway County the disgrace of mob violence. I regret to allude to this at all, would much rather pass the incident by in silence forever, but gentlemen, I cannot afford to do it. Neither can you.

Perish the thought. A decent respect for our institutions pertaining to both church and state, our instinctive love of simple justice, law and order, our regard for the welfare and protection of society; the sanctity of our homes, and the happiness and prosperity of our beloved ones demand that we should be equal to the emergency. The law has been ruthlessly violated without the semblance of excuse. Your temple of justice desecrated and profaned, and it is for you to say whether there shall be any atonement for it.

The grand jury has to take the initiative. It may be, and doubtless is, an unpleasant duty. But you cannot afford to shirk it. This is a good county full of good noble people. I have personal esteem for them all. I seek no personal revenge. That is contrary to a cardinal doctrine Him to whom we should all bow in humble submission. I am prompted by a sense of duty as an officer of the law and I appeal to you and the good people of Calloway County and of this judicial district to co-operate with me and hold up my hands.

It is through the instrumentality of the courts that the inestimable blessings of life, liberty and the pursuit of happiness are to be preserved and perpetuated and unless the courts are supported and sustained by the people in upholding and enforcing the law, all that is best in our splendid civilization will perish. The law is plain that if persons band themselves together for the purpose of intimidating, alarming, disturbing or injuring any persons, they are guilty of a felony and punishable as described in Section 1341 (A) Kentucky statues. This is the law, and it has been violated and trampled underfoot. It is your duty to make it known. I call upon you gentlemen to rise up in the majesty of your sovereignty and indict the guilty parties, thereby doing what you can to wipe this stain from the annals of Calloway County.

One of the last messages from David to Solomon was 'I go the way of all the earth. Be strong. Show thyself a man.' Gentlemen, I commend to you these divine words of the Lord's appointed.

Almost ten days later, on Wednesday April 18, after hearing 22 witnesses, including Judge Bush himself, the grand jury returned.

Incredibly, it indicted no one. Not one single soul.

Understandably, Judge Bush was outraged.

If the veteran old trial lawyer had been beaten down by the mob in January, his old fighting spirit was now returned.

Upon motion from Commonwealth Attorney Smith, he threw out the whole batch of grand jurors and summoned in a new panel.

On that same day the United States incurred its very first casualty of World War I when American aviator Edmond Genet was shot down over France. Ironically, Genet himself was a great-grandson of the famed Edmond "Citizen" Genet, French minister to the United States during the French Revolution.

By Friday morning, April 20th, 1917 dutiful Sheriff Patterson had gathered 44 potential jurors in the courtroom. Twelve Calloway County men were then selected as the new grand jury. Once again Judge Bush gave them the strict admonition as to what he expected. This time however, he ordered them locked in the room during the consideration of the evidence. It was clear that the testy old jurist now meant business.

So, the grand jury rolled up their sleeves and went right to work, undoubtedly concerned that the irate judge might just keep them there for the whole weekend if they didn't dispatch of the matter quickly.

By five o'clock that afternoon, they had examined 24 witnesses and returned to the courtroom.

Say the official court records:

This day the foreman of the grand jury in the presence of the entire jury returned into open court the following indictment which was received by the clerk from the Judge and filed in open court:

One against Sam Byrd, Will Starks, Ewin Bourland, Burnett Waterfield and Dick Vance, charging them with the offense of "Contempt of Court" upon which bail is endorsed in the sum of $500 each......

Sam Byrd was then a candidate for jailer. Guthrie Diuguid's brother, Ed, posted his bond. Edwin Bourland, was a nephew of Guthrie Diuguid.

To Bush's chagrin, the men were not indicted on the felony charge that he had requested. Thinking he had done the best he was going to do however, he dismissed the grand jury and ordered the arrest of the new defendants, setting their bonds at $500 each.

Bush also announced the obvious. He would have to recuse himself from their trial and request another judge, since he would be a primary witness.

When the grand jury returned indictments only for misdemeanors instead of felonies, both Bush and Smith lost interest. The cases would eventually fizzle out with a mere whimper.

Over the next several months Vance, Starks, and Byrd pled guilty and paid meager fines. In November 1919, over two and one half years later, the cases against Bourland and Watterfield were quietly filed away.

The trial of Lube Martin's co-defendants was almost an afterthought in that April term. When they were brought to court for a definite day to be set, the commonwealth attorney requested that their cases be continued generally until the state's highest court had ruled on Lube's case. If there were reversible mistakes in that case, he did not want to repeat them in a trial with the rest of the defendants.

Ed Jordon was free on bail. But the Martin brothers would have to vegetate the entire time in the McCracken County Jail where they were being held for safekeeping.

In March of 1917, an interesting sideshow to the whole Lube Martin story was taking place in Hopkinsville, home of Judge Bush and Commonwealth Attorney Denny Smith.

Safely back in his home town after taking a shellacking from the press for his role in the January lynch mob mess, Bush decided to go on the offensive in an attempt to restore his battered reputation. He, along with Denny Smith, had lost little time in marshaling the forces of the local bar in giving written support in the newspaper as to their courage and integrity. After all, what lawyer in his right mind could resist the pressure of both the circuit judge and the commonwealth attorney?

Bush was convinced that he had been wrongly, and falsely maligned by all of the negative newspaper reporting. And the most culpable of those papers had been the Louisville *Courier Journal.*

In the January 12, 1917 edition of that paper reporter Claude H. Perry had written of a telephone interview the night before wherein Judge Bush had reportedly told him that "he was compelled to issue an order of return for Martin to save his own life, and that the mob had threatened to blow him up if he did not comply with their request." Bush declared that he had never talked to Perry and had never made such a statement.

Prosecutor Denny Smith, no doubt at the behest of Judge Bush, obtained an indictment from the Christian County grand jury on March 10, 1917 against both Perry and the *Courier Journal* for criminal libel.

Of course Judge Bush would not be able to preside over the criminal prosecution, since he would be the main prosecution witness. As was the procedure of that time, Bush certified to the circuit clerk a need for a special judge, and the clerk in turn petitioned the governor to appoint the replacement.

Stanley ignored the request, and the case had to be continued from term to term for lack of a judge. Repeated requests were made through June 1918.

Still Stanley refused to act. If no special judge was appointed, then Perry and the *Courier Journal* could not be prosecuted.

It might appear on the surface that the political Stanley was simply attempting to curry favor with *The Courier*, a paper that went into all of the hills and hollows of Kentucky. And he could use a favor, since it was a paper that had repeatedly given the governor rough going.

But the toughened old statesman was more principled than that.

There was a very good reason why Stanley did not give in to prosecute the *Courier Journal*. He knew first hand that the story written by Perry was essentially true.

Right after Stanley's rescue of Bush and Smith from Murray in January, and the universal condemnation the judge took by the press, including the *Courier Journal,* Bush had requested the governor's aid.

He wrote to Stanley, "A very great wrong has been done me. Your name has been invoked by the *Courier Journal* to justify it." The old jurist, who had owed his job to Stanley who appointed him after Judge Adolphus Hanberry's death, was inferring that Stanley was responsible in some way for his brutal treatment by the media.

The insinuation infuriated the governor.

In his written response to Judge Bush's January letter, the governor wrote in part:

The civil authorities of Calloway having wired that they were utterly powerless to control the situation and requesting my immediate intervention, citizens from adjoining counties, by telephone and telegraph confirmed the truth of these statements.......I immediately advised the long-distance exchange of the situation, urgently insisting that I get in immediate communication with Judge Bush, without regard to inconvenience or expense. In the meantime I prepared to leave Louisville for Paducah within the hour, having secured a special train over the N.C. & St. L. from Paducah to Murray. This was done, not so much to save the life of this Negro, who was for the time being secure, but to save your own, which I have every reason to believe was in imminent danger.

About an hour after putting in the call, I was advised that you were on the line. I went to the telephone and asked, 'Is that you, Judge Bush?' The voice cried 'yes.' I then reiterated what had been said...the answer came, 'governor, it is worse that that.' I then said, 'My God Judge Bush! Is it possible that you have, at the instance of this mob rendered the return of the prisoner to Murray,' and the answer was, 'yes.' I exclaimed, as I remember, 'the hell you did!' Then the never to be forgotten reply, 'I had to do it to save my own life; if I had longer refused they would have hung me.'

There it was, exactly as Perry had reported. So as there was no mistake about his recollection of that fateful evening, Stanley went on:

We have known each other intimately for thirty years. Are you surprised, under such circumstances at my absolute certainty that you were at the other end of that telephone line?

In reminding Bush as to what happened when he arrived at Bush's hotel room that night, Stanley wrote:

......when I arrived at Murray you were in bed. I came in with Tom Pannell, Henry Hines and Dr. Larue. You sat up on the side of the bed and talked to us a few minutes, and I then referred to the telephone conversation and the difficulty I had in getting you, and you replied that the delay was caused by the fact that a relative of Diuguid's was at the switchboard and you hesitated to use the telephone unless it was absolutely necessary.

And to clinch the veracity of his memory:

.......For fear that my memory might be at fault in this particular, I have spoken to Henry Hines, Tom Pannell and Dr. LaRue, and they all vividly remember the entire conversation.

Finally on June 24, 1918, Commonwealth Attorney Denny Smith filed a long, narrative motion asking that the indictment be dismissed. (It's a puzzle as to how Smith remained on the case since he, like Judge Bush, would have been a material witness.)

In the motion Smith related how repeated attempts to get the governor to appoint a special judge had been rebuffed. And then the motion recited from a June 22nd editorial from the *Courier Journal* where it was apparently admitted that the reporter had in fact talked to an impostor, and not Judge Bush, on the evening in question. In other words, the *Courier Journal* ran a recantation and retraction–over a year after the event.

So, that must have been the deal. The Commonwealth would dismiss the charges, and *The Courier* would admit that it had been someone else who had talked to the reporter and not Bush.

Had the *Courier Journal* known of the content of the letter from the Kentucky governor to Bush of January 24 of 1917, it might not have been so inclined to admit that there had been a mistake.

It apparently seemed like a small price to pay to break loose from the criminal prosecution way down there near the god forsaken Jackson Purchase.

Bush had not fared well in his attempts to either redeem his reputation or to punish the guilty mobsters.

CHAPTER 12

CLOSURE

On December 21, 1917 the hammer fell on Lube Martin.

On that day the Court of Appeals affirmed his conviction and sentence out of the Calloway Circuit Court.

It was a unanimous decision written by Judge Rollin Hurt. One by one, the court methodically discounted each of the seven points of appeal. In upholding Bush in the exclusion by Bush of Lube's mother's desperate letter Judge Hurt wrote:

> *An examination of the letter however, shows, that it did not contain a statement to the effect, that the deceased, Diuguid, had made any threat against appellant. The evidence does not disclose, that appellant's mother ever had any information to the effect, that Diuguid had made a threat of any kind against the appellant, and hence it can not be assumed that the party to whom the letter makes reference, as having made a threat of violence against the accused, was the deceased, Diuguid. A threat made by someone, other than*

deceased, and communicated to accused, would not be any ground for the accused apprehending danger from the deceased.

The distinguished judge speaking for this august body then went on to make a totally erroneous legal deduction considering the totality of the case:

The letter refers to the party, who made the threat as that 'old man.'.............The circumstances of this case do not justify the conclusion, that the deceased was the 'old man' referred to in the letter, as it might have reasonably been another as the deceased.

This, of course, was pure fiction.

Even so, it would have still been a jury's job to decide the identity of the "old man." It could have been Robin Hood. But if Lube thought it was Guthrie Diuguid, it would have still been relevant to his fearful state of mind at the time of the shooting.

But the big boys said otherwise, and that was the final say.

Lastly, the high court dealt with what was the central flaw in the due process–the failure of the case to be moved from Calloway County:

The argument offered, that the judgment should be reversed, because of newspaper reports, which would indicate such a bitter state of feeling in the county of Calloway, against the appellant, that he was prevented from having a fair trial, and that, for such reason, the judgment should be reversed and a change of venue ordered by this court cannot be accepted. This court is a court of review, and upon appeals, it is restricted to the duty of determining the soundness and correctness of the decisions and actions of the tribunals of original jurisdiction, from whose judgments appeals are prosecuted. The record does not disclose, that any motion was made or petition filed for a change of venue, in the trial court, and without such the trial court was powerless to order a change of venue, and such question cannot be before the court for review, as neither the trial court nor this court could order a change of venue, in a criminal prosecution, when it is not desired nor sought by one or the other of the parties. The record shows, that in place of asking for a change of venue, the appellant moved the court to order a jury brought from the county of Christian to try him, which motion was acceded to, and the jury, which tried him was summoned and impaneled out of the citizens of Christian, which is not an adjoining county to that in which the action was tried, and no fact is shown or relied upon, in the record, which would indicate, that the jury was anything, other than an impartial one.

So, in a final wave to the case, the Kentucky Court of Appeals said, in essence, to Pat Holt, "this is what you wanted, so this is what you got."

Never mind that someone else–not Holt–would pay with his life for this decision.

For whatever reason the fine defense lawyer had chosen the course he took, however sensible and sound it may have seemed to him and his co-counsel Thompson at the time–the words of Judge Hurt must have echoed across the vast canyons of Holt's soul for the rest of his life.

On December 4, 1917 and some two weeks before the decision upholding his conviction, Lube was quietly moved from his jail cell in Paducah to the Kentucky State Penitentiary in Eddyville.

The day before, just a few miles down the road from Murray in Dyersburg, Tennessee, a Negro by the name of Lation Scott was taken in custody for the alleged assault on the wife of a prominent white farmer in the community. A lynch mob gathered and swelled into the thousands, quickly snatching Scott away from the officials. He was taken to a vacant lot where he was tied to a stake and tortured with hot irons. His eyes were punched out and then he was burned at the stake.

With such an atrocity taking place so close to home, and the final decision on Martin's case due any day from the state's highest court, the Paducah officials decided to take some precautionary measures. They did not want to have the unpopular Lube Martin on their hands if his conviction was reversed. Better get him behind the stone walls at Eddyville while the "getting was good."

So on December 4, 1917 Lube was taken by car to the medieval-like fortress overlooking the Cumberland River in the little county seat of Lyon County.

On arriving at the prison he was taken to three cell house which was the Negro unit at the segregated prison. He was assigned to remain there until the night of his scheduled execution. The white prisoners condemned to die were kept together in the "death house," a small block building attached to the Negro cell house.

When Martin arrived in Eddyville, 24 men had died in the electric chair since it was installed in 1911. Eighteen of them had been black, including 16-year-old Silas Williams who on March 21, 1913 was executed the same day he arrived at the prison.

Lube had the dubious distinction of being the first from Calloway County to arrive in the land of dead men walking.

So, it was there, just before Christmas, when he received word that his conviction and sentence had been upheld.

But there was still a faint ray of hope for the killer of Guthrie Diuguid.

Executive commutation. That hope would remain as long as Lube Martin had breath, and as long as A.O. Stanley was governor.

As soon as he had returned to Frankfort after his dramatic rescue in Murray, the colorful governor was called to other tasks.

At the special legislative session called in mid-February–about the time the Lube Martin trial was taking place in Murray–Stanley was able to get his controversial tax reform package passed. The new laws established a system for classifying property for tax purposes, lowered the tax rate, and established a tax commission of three members to supervise the administration of the tax laws and to make assessments on certain kinds of property.

This was all dry stuff to most Kentuckians, but vital to the economic growth of the state.

The new tax laws were understood by few, and criticized by many who did understand them. So, he hit the hustings in the fall election in defense of his own Democratic candidates for the general assembly.

Riding on that election also was the success or failure of the 18th Amendment to the U.S. Constitution which would be up before the general assembly in January for ratification or defeat.

That of course was the Prohibition Amendment. And although Stanley had long been "wet" on the issue, he wisely stepped aside to let the voters decide without his executive guidance. In an open letter to the public he expressed this decision to let the matter be resolved in an honest election "without joker, equivocation or delay."

So, in January 1918, the legislators ratified the 18th Amendment.

That same general assembly passed a number of other laws under Stanley's leadership including a bill strengthening the Workmen's Compensation Law, a legislative redistricting bill, and various increased appropriations for the state's social services, penal institutions, and education.

But one bill which was passed against the wishes of the state's chief executive would lead to a dramatic clash between the lawmakers and him. And it would once again test and reveal the fierce courage of the governor from Henderson.

The general assembly, as one would expect, had become completely caught up in the patriotic war spirit of the entire nation. Red, white, and blue bunting was everywhere. Inspirational speeches for God, country and motherhood were being given by every politician in the state and at every opportunity. Bands blared rousing numbers including the popular "Over There" to stir listeners into a frenzy. Mass meetings were held in each community to show support for the troops and to pour venom upon the Kaiser, and the Huns.

And almost overnight, everything German became odious and despicable.

The anti-German sentiment sweeping the country, including Kentucky, became first intense and heated, and then senseless and irrational.

In March of 1918, with almost no opposition at all, a bill was passed by the general assembly outlawing the teaching of the German language in all public schools in Kentucky.

With a whoop and a holler for the grand ole flag, the boys in the state legislature adjourned, threw the freshly cut bill into the lap of the governor, and went home.

There in the quiet reflection of the governor's study, removed from the war hysteria sweeping the state by storm, Stanley calmly considered the bill.

And he thought of the Germans. Not across the sea, but here in Kentucky.

The well-traveled governor knew every nook and crevice of the wide ranging Commonwealth. Unlike the provincial legislators constrained by the narrow views and experiences of their restrictive constituencies, he had not only a fuller knowledge of the geography of the state, but its history and culture as well.

Germans had been some of the earliest explorers and settlers in Kentucky. In 1790, just two years before statehood, almost 14 percent of the population were German-Americans. As far back as 1854, the "Herald of the West," a German publication out of Louisville had taken a bold stand for rights of women, minimum wage for workers, and abolition of the death penalty.

They had not been without a different sort of persecution. In 1855 the Know Nothing Party in Louisville had targeted these "foreigners" in an attempt to keep them from voting, a battle which led to bloodshed and several deaths.

By the turn of the century, there were small German settlements reaching from the far western "land between the rivers" in Lyon County, to eastern and northern Kentucky.

Governor William Goebel, martyred in 1900, had been the son of German immigrants.

At the time Stanley was confronted with the latest anti-

German action by the state legislature, the heaviest concentrations of Germans were in Louisville, and the northern Kentucky cities of Covington and Newport.

Stanley was aware that in these German settlements, some newspapers were still printed in German. More significantly as to the matter at hand, there were some schools where courses were still taught in the German language.

This new law would not do.

So, he vetoed the bill.

With this bold stroke of his pen, his life immediately became endangered. The bitter outcry against him across the state was ferocious.

His action was called treasonous, disloyal, and worse. On April 3, a mass meeting was held in Covington where a resolution was adopted declaring the governor's veto "un-American and unpatriotic." One Protestant minister branded Stanley a "traitor and coward." In Campbell County another organization adopted a resolution accusing the governor of having "countenanced and aided the spreading of disloyalty, sabotage, and treason."

But, once again the eloquent Stanley rode out the storm with his words.

In defending himself he said, "We are at war with an armed despotism, not a language. We injure ourselves, not another, by shutting our ears to the melodies of Mendelssohn and Mozart, or Wagner and Beethoven. This nation in her righteous wrath will not cease to be just or magnanimous. We are at war with Germany's evil political institution and her ruthless and domineering war lords—not her art, her literature or her marvelous scientific discoveries."

Like the blue-heat emotions of the lynch mob at Murray, the stormy and venomous outcry against his veto slowly wilted and faded away into history.

The combination of courage and eloquence is an implacable foe to bigotry and hate. It's an extraordinary leader indeed who is armed with both. Stanley was such a man.

On August 28, 1918 the Commonwealth of Kentucky lost one of the bright stars of its political firmament. U.S. Senator Ollie James from Marion, Kentucky collapsed and died at the meager age of 47.

James, a brilliant orator, had been a friend and political ally to Stanley. His illustrious career included serving in the U.S. House of Representatives for five successive terms beginning in 1903. He was elected to the U.S. Senate in 1913 where he served with distinction until his untimely death. James served as chairman for the Democratic National Convention of 1912. At that convention he brought great honor to his beloved Kentucky by giving a stirring and eloquent keynote speech supporting Woodrow Wilson as the party's candidate for the presidency. James was back at the convention in 1916 speaking once again praising Wilson's record.

Many considered him a rising star upon the national political scene.

But his health faltered, and death cut him short of his promise.

His death was a blow to the Commonwealth of Kentucky.

As it turned out, his death would also have a tremendous impact upon the fate of Lube Martin.

A.O. Stanley had always wanted to go to the United States Senate. Now with his politically invincible friend, Ollie James, gone, the way lay open for him.

After securing the nomination of Democratic Party State Central and Executive Committee, he was thrown immediately into a fall campaign against the Republican party nominee, Dr. Ben L. Bruner, a Louisville physician.

It was a brutal and bruising campaign. All of the unpopular decisions Stanley had made as governor, including the veto of the anti-German bill, were flung back into his face. Stanley campaigned hard on his record, as well as declaring that a vote against the Democratic Party at this crucial time would be a vote against

President Wilson and his war efforts against Germany.

In the end, Stanley narrowly prevailed in one of the closest general elections in the state's history. However, his 5,590 statewide margin against Bruner must have seemed like a landslide to Stanley compared to his margin of less than 400 votes in the previous governor's race against Ed Morrow.

So, on May 19, 1919, with Lube Martin still on death row at Eddyville, Governor A.O. Stanley resigned the governorship of Kentucky to be sworn in as U.S. Senator.

Lt. Governor James Dixon Black from Knox County, was sworn in as governor to serve out the remaining seven months of Stanley's term.

Lube Martin's previous execution date had been postponed. Now he was scheduled to die in the electric chair on July 11.

It was universally agreed that Lube Martin's last chance had just departed for Washington, D.C.

Governor James Black was of relatively unknown quality, especially to the people of far west Kentucky. Most would not even recognize his picture if they saw it in the paper—which they rarely did. His cameo appearance upon the statewide political stage of Kentucky would turn out to be short, and unremarkable.

A good man no doubt, he lacked the ebullient charisma of his predecessor. A lawyer and educator from Knox County, 67-year-old Black had only served one term as a state representative way back in 1876, and then as assistant attorney general in 1912 before being elected lieutenant governor with Stanley. His real love was academia; he taught school and helped to establish Union College in Barbourville and became its first president. He also served as superintendent of schools in Knox County.

Stanley was a hard act to follow. Well intended as he no doubt was, Black failed to instill much confidence in the citizens of the Commonwealth.

And of course he inherited all of the condemned men on death row in Eddyville. For them he was the last resort, the last chance for reprieve and pardon.

At the time Black took office, there were four men under sentence of death at Eddyville. One was Martin, whose execution date was less than two months away.

On June 6, two of the four–James Howard, of McCracken County, and Lewis Harris, of Mason County, both black–were electrocuted. The next scheduled to go was Lube Martin.

All eyes turned to Governor James Black to see if he would wave him on into eternity, as he did Howard and Harris.

On July 8, as the warden at the Kentucky State Penitentiary and his staff made ready for the 30th electrocution at that prison, Martin received good news.

Black had ordered a stay.

In the order postponing the execution, the state's chief executive stated:

Since the undersigned became governor of Kentucky, more than one delegation of earnest and intelligent men have asked me to grant some relief to Martin against the carrying into effect of the said death penalty, either by the commuting of said sentence to imprisonment in the penitentiary for the remainder of the natural life of the said Lube Martin, or some other relief within the power of the governor to grant.

After having heard the earnest plea of the said delegations, I have decided to examine the court record in the said case against said Martin, in order that I might be prepared, as thoroughly as possible, to pass upon the said application properly, and as becomes the seriousness of the matter involved; but, because of very great pressure of official business it has not been practical for me to make the examination of the record, as I determined as aforesaid, and in order that I may yet make such examination of said record, I have determined to stay the execution of the said death penalty against the said Martin until the morning before sunrise of July 25, 1919.

So within a very short time, during his first 45 days in office, Black had received "more than one delegation" to Frankfort pleading on behalf of Lube Martin's life.

Who were these men? Who were the delegates who made this long and laborious trip to the state capitol from Murray to beseech the governor to spare Lube's life? One must assume the petitions were coming from Murray, as there is no evidence of any other interest shown in Martin's plight by any other group from any other part of the state.

The dusty vaults of government give no clues. Knowing hands which could have written the names have long been stilled. Lips which could have spoken to the mystery are now sealed in death. Answers to these questions stand like solemn sentinels down through the long silent canyon of history. We are left only to know that some "earnest and intelligent men" pled for the condemned Negro assigned to the bowels of the "Castle on the Cumberland" in Eddyville.

For seven days Lube Martin waited in his cell in Eddyville.

What thoughts went through his mind were not recorded. Men in Frankfort toiled over paper and pleadings, briefs and trial transcript. Phone calls made and received, the raw grinding of politics and conscience brought to bear upon a life and death decision. Men without names now lost to history, thoughtful, pondering, considering the options, feeling the push and pull of justice being distilled from chaos. Some motivated by good. Some motivated by less than good.

But alas Lube Martin lost.

On July 15, Governor Black denied any further stays, any reprieves, any pardons, any commutations. The execution would go forward on July 25.

Summer on the banks of the steamy Cumberland River could become very humid with the tepid river easing by like larva. Simmering at low water the stream released its invisible sweat into a sweltering blanket of humidity.

On the evening of July 24, 1919, the steamy summer day gave way to the humid darkness. The huge granite "Bastille on the hill" in Eddyville imprisoned not only men, but the scorching heat of the season into its vast confines.

As darkness came late, near 9 p.m. crude electric lights began to snap on around town. The artificial lamps did not deter the people of this small village from settling in for the night's nocturnal, ritualistic sense of melancholy and foreboding.

Even with a dying body, wracked by disease withering on a bed of sweat and excrement, no one knows for sure–absolutely for sure–when that life will expire. Or, allowing for the miraculous, even if the life will expire.

But a state execution defines the moment when someone in our midst will be called to meet their Maker. This awesome event summons up a collective feeling of mortality, of gathering your kin around you–of settling into the stifling sleep of a midsummer night, knowing that before the bacon sizzles and coffee lends its wonderful fragrance to the morning, one certain human being will no longer be with us.

A somber knowing that in the night, when the electric dynamo at the death house in the prison begins to churn into a low whine, storing up the awful thrust of death within its sounds, the street lights in town will quiver and dim, blinking a lonely farewell to a fleeting soul.

Granted, at this dreadful hour men have been saved by mortal hands–a governor's late hour change of heart. But such interventions were mostly in the make believe world of novels and movies, especially if the condemned was black.

So the little town of Eddyville, 45 miles northeast of Lube Martin's home, prepared for his last night.

During the early hours of the 24th, Lube was taken from his cell in the segregated unit and escorted to a cell in the death house. This block-shaped building was tacked on to the end of three cell house. Black faces peering from the bars, stacked in narrow cells on walks all the way up to the high vaulted ceiling, movingly sang out a Negro gospel song, bidding adieu to their departing friend.

It is not known, and it is not recorded whether any of Lube's family or friends were on hand when he ate his last supper, said his last prayer, muttered his goodbyes and shortly after midnight–July 25, 1919–was led to the electric chair.

All that is known is what was succinctly written in the newspaper later that day:

> *Lube Martin, slayer of Policeman Diuguid at Murray, was executed in the prison here this morning.*
>
> *Execution of Lube Martin for the murder of Officer Guthrie Diuguid closes one of the most interesting chapters in west Kentucky criminal history.........*

As to Martin's brothers and co-defendants, their fate was finally decided before his.

Back in April, 1918, few people were even thinking of Lube Martin and Guthrie Diuguid, let alone the much lesser known co-defendants. However, Judge Bush was taking no chances.

On April 15, 1918 he commanded:

> *....the jailer of McCracken County is ordered and directed to deliver said prisoners to the said sheriff and deputies, and it is further ordered that the said sheriff in addition to his regular official force appoints as many as eight sober, discreet and brave men to meet him at the depot in Murray, Ky. upon the arrival of said prisoners from Paducah who shall be prepared to assist in guarding said prisoners and protecting them while being conveyed from the depot to the courthouse and who shall if necessary assist in guarding them at the courthouse during the trial and in preserving order and who shall also assist in guarding and protecting said prisoners during their stay in Murray...*

There would be no "doughboys" in Murray this time. They were all in Europe. They were needed there much more than they were in the Calloway County capital.

Few people were interested in the plight of these co-defendants as they were brought into the courtroom to join up with their dauntless attorneys Pat Holt and A.D. Thompson. At last, Holt had made a motion for change of venue for his clients. But by April 16 that was made academic as he and the commonwealth attorney had worked out a deal. The case against Jordon would be dismissed. The Martin brothers would plead guilty to the reduced charge of manslaughter and have their sentence set by the jury.

In short time, the jury returned a maximum sentence of 21 years in prison for each of the remaining defendants. Judge Bush perfunctorily sentenced them, and they were sent on their way to the Kentucky State Penitentiary in Eddyville. There, one must assume, they were part of that doleful chorus of Negro voices in three cell house who sang a mournful farewell to their brother.

Unto this day, there hovers a haze of mystery over the Lube Martin case. There are many unanswered questions that only lips now silenced by death could answer. The killing of Guthrie Diuguid by Lube Martin is known. The date is fixed, and the cause of death is unquestioned. Beyond that, we wander into a maze of speculation, intrigue, and darkness.

The date of Lube Martin's execution was first fixed for July 8, 1918, over 17 months from his conviction. But he would not die for over a full year from that date.

Neither the public records nor the newspapers of that time reveal what went on with the Lube Martin case during that time.

We do know that according to Governor Black, who took office less than two months before the execution, at least one delegation paid a visit to Frankfort on his behalf. It must be assumed that Stanley, who moved on to the U.S. Senate in May of 1919, extended at least one stay of execution for Martin.

What was this political tug-of-war that was going on with the life of Lube Martin? Who were the forces on the ground in Murray who pushed for his demise? Pushing for his reprieve? What were the motives of these contending forces that leave no trace of their deeds?

Wells Lovett, distinguished lawyer from Owensboro, Kentucky, and grandson of Rainey T. Wells relates an intriguing story. His grandfather only mentioned the Lube Martin case to him once, and from a rather oblique angle.

Said Lovett, "My grandfather and Governor Stanley were of course good friends. My grandfather said he went to Frankfort to get a pardon for George Diuguid who had gotten into some trouble. He and Stanley were relaxing at the governor's mansion when Wells broached the subject. When Governor Stanley heard it, he roared with laughter and called to his wife, 'Hey Sue! Guess who Rainey wants me to help?' "

Like, can you believe that troublemaker who helped cause us so much grief now needs a favor from me?

But there is no record this writer can find anywhere—including the state archives—where George Diuguid was ever in trouble or in need of executive pardon.

Has the story been twisted by time? Was Rainey T. Wells in the governor's mansion on some other mission regarding Lube Martin? Was he there on behest of the Diuguid family to push for execution? Was he there pleading Lube's case for a stay of execution?

It is highly doubtful that we will ever know.

At the trial of Lube Martin did Felix Skinner perjure himself when he testified about the conversation he had with Lube Martin in the fall of 1916? Felix reported that Lube had shown him the pump shotgun given to him by City Judge Harold Schroader for the purpose of killing Guthrie Diuguid. What would be a fellow black man's motive to lie, especially when he was dangerously implicating two of the leading white politicians of the town.

Guthrie's brother, George, had announced to the press before the trial that the killing was part of a larger conspiracy, seeded no doubt by Guthrie's political enemies.

Of course Lube denied any of it.

But still, one wonders. To have admitted it would have confirmed premeditation, a lethal blow to his claim of self-defense.

Perhaps nothing denotes the persistent puzzle of this event as much as the state of mind of the black community in Murray today.

They know nothing.

Even the children of Queen, Lube's daughter, never heard her mention it. Old-timers have only heard that the shooting was "over Lube's wife."

The Diuguid family, as a political and social force, has disappeared from Murray. But several descendants, good and decent people all, still live in western Kentucky.

They know nothing.

No one remembers hearing anything about the shooting. "Perhaps parents were careful about what children heard discussed," says one family member.

In fact, there evolved an ironic meshing of the two families affected by the tragedy. In later years, Lube Martin's sister-in-law, Duma, who was Chester's wife, worked in the home of Edwin Diuguid, Jr.'s widow after she remarried Ed Filbeck.

"Chester was custodian at the Bank of Murray and highly respected," reports Eleanor Diuguid, the surviving daughter-in-law. "Duma was loved by the family and there was no animosity or resentment toward her whatsoever."

It is like both the white and black communities of that day struck an unspoken bargain, that the truth of the whole sordid affair would disappear into the graves of those who lived through it. Like a pebble dropped into the sea, the tragedy has sunk beneath the ocean of time, leaving not a trace upon the surface.

Lube Martin may have died for the sins of those on both sides of the color barrier, including those of his wife.

CHAPTER 13

CHANGING TIMES

The immaculately dressed elderly man made his way through the lobby of the Capitol Hotel in Frankfort, Kentucky. It was March 1954, and 85-year-old A. O. Stanley headed directly to the dining room. Rotund and bald, very few people now recognized him, although he greeted each and every one as if he knew them well. His quick step and sparkling eyes belied his advancing years. It was if he was late for his next appointment, and had a full day scheduled after that.

Recent prostate surgery had not slowed his gait nor dampened his spirit.

He was in Frankfort for the political kick off of former Vice President Alben Barkley's campaign for the U.S. Senate.

The Capitol Hotel was a gathering place for members of the general assembly when it was in session. There, throughout the lobby, dining room and bar, the air was thick with cigar smoke and talk of pressing matters of state. Legislators, bureaucrats, lobbyists, constituents, and even a few luring women mingled and plied their respective trades amidst a low roar of conversations and deal making.

As Stanley appeared in the door of the dining room, two people waited for him at a table. One smiled knowingly. She was Pearl Runyon, Kentucky's state treasurer. It was a reaction that the old gentleman generated these days. Everyone who knew him looked forward to his visit with eager anticipation, knowing that it would not be lackluster or boring.

The other person at the table was young Ned Breathitt, a 29-year-old state legislator from Hopkinsville, Kentucky. This meeting had been arranged by Runyon, who wanted her young friend with a bright political future, to meet a Kentucky political legend. Breathitt was also eager to meet Stanley. As a history student at the University of Kentucky under the eminent Dr. Thomas D. Clark, he had heard plenty about the colorful politician.

Upon seeing Stanley approach the table, Runyon and the baby- faced representative jumped to their feet, extended their hands which the ebullient former governor began to shake with warmth and vigor. Before they were even seated again Stanley had launched into conversation, gesturing and animating with great enthusiasm.

The two admiring moths were drawn immediately to the flame.

It would confound the young legislator later when he reflected upon the meeting, how a man so old, and beyond his time, even speaking in a bygone idiom, could still be so charismatic, energetic and full of life.

Topics bounced around the table as they placed their orders.

In his later years, when eating in places with cloth table coverings, Stanley had a habit of becoming so involved in his storytelling that he would grab hold of the hem of the cloth near the seat of his chair. As he tugged and pulled with the drama of his tales, his dining companions became concerned that he would pull the dishes and silverware right off the table.

The two west Kentuckians, Stanley and Breathitt, old and

new—spoke of their shared west Kentucky and swapped names of mutual acquaintances and friends. Stanley knew the politics of Ned's home county and commented on how Franklin Roosevelt had turned the area into a "Gibraltar" for the Democratic Party. Stanley idolized Roosevelt. So did Breathitt.

The two men had a lot more in common than they would ever be able to know, or to share, in their short time together.

Stanley was asked about his current health, and in a subtle way, what he had been doing for the past fifty years or so.

Time would not allow a full answer to that question.

The fickle winds of politics had not been particularly kind to Stanley. He eventually paid for his unpopular positions on highly emotional issues. His loyal constituency made up a patchwork of supporters. His strongest base were the farmers, who loved him for his fight against the despised monopoly, the American Tobacco Company, which had played a role in driving prices to the bottom for their tobacco. He successfully fought in Congress for the repeal of the onerous tobacco tax, which was a boost to consumption and thusly the production of tobacco.

But when these men of the soil scrubbed themselves to Sunday sheen and went to church, they heard preachers lambaste Stanley because of his strong "wet" position in the ongoing battle between the prohibitionists and the liquor people. For Stanley, it wasn't his strong love for Kentucky bourbon which fueled his fight against banning the sale of alcohol, although his love for it was great, but his strong belief in the right of the individual—not government—to choose. His position on the liquor issue had remained consistent over the years, going back to his days in the state house. And it placed him high on the enemy list of the powerful Anti-Saloon League lobby.

His noble stand for individual freedoms was lost on many who saw him as unpatriotic, or somewhat of an infidel. His position on civil rights roused the ire of the Ku Klux Klan which still wielded considerable political clout in the state. While in the U.S. Senate Stanley loudly spoke out on behalf of women's suffrage. He opposed the heavy hand of industry and corporations, especially the railroad, on behalf of labor.

Many things could be said of Stanley concerning his tenure in the U.S. Senate. But everyone–friends and enemies–had to agree, he never dodged difficult public questions, and he always let people know where he stood.

But in 1924, the chickens came home to roost. Popular as he was among a devoted segment of the electorate, Stanley went down to defeat in his bid for re-election to Republican Frederic M. Sackett.

Said the wounded political soldier in losing:

The day must come in the life of every honest public servant when he must choose between right and being popular. My friends and foes alike must admit I was true to my convictions; that like Paul I 'bore witness to the light' as God gave me to see the light. He who lives by the sword must fall by the sword.

The former governor and U.S. senator then took up the practice of law in both Washington and Louisville. He was mostly a rainmaker, able to bring cases into his firm by his reputation, personality, and charm. While living in D.C. Stanley made frequent trips back to Kentucky to keep his name alive in political circles "just in case" the old war horse was called upon again to do battle. But even though he came close to entering senatorial races to reclaim his old seat, the colorful lawyer never made another political race.

On May 29, 1932, personal tragedy struck home when his 20-year-old son, Marion Shelby Stanley, was killed in an airplane crash at Bluegrass Field in Lexington. He was flying without a student permit, a common practice at that time.

In 1930 Stanley secured an appointment by Republican President Herbert C. Hoover to the International Joint Commission, which was charged with the responsibility of arbitrating boundary-line disputes with our northern neighbor. Needless to say, there weren't many and the job was primarily ceremonial with pay. How the controversial Democrat secured this appointment from a Republican president would no doubt be an intriguing story.

In explaining his duties with the commission to his friends at the Frankfort luncheon, he described it with a wink and twinkle in his eye.

"There was no heavy lifting."

He held this position until 1954 when he resigned.

During his 24-year tenure with the commission, he and Mrs. Stanley resided in Washington, D.C. For four years, 1930-34, he was joined in the nation's capital by his old and dear friend, and political nemesis, Edwin P. Morrow.

Morrow had managed to unseat Governor James D. Black, Stanley's successor. The Somerset native made a good governor, sharing many of the core political beliefs as his friend A.O. Stanley. The two especially shared strong convictions in regard to their opposition to the Ku Klux Klan. While in office Morrow himself was confronted with a racial crisis not greatly unlike the Lube Martin affair in Murray.

In February 1920 Morrow sent the National Guard to Lexington to protect a black man charged with murder and on the verge of being strung up by a mob. A year later Morrow removed a Woodford County jailer who had allowed a black man to be lynched.

In 1926 Morrow was appointed to the U.S. Railroad Labor Board, later to be known as the U.S. Board of Mediation.

The four years that Morrow and Stanley both lived in D.C. were the most enjoyable of their lives. Frequently visiting each other in their respective homes, they would stay up 'till the wee hours downing good Kentucky bourbon whiskey and spinning one tale after another as their devoted but exhausted wives fell asleep in their chairs.

On June 15, 1935 Stanley's old friend passed away. Stanley would dearly miss him for the rest of his life. Many years later he would still lament, "His death was a tragic loss to Kentucky. To me, it has been depressingly harder and harder to endure. There'll never be another Ed Morrow."

All of this was behind the old man as he sat dining and holding court at the Capitol Hotel with his two friends.

A highly dramatic trip to Murray and a spell-binding speech to save the lives of Judge Bush and Denny Smith, now so many years in the past, was a story few people remembered.

"That was the most picturesque thing in my public life," he would recall for a newspaper reporter in 1950. "It's a story I've seldom told. I had to watch my step. If I had shown the flicker of an eyelash, I wouldn't be here. It was in the days of night riding, and they weren't used to law."

Then the governor proceeded to give his own account of that historic event. While time had muddled his mind as to some of the factual detail, it had not dimmed his recollection of the main event:

We had a fight on to control the new legislature and with 25 or 30 leading Democrats I was in a meeting at the Seelbach Hotel in Louisville. The telephone rang. It was some fellow scared to talk at Murray, so he had slipped over to Paris, Tennessee. His tongue was so thick he couldn't talk. He told me Judge Bush had entered an order removing a Negro, charged with killing the sheriff, from Murray to Paducah. He said a mob had surrounded the Murray Hotel and told the judge if he didn't reconvene court and rescind that order, they'd kill him. He had reconvened court and ordered the Negro back from Paducah.

I called Bush at Murray and told him I couldn't believe it, it was so fantastic. He warned me there would be violence and the mob was liable to hang him, "They can hang you and me, too, but I'll be damned if they'll hang the Negro."

Stanley would go on to recount his hurried jaunt to Murray

and what he found when he arrived there:

> *I went to the hotel. The commonwealth's attorney, Denny Smith, was hugging the fire in a small stove. He said, 'Governor, did you bring the Negro back?' 'No,' I told him. He asked me if I thought public opinion would stand for a white man being hanged to let a Negro go free. 'If they hang you, they'll probably hang me,' I replied.*

As to the effect his dynamic speech had on the gathering at the courthouse, the old governor remembered, "Some were wiping their eyes. You could hear a pin fall."

The young representative from Hopkinsville hung onto every word.

This short meeting was the one and only time the two men would ever see each other. One, an old, battered war horse, having outlived most of his friends and enemies, the other a young colt kicking up its heels in the fresh, spring meadow of Kentucky politics—one passing from the scene, the other just arriving.

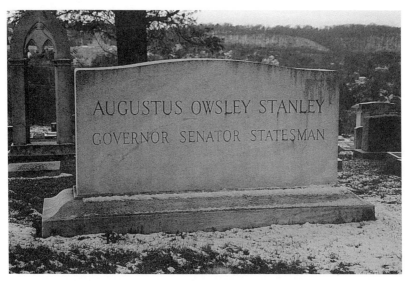

Tombstone of Augustus Owsley Stanley, Frankfort, Kentucky.

Outside the front of the old Capitol Hotel, while state legislators and power brokers of the general assembly scurried by, Breathitt and Stanley stood and said their goodbyes. With a final handshake Ned Breathitt saw the old man walk away into the pale light of the March afternoon sun.

Stanley lived four more years. In the beginning months of 1958, his health declined rapidly. Then on August 12 of that year he died at the age of 91, in Washington, D.C. After a funeral service in the nation's capital, he was brought to the Capitol Rotunda in Frankfort where his flag-draped casket lay in state. He was buried in the picturesque and historic Frankfort Cemetery overlooking the capitol and the scenic Kentucky River.

While speaking on behalf of the impoverished tobacco farmers of west Kentucky, A.O. Stanley had spoken his political epitaph:

The purpose of government is not to make a few men rich; but to make all men free.

After his meeting with Stanley the young lawyer from Hopkinsville turned and walked away toward a meteoric rise to the governorship of Kentucky.

Edward Thompson Breathitt, Jr. was born at 1804 Hopper Court in Hopkinsville, Kentucky on November 26, 1924.

A.O. Stanley was then serving in the United States Senate.

Just a short mile away down at the Christian County Courthouse, Judge Charles Bush was still on the bench, struggling daily with the balance of right and wrong. Denny Smith still labored in the vineyards of Calloway, Christian, Lyon and Trigg counties.

Hopkinsville, a town of about 10,000 people, was the county seat of one of the richest agricultural counties in Kentucky. Tobacco was the main crop of the county, and the town itself was a hub of commerce invigorated by the Louisville & Nashville and the Illinois Central Railroads.

Growing tobacco was labor intensive and the antebellum plantations of the rural community had supported a large slave population.

At the time of Breathitt's birth, Christian County had the highest percentage of blacks in the state, accounting for 36 percent of the population.

So even in the strictly segregated society of that day, Ned, as he was labeled by his parents, became intimately familiar with that race at a very early age.

Being the only child, five-year-old Ned searched out the neighborhood for other playmates. He found one down by the railroad tracks where he met a little boy his same age. Ned paid no heed that his little friend's skin was black. There they would meet every day and play and romp in a sand pile left behind by a railroad maintenance crew.

Then one day his father came to fetch him.

Brusquely and with searing insensitivity, his father sent Ned's little playmate home. His father made it brutally plain that the two boys were not to play together anymore.

Even at that tender age, Ned felt embarrassed and humiliated by his father's treatment of his friend. It became a searing memory forever etched upon his soul. A lasting question was planted in his young mind as to why anyone should be treated so rudely simply because of their skin color?

His father, Edward Thompson Breathitt, Sr., was a World War I Navy veteran who returned home to Hopkinsville after the war to go into the tobacco business with the Tennessee Tobacco Company which bought the dark leaf for export to Italy. After Mussolini nationalized the Italian tobacco companies, no more tobacco was bought from America. So Ned's father lost his job and bought and sold tobacco on his own. "Pinhooking" it was called.

Ned's father, Ed, was a Republican, the party which made up a sizable majority in Christian County at that time. While he was politically inactive, he came from one of the most politically active families in west Kentucky. Ed's father, James Breathitt, Ned's grandfather, had been circuit judge and Republican attorney general of Kentucky.

At the time of Ned's birth and throughout his early years, his father's brother, Jimmy, would play a prominent role on the state's political scene.

Oddly, a Woodrow Wilson Democrat in a family of Republicans, Jimmy became lieutenant governor in 1927 and in a peculiar arrangement, possible in those days, served with Republican Governor Flem Sampson.

Jimmy was a popular Democratic prospect for governor in 1931 as Republican Sampson was limited by the state's Constitution to one term.

That was the last year for the party candidate to be selected by convention, which was held in Lexington. Jimmy had strong support throughout the state, and would have easily won a primary election. However, in the convention the political powers of the Bluegrass controlled the delegates and Jimmy came up wanting. Ruby Lafoon of Madisonville got the nod, and Ned's Uncle Jimmy was sent home empty-handed.

Undaunted, Jimmy came home and ran for the state senate and was elected. He was a thorn in the side of Governor Ruby Lafoon, bitterly opposing proposals in the 1934 session of the general assembly, including a controversial three percent sales tax bill which passed.

But Senator Breathitt was able to pilot several pieces of legislation of his own through to enactment, two of which had far reaching effects upon the justice system. One Breathitt bill created the State Bar Association under the jurisdiction of the Court of Appeals. Another was a measure setting up a probation system for first time offenders.

In October 1934, the son of a former governor and great lion of the Democratic party, J.C. W. Beckham, Sr. passed away. Loyal and true a Democrat as he was, Jimmy rose from his sick bed to attend the younger Beckham's funeral in Frankfort.

He caught pneumonia and died shortly thereafter at the

young age of 44.

So beloved was Jimmy Breathitt that Lawrence Haggar, owner of the Owensboro newspaper wrote a stirring and inspiring benediction to his life entitled "Fondly, Jim, Farewell."

James Breathitt, Jr. was a partisan not afraid to fight the entrenched leadership of his party. Its integrity was of more concern to him that the fortunes of any individual, including himself. He distinguished himself as lieutenant governor when a mere lad of 38 by quality of the Democratic legislative program he initiated. He distinguished himself further by the quality of leadership he gave in effectuating a reorganization of the State Highway Commission, resulting in the dawning of a new day for western Kentucky, against which grossest discrimination had been practiced in previous road building.

Even the front page news coverage of the fallen Breathitt was effusive in its praise of Ned Breathitt's uncle:

By his nature, the former lieutenant governor and potential candidate for governor was one of the best-liked men that ever served in public life in the capital. His political foes were numerous, especially during the 1934 sessions of the general assembly in which he took an active part and was a leader of the so-called anti-administration faction. But if he had any personal enemies in Frankfort, no one knew about it.

Jimmy Breathitt had become a sculptor of sorts to the yielding stone of his young nephew–a beacon for the youngster's future political life.

But Ned's father was bitter and disenchanted with politics. Because Ned's grandfather, then Kentucky's attorney general, was passed over and denied his dream of an appointment to the federal bench, and his brother sold out in the smoky back rooms at the convention–the last thing he wanted was for his only child to become interested in politics. The sad fact that both his father and brother passed away within a few short months of each other served to further embitter Ned's dad.

In 1932, when Ned was 8 years of age, America was in bad shape.

The Great Depression had settled in so deep that all of west Kentucky was suffering from the most deprived poverty.

Ned would remember his father coming into his room and opening his closet and surveying what was inside.

"I'm just checking," Ed explained to his curious young son, "if we have enough clothes to make it through the winter."

President Herbert Hoover and the Republican administration in Washington were not only in severe disrepute, but much maligned and despised by an overwhelming number of the rural citizenry of west Kentucky.

It's undoubtedly a mythical story, but worth telling, nevertheless.

President Hoover paid a visit to west Kentucky to speak at the dedication of a public landmark. He was given the usual 21-gun salute.

After the last rifle had fired its blank, some old farmer in the rear of the congregation shaded his eyes and peered toward the platform where Hoover was standing.

"By gum!" he exclaimed, "They missed him!"

But then, a bright, smiling face came upon the scene.

The great Democrat, Franklin Delano Roosevelt.

He won by a landslide in 1932, and immediately after taking office he lifted the spirits of the fearful and impoverished of the rural South by promising federal programs and assistance.

His personality instilled hope. The federal programs which followed put men to work. Raised their self worth, and west Kentucky was poised, with the entire southeastern United States, to be electrified by TVA.

By 1937, Christian County had shifted from Republican to Democrat.

In the summer of 1937, 13-year-old Ned Breathitt went by train with his local Boy Scout troop to attend the National Jamboree. While there, he was taken by Hopkinsville native Colonel Will Starling, then serving as the head of the Secret Service, to the White House.

Moving through the back corridors, Colonel Starling gingerly led the boy into the Oval Office to meet the great FDR. The President was between appointments and the meeting would be limited to a quick handshake. But this most-fortunate young lad from Kentucky was, even if just for a moment, personally exposed to that magical grasp of the hand, and the sunny smile of the American savior.

That moment, like the painful break up with his little black friend, would be one of the defining moments in young Ned Breathitt's life.

Ned's mother, Mary Josephine Wallace, was from the small village of Cerulean, in Trigg County.

Her grandfather, Abithal Wallace, was a veteran of the Confederate forces of the legendary General Nathan Bedford Forrest. He had been part of the forces, who along with Forrest, had broken out from Ft. Donelson on the Cumberland River before it fell to the Union gunboats. The evacuation had been an incredible, almost super-human effort at getting a large number of Calvary men through the icy backwater of the Cumberland River, which in some places ran saddle deep.

"I'm a card carrying member of the Sons of Confederate Veterans," Breathitt would unabashedly proclaim in his later years as he recounted his heroic struggles for the Negro race.

It was from his mother that Ned would acquire his polite and graceful personality. It was also from Mary Josephine that little Ned would acquire his intellectual curiosity for things beyond the boundaries of the rural, Southern culture.

The Wallace's were a highly respected family of Trigg County, many of them excelling in the field of education.

Ned's mother was educated in the Hopkinsville school system, because of its close proximity to Cerulean. After graduating from high school she was sent to Brenau College in Gainesville, Georgia for four years. The finishing touches to her refinement were added by attending the Maret School for Women in Washington, D.C. Needless to say, for that time she was exceptionally educated when she returned to Hopkinsville to work as a teller at Planter's Bank & Trust Company. It was while working there that she met and married Ned's father.

After graduation from Hopkinsville High School, Ned enlisted in the U.S. Air Force serving throughout most of World War II. In the service, he once again faced the troubling question of race relations in the South. He got to know and became good friends with Americans north of the Mason-Dixon Line who considered the South's segregated treatment of Negroes not only antiquated but inhumane. These varying views served as a window for Ned to other more liberal and tolerant ways of looking at race relations.

Leaving the service in 1945, Ned began to think seriously about a career in law and politics.

After enrolling at the University of Kentucky in 1945, he met a pretty young coed from Mayfield, Kentucky, Frances Holleman. They married in 1948 when he was in law school at the university. The future governor got his first taste of statewide politics while still a student at UK. At the behest of professors Dr. Jack Reeves of the Political Science Department and Dr. Thomas Clark of the History Department, he became campus chairman of the campaign to persuade voters to pass a new State Constitution. While that effort failed statewide, the eager and charming young student gained much experience in public speaking and in the nuts and bolts of state government.

Upon graduating from law school in 1948, he became a member of the law firm, Trimble, Soyars, and Breathitt in Hopkinsville.

Breathitt's early recognition of the injustice of racial bias continued on into his early years of practicing law. As the "new kid" on the block with the Christian County bar, he was often appointed to represent pro bono, those blacks charged with crimes in Hopkinsville.

"I was distressed about the double standard of justice in murder cases," he would later recall. "If you were black and were charged with killing a white person, justice was swift and severe resulting in a death sentence. If you were a white person accused of killing a black and could hire a good lawyer, you had a good chance of being acquitted or receiving a light sentence."

He also noticed that in crimes of violence of black on black, a casual indifference prevailed and they were routinely treated as low-grade offenses, and of little importance. Often the defendant would be released from custody if a white farmer needed his labor.

In those early years of law practice, Ned's family grew quickly as Frances gave birth to three girls and a boy. He was also active in the community becoming a member of various civic groups as well as serving as the attorney for the Christian County School Board.

Soon he plunged into politics with a vengeance, running for and being elected as state representative from the 9th Legislative District in 1951. At the age of only 27, he was the youngest legislator in the state.

His oratory skills improved dramatically in 1952 when he served as speaker chairman for the losing cause of Democrat Adlai Stevenson for President. His efforts were more successful two years later as he worked hard for the return of fellow west Kentuckian, former Vice President Alben Barkley to the U.S. Senate.

This young, handsome man from Hopkinsville was catching the eye of the leading Democrats of the state. He was a comer. His hard work was also valuable experience for this young politician. He possessed loads of charm to go along with a burning ambition for higher office.

It was as president of the Young Democratic Club of Kentucky that he became acquainted with another young Southerner with just as much ambition and charm–George Wallace of Alabama.

As a member of the national committee of the Young Democrats of America, Ned met Wallace in 1952 at the National Young Democrats Convention in Minneapolis, Minnesota. Ned was the president of the state Young Democrats club. George was a young circuit judge from Alabama.

There in the heady atmosphere of youthful ambitions and dreams, these aspiring, fresh political faces took on the vital issues of the day.

And there were speeches–many of them.

Eugene McCarthy spoke. Spell-binding liberal, Senator Hubert Humphrey gave a stem-winding civil rights speech.

Apparently in the mood of the moment, the young circuit judge from Alabama–George Corley Wallace–to no one's particular surprise at that early date of his career, gave a sterling and rousing endorsement of civil rights and full support for the Negro.

Ned Breathitt gave him his hearty applause.

On his return home Breathitt quickly showed that he had the courage of his conviction to go along with his winning personality. In the state general assembly he bucked the all-powerful coal industry by supporting passage of the Commonwealth's first strip mining legislation. He also made an unsuccessful bid to establish a merit system for state employees.

In 1959 ingoing Democratic Governor Bert T. Combs had been so impressed with the Hopkinsville native, that he appointed him as his personnel director, and later as a member of the powerful Pubic Service Commission.

In the spring of 1963, John F. Kennedy was president. His youthful vigor and attractive young family had captured the country's attention. While his administration had received a mixed review by the American public at the time, one thing was certain, he had inspired a new generation of politicians, who at an early age were called to the idealism of his New Frontier.

Younger, handsome faces from both parties began to appear upon the political scene across the land: Governors Mark Hatfield in Oregon, Dan Evans in Washington, Terry Sanford in North Carolina, Carl Sanders in Georgia, John Chaffee in Rhode Island, Senator Charles Percy in Illinois and Mayor John Lindsay in New York, to name a few.

In Alabama George Wallace was young but he lacked the shining rhetoric of a bold new course. Instead, he held to the ancient prejudices and dogma of the past, especially in the area of race relations.

In Kentucky, Ned Breathitt was the right man at the right time.

Young, buoyant, and energetic with a pretty wife and four young children, he gave Kentuckians the vision of "Camelot South." He got the nod from sitting governor, Combs, who could not succeed himself.

Breathitt was only 38 years of age.

Running against Breathitt that spring, in the Democratic primary, was the venerable old war horse of Kentucky politics, Albert "Happy" Chandler.

At first, most courthouse politicians and prognosticators thought the young upstart was overmatched by Chandler, even if he did have the full endorsement and support of Governor Combs.

Chandler was practically a legend. A two-time governor, and former Major League Baseball Commissioner, Happy, even at almost 63 years of age, was a dynamic and electrifying campaigner.

Chandler had a great gift for remembering names. He could show up in Hickman for the first time in years and greet enough locals by their first name to make one think he lived there.

He was also master of the caustic, if humorous, political one-liners.

Once, while running against fancy city-slicker Wilson Wyatt, who wore spats in one of his gubernatorial races, Chandler referred to the dapper Louisvillian as "ole ankle blankets." It always caught a chuckle and a vote in the rural areas of the state.

Contrasted with the fresh, young face and upbeat style of Ned Breathitt, however, it soon became apparent to Kentucky voters that Happy's time had passed him by.

In the May Democratic primary, Breathitt trounced Chandler by over 60,000 votes. His lieutenant governor running mate for the fall election was Harry Lee Waterfield of Hickman, Kentucky.

Waterfield was the son of Burnett Waterfield, a Murray taxi cab driver who was one of the lynch mob members indicted in the Lube Martin episode.

The day following his primary victory, Breathitt got a congratulations phone call from the president of the United States.

It was the first time the two men ever talked, and the young country lawyer from Hopkinsville, Kentucky was impressed, even awed by John Kennedy's call.

The Kennedy administration had remained neutral during Kentucky's Democratic Primary. Not without some effort however. The Breathitt people had been deeply concerned. Although the Kennedy administration was not particularly popular in Kentucky, or throughout the South at that time, he was still president of the United States, and possessed the glamour and charisma of a movie star.

Jack Kennedy's father, Joe, was a good friend of Happy Chandler. Other men in the administration had known Happy previously. So, the administration was on the verge of endorsing the former Kentucky governor when Ed Pritchard heard of it.

Pritchard, a Bourbon County native, was at one time considered to be the brightest young star in the political firmament of Kentucky. Gifted with the mind of a genius, he attended Harvard, and clerked for Felix Frankfurter on the U.S. Supreme Court. During his days at Harvard and while serving in Franklin Roosevelt's administration he became close friends with many of the powers in Washington. But he fell from the heavens when he returned to Paris, Kentucky and foolishly committed an election-fraud crime in a rather inconsequential local election. He ended up in jail, later to be pardoned by President Truman. Though out of favor with the public because of the scandal, "Pritch," nevertheless, stayed close to politics as an advisor, using his incredible mind and bulging stable of contacts to assist his friends.

Ned Breathitt was one of those friends.

Pritch got on the phone to the Kennedy people. Talking to Arthur Schlesinger, a close friend and aide to Kennedy, Pritch railed against the prospects of the young, progressive president endorsing Chandler. Yelling and pounding his fist upon the table, he spelled out all the reasons why the Kennedy people should be for Ned instead of Happy.

Pritch managed to keep the John F. Kennedy presidency neutral during the 1963 Democratic Primary for governor.

During Ned's congratulatory phone call from Kennedy, the President had said, "I'd like for you to come up and talk to us."

The implication was clear: we might help you in the fall election.

Excited about the prospects of going to Washington to meet the president of the United States, Ned and Frances quickly made plans for the trip. Louis Cox, a Frankfort attorney and the Kennedy man in Kentucky made the arrangements.

At the White House Breathitt was escorted into the Cabinet Room where he was cordially greeted by the president's brother-in-law, Steve Smith. Soon Bobby Kennedy arrived.

It was exam time.

In a polite but direct manner, the two men grilled the young, Democratic nominee for governor of Kentucky.

Would he be for them in '64?

Absolutely.

Could he control the Kentucky delegation to the convention?

Absolutely.

This was crucial to Kennedy as he was losing most of the state houses in the South because of his stand on civil rights.

And civil rights were also on the agenda that day.

Bobby Kennedy wanted to know where Breathitt stood on

the issue.

Ned's answer to the U.S. attorney general took him way down to Christian County, Kentucky.

"I was the attorney for the school board in Christian County and wrote the integration plan, and then supervised it with the superintendent, and made sure the Brown Decision was implemented."

After a long time, the men seemed to be satisfied with this young prospect from the South. They took him and Frances into the Oval Office.

There, to Ned's surprise was the entire Kentucky delegation from the House of Representatives along with the president to greet them. Kennedy was "all charm" that day and the two young politicians–poles apart culturally and geographically–warmed to each other immediately.

"Would you like for me to come to Kentucky and campaign for you?" the president asked.

"Not really. I'd rather you come to Kentucky after I'm elected," was Breathitt's reply, which seemed to surprise some in the room.

But not the politically astute Kennedy, he laughed with appreciation and understanding of Ned's candor. As a liberal and a Catholic and because of his stand on civil rights, Jack Kennedy's presence in Kentucky would cost Ned as many votes as it would gain.

Kennedy then asked about another high-profile politician from the North.

No thanks.

"Mr. President, just send money. When I'm elected I'll be your strong supporter and we'll be glad to welcome you to Kentucky any time you want to come."

Kennedy seemed to have been impressed by Breathitt's candor, spoken in his easy drawl and packaged in the gracious and genteel personality of a Southern gentleman.

He would later comply with Ned's request by having the

Democratic National Committee send down to Breathitt's campaign $50,000 in cash. It was a sizable contribution to a candidate whose party would spend less than a half million dollars in the general election.

In those days in Kentucky, the Republican Party hardly bothered to show up in the general election for governor. In the predominantly Democratic state, the state house belonged lock, stock and barrel to the party of the rooster. The Primary election was, in effect, the whole ball game. The Republican nominee on the ballot for governor in November was usually less known to the Kentucky voters than the U.S. Ambassador to Senegal.

But in 1963, something quirky happened, something which would give the young Ned a peck of trouble.

After Breathitt had soundly disposed of Happy in the May Primary, Governor Combs, without conferring with the Democratic nominee, immediately issued an executive order that desegregated all public accommodations in the state.

The proclamation immediately raised a political firestorm within the Commonwealth.

Breathitt and his closest aides were bewildered as to why Combs did not wait 'till after the November election and before he left office.

Combs thought the timing was perfect. It was after the hotly contested primary against a most formidable foe. The race in the fall against a token Republican would be a cakewalk. No need to worry.

Or so he thought. But Combs had badly underestimated both the magnitude of the racial invective in the state, and the political savvy and adroitness of a young county judge from Barren County.

Louie B. Nunn, of Glasgow, was the same age as Ned Breathitt. He was the Republican nominee for governor in the fall election. Nunn saw the Combs desegregated edict as just the hot-button issue to turn what would have ordinarily been an easy and lopsided victory for the Democrats into a dog race.

And a dog race it became.

Nunn cleverly managed to arouse the racial fears and resentment of the voters of Kentucky. Appearing on television with the American flag, a Bible, and a copy of Combs' executive order, Nunn proclaimed, "My first act will be to abolish this," pointing to the Combs' edict.

Nunn's henchmen played upon the base prejudices of those most directly affected by the Combs' order.

They went to barber shops, restaurants, hotels and motels, and somberly advised their owners that if they were required to service Negroes, their places of business would be contaminated with lice and that it would take extra costs to clean and maintain them. Whites, they asserted, would stay away in droves.

The New York Times in following the highly heated race called it a "reversal for the forces of racial moderation."

Soon the Democrats were beginning to dread the unthinkable, and the Republicans smelled blood in the water, and just a slight whiff of victory in the air.

To make matters worse, Chandler, who had been Major League Baseball Commissioner when Jackie Robinson had broken the color barrier, bolted the party and endorsed Nunn. It was primarily a slap at Combs, his long-time political enemy.

In the summer of 1963, the race war was raging across the entire South. It was a long, hot, violent summer of civil unrest and bloodshed. And it was a summer which in a most subtle and unexpected way, changed the way white Southerners looked at race.

President Kennedy had taken aim against the segregationist South, with his main focus being directed toward Alabama, and its little governor, George C. Wallace.

After his progressive stance on civil rights in 1952 at the Young Democrats gathering in Minnesota, Wallace returned to Alabama and ran for governor. He found that his position on the racial question voiced way up North among bright, young politicians from across the country was not hardly as popular in

Alabama. However, Wallace still managed to remain somewhat of a moderate on the racial issue. In his campaign for governor in 1958 against the state's Attorney General John Patterson, an opponent who took the low road on the race issue, Wallace even attacked the Ku Klux Klan. "There are a lot of pistol-toters and toughs among Klansmen," he warned.

In that campaign Wallace was almost statesmanlike, pressing the issues of improved roads, better education and industrial recruitment. His position on race was what historian Dan T. Carter called a "dignified defense of segregation."

And Patterson beat him soundly.

The outcome changed and embittered George Wallace, and in the process, changed the course of civil rights throughout the South and the nation.

He would later deny even making the remark that "he would never be outniggered again." But his future positions and rhetoric on the matter would prove that was exactly his sentiment.

It was the crossroads of the political life of George Wallace. Two roads diverged into the political woods and he took the one most traveled.

By 1963 Wallace had rebounded and was the sitting governor of Alabama.

On Tuesday morning, June 11, while Ned Breathitt was still contemplating with mixed emotions his big victory over Happy Chandler and the effect the Combs desegregation directive was going to have on his campaign in the fall, Governor Wallace was making his way to the steps of the administration building of the University of Alabama in Tuscaloosa.

There he would make his historic and symbolic stand against the federally enforced admission of black students Vivian Malone and Jimmy Hood into the University. While tension was running high, and with U.S. Marshals and the National Guard ready in the wings for whatever might come, the actual event was the culmination of many hours of negotiation between the president and the U.S. Justice Department led by Robert Kennedy, and the governor's office. George got to make a scripted statement for local consumption of his opposition to the federal encroachment of states rights. In turn, the black students got to enter school and violence was averted.

In truth, it would have been hard to determine that night who was the most relieved–John Kennedy or George Wallace.

But the rest of the summer did not go so well in the South.

The very next day, June 12, 1963 in Jackson, Mississippi, a young, black army veteran of Normandy was gunned down in front of his home. Medgar Evers was a well-educated civil rights worker who was establishing local chapters for the National Association for the Advancement of Colored People (NAACP) through the Delta region. He had organized boycotts of gasoline stations that refused to allow blacks to use their restrooms. At the time of his death Evers was serving as Mississippi's first field secretary for the NAACP. It would be over thirty years before the killer would be brought to justice.

Meanwhile in Ned Breathitt's hometown of Hopkinsville, Kentucky, Negroes were picketing the downtown movie theater, demanding they be allowed to sit on the main floor and not be forced to sit in the balcony.

The *Paducah Sun* reported that two western Kentucky Negro schools, Princeton Dodson and Murray Douglas, would not open their doors in the fall. Their student bodies would instead be integrated with the neighboring white schools. They were among at least 26 black schools in Kentucky that in the spring of 1963 graduated their last class.

In Birmingham, Alabama–one of the most severely segregated cities in the U.S.–violence erupted. Martin Luther King, and other leaders of the NAACP led demonstrations against the discrimination against blacks in public places–the exact same practice the Combs executive order had addressed. On their black and white television screens that summer Americans saw grainy images of black citizens being washed along sidewalks and streets, their bodies tumbling like rag dolls from the powerful surge of fire hoses being turned upon them by law enforcement officers. The snarling and menacing teeth of police dogs were seen by the American public via news film, tearing away clothing and even flesh of the black protesters. These were not pretty images being shown to the world.

As the summer heat of 1963 boiled, politicians in Kentucky gathered at Fancy Farm on the first Saturday in August. The political picnic which begun just after the Civil War is traditionally considered to be the kickoff for November elections, after the relative calm which follows for a few weeks after the May primaries.

It was August 3, 1963 and at Fancy Farm it was 96 degrees under pale blue skies in a day before heat indexes were invented. Few had air conditioning in their cars. There at the political Mecca of Kentucky politics, the sweltering crowd of thousands gathered under the giant oaks of St. Jerome Catholic Church. Men were in short sleeves, women in bare-back sun dresses, and small kids dressed in practically nothing. Funeral home fans were vainly flailing at the humid air. Barbecue was once again consumed by the truck loads, bingo was played with relish, and politicians of all levels pumped hands.

A governor's race always brings out a bigger crowd than usual at Fancy Farm. This time the crowd was expecting a dramatic face-off between two young candidates. Even in this Democratic Gibraltar of far west Kentucky, it was generally accepted that Combs' order and the race issue had turned the fall campaign for governor into a barn-burner. There were an estimated eight to ten thousand people in the little Graves County hamlet on this blistering August afternoon.

Like heavyweight boxers making their way down the aisle to the ring, each candidate arrived on the grounds in dramatic fashion with their retinue of aides, advisors, and local political wheels. Smiling, perspiration pouring from their faces, both Nunn and Breathitt shook hands and kissed babies on their way to the podium which set under the shade of two ancient oaks.

By luck of the draw, Republican Louie Nunn went first.

As expected, he went to the issue which was giving him the

chance to be the first Republican governor of Kentucky in many years.

He lambasted Governor Bert Combs' order banning racial discrimination in state-licensed businesses as a "hoax" and called it the "greatest question that has confronted voters in your lifetime, in my lifetime."

According to the Republican standard bearer the "Combs-Breathitt" order was simply a "move to buy a few Negro votes" directed by the Democratic administration in Washington, D.C.

To thunderous applause he proclaimed, "When I'm elected as your governor, I'm going to rescind that order."

At the completion of his speech, Nunn proceeded to leave the platform, and move with his entourage toward his car–a move which clearly angered the young Hopkinsville lawyer.

"Loud Mouth Louie!" Breathitt shouted, as he came to the podium, "Look at him go. He didn't have the courage to stay here and hear what I had to say."

And the Democratic candidate had plenty to say. He didn't dodge the race issue. Instead, Breathitt launched into a fiery defense of civil rights.

"Civil rights has never been a partisan issue in a Kentucky campaign," he declared, "until my opponent made it so. Kentucky has had an outstanding record in this field because leaders of both races and both political parties have worked in harmony and good-will toward solving these problems."

As Nunn drove away, Breathitt stated, "I do not intend to conduct this campaign on racial prejudice. The issue of civil rights should not be a partisan issue. It is a human and moral issue. If my opponent continues to make racial animosity his only issue of this campaign he may find that he has sown the wind and reaped the whirlwind."

Breathitt concluded his speech by challenging Nunn to a series of televised debates.

So the main event of the Fancy Farm picnic of 1963 came to a close. People would linger into the night, visiting and listening to the country music of a local band. Darkness would finally bring down the curtain upon this hallowed ground, where religion and politics mix so well. On this day, the ancient issue of the South had once again raised its head in the political arena. Here under the towering oaks which had served as sentinels of past gatherings of graying old Confederate veterans, the question of race, and the proper place of the Negro in an evolving Southern society had once again been debated.

The sounds of crickets and katydids slowly replaced the strident rhetoric of politicians, the softening shadows of a summer gloaming fell upon the deserted battle ground of discarded placards, signs and paper plates. Quiet returned to the church yard, as workers moved in to clear the debris as this peaceful and idyllic land was reclaimed by its strong and endearing people.

Nationally, the whole cauldron of civil rights came to a boil on August 28, as the long hot summer of discord was punctuated by a demonstration of over one quarter million marchers, mostly Negro, in Washington, D.C.

It was an impressive gathering put together by the leading civil rights organizations of the day and leaders such as Whitney Young, Roy Wilkins, Martin Luther King, Jr. and others. Contrary to dire and dark predictions of many, the event remained peaceful and without violence.

It provided the venue for one of the most memorable speeches in American history. Standing on the steps of the Lincoln Memorial, and on live national television, King brought not only his own race to the mountain top of racial relations, but millions of whites as well:

I have a dream that my four little children will one day live in a nation where they will not be judged by the color of their skin but by the content of their character.

I have a dream.......where little black boys and black girls will be able to join hands with little white boys and white girls and walk together as sisters and brothers.

I have a dream.......

On the very day of the massive march in Washington, W.E. Dubois, one of the founders of the NAACP, died in Ghana.

But as powerful as the words of King were on that late summer afternoon, it would be an incident of a totally different kind which would begin to turn the hearts of Americans in the great upheaval of integration and civil rights.

On a quiet Sunday morning, September 15, 1963, members of the 16th Street Baptist Church, a black church in Birmingham, Alabama, began to gather. It was Youth Day at the church, as the Sunday school rooms began to fill. Four little black girls, Denise McNair, Carole Robertson, Cynthia Wesley, and Addie Mae Collins–ages 11 and 14–dressed in their frilly dresses settled in with their classmates for the Sunday school lesson.

Suddenly there was a tremendous explosion which ripped through the basement of the church blasting brick and mortar and splintering furniture and door facings. The shock was so intense that it blew out the face of Jesus in the stained-glass window and stopped the church clock.

When the eerie quiet descended upon the dust and rubble, these four innocent children lie dead under the debris.

The dastardly deed was the work of segregationists designed to kill and maim innocent members of a church which had been used as a meeting place for civil rights activities. The blast also followed many tense weeks of desegregation in the Birmingham schools.

Birmingham erupted in violence and other victims lay dead before the day was over. It would be many years before anyone would be brought to justice for the murders.

McNair, Robertson, Wesley, Collins. Names lost now to the nation became the most influential martyrs of the civil rights movement.

To understand the full significance of their supreme sacrifice, one has to understand the whites of the South at that time.

Unrecognized by the unknowing North, there was a broad swath of benign segregationists in the South. Their numbers made up the vast majority of the population. These were well-intended, if misguided, men and women who had been brought up in the ancient mores and customs of the separation of the races. There was no particularly animus borne toward the Negro, as long as members of that race kept their place. It was believed, in good conscience, to be the natural order of things. These same people–good people for the most part–did not condone the atrocities committed against the blacks, but did very little to stop them. Their sins were those of omissions, and up to that time, served to be just as lethal. Bad things happen when good people do nothing. The vast majority of white Southerners, including Kentuckians, saw Martin Luther King and others of his ilk as troublemakers, stirring up civil unrest and disturbing the status quo. The whole onslaught against the customs and laws of the Jim Crow South by the Negro was intimidating and frightening.

So they resisted, with minds totally closed to change. "We didn't know any different," says a ninety-year-old white North Carolinian today, "because it was the way we were brought up. It took a while for us to learn it was wrong."

Until September 15, 1963.

Innocent little girls, in their frilly dresses, murdered in Sunday school.

White faces could not turn away from this appalling atrocity. The Bible Belt of good Christians of all colors was inescapably connected to the blood, the smoke, the deadly debris of that Sunday morning.

> *Jesus loves the little children,*
> *All the children of the world.*
> *Red and yellow, black and white,*
> *They are precious in His sight.*
> *Jesus loves the little children of the world.*

Other victims of violence perpetrated by white racists were either ignored, or rationalized by the ill-informed. The dog victims of that summer in Birmingham might be seen as delinquents looking for trouble. Evers could be imagined as part of some Communist conspiracy. Any twist to maintain their comfortable perspective on race and change would suffice. Even the victims of the scores of awful lynchings were usually guilty as charged, and somehow this fact skewed the moral compasses of otherwise law-abiding citizens.

And of course there were the less-numbered "white moderates" who believed in integration but thought that the civil rights leaders were pushing too hard and too fast. It was this smaller group with which King became the most irritated because they would not openly come to the aid of the Negro.

But the inner goodness of these people, sleeping until now, could find no redemption to the killing of innocent little girls in their Sunday worship. If the cause of segregation had stooped to this cowardly and dastardly deed, then there must be something inherently wrong and misguided with the cause.

"The arc of the moral universe is long, but it bends toward justice."

These words were spoken by King, and it professed an underlying optimism that sooner or later, the good white people of the South would finally see the light.

With the tragedy of September 15, in Birmingham, there was no sudden running out of doors by Southern whites, to repute their segregationist ways. No overnight conversion. No bright line, across which a social metamorphosis took place.

But deep within the earth of racial bias, layered underneath generations of prejudice and ancient codes, imperceptibly and unknown to the people of America, the plates shifted on that early autumn Sunday, and the mind of the segregated South began ever so slowly to quake and change.

A long and bloody road still lay ahead for the American

civil rights movement. But on September 15, 1963, the road turned.

Within a year, the country's young president would become a martyr to the cause. The revolutionary Civil Rights Act of 1964 would be passed by the U.S. Congress under the leadership of a Southern president who heroically rejected his segregationist past.

On November 5, 1963–just 45 days after the evil crime at the 16th Street Baptist Church in Birmingham–Kentuckians would give Ned Breathitt a razor-thin margin of victory over Louie Nunn in the race for governor.

That fall at Murray State University, a lanky Negro from Pittsburgh, Pennsylvania by the name of Stu Johnson would become the first black ever to play basketball in the Ohio Valley Conference, a league made up solely of schools from Kentucky and Tennessee.

And Bob Dylan's lyrics blared out from college campus juke boxes across the country, "the times, they are a changin'."

CHAPTER 14

THE TORCH IS PASSED

After the dust had settled from the narrow win over Nunn, Breathitt received a congratulatory telephone call from President Kennedy. The Boston accent meshed with the soft drawl of Christian County, Kentucky.

"Well, I'm sorry, Mr. President, that I didn't win by more votes," said the apologetic governor-elect.

"Ned, compared to my election, yours was a landslide," responded Jack Kennedy with his typical wit.

They then turned to the future, and the conversation took on the more intimate and personal tone of two kindred spirits, two young political warriors taking on the ills of the world. Kennedy was obviously heartened by having a personal ally for his own agenda below the Mason-Dixon Line.

They made plans to hook up soon.

"I want to come down there right after you are sworn in and announce my support for the Appalachian Bill," Kennedy said. "I've studied it, and the report of the Appalachian Commission and I'm coming down there,

West Virginia and North Carolina and endorse it. I'll go to West Virginia and announce my support and then I'll come over to Kentucky and announce it with you."

But first the president had another trip to make.

"I've got to go to Florida and then I've got to go to Dallas. Lyndon and I are going down there to try to pull that state together. If I don't carry Texas, I can't win. When I get back Mrs. Lincoln will call you to set up the time and place for us to get together."

It was the last conversation they ever had. In Dallas, Texas, just two weeks later, Lee Harvey Oswald took care of this brief alliance.

Flags still flew at half mast for the recently fallen president, and the state of Kentucky, was in a doleful mood as young, vibrant Ned Breathitt took the oath of office on December 10, 1963 on the steps of the capitol in Frankfort. At age 39, he was the youngest governor in the United States.

The sun peeked through leaden skies, and spots of snow still lingered on the hills hovering over the capitol. While the state may have still been mourning the tragic death of their young president, thousands of Kentuckians came to pay homage to their new young leader.

The *Paducah Sun* reported, "His grin as wide as the old-fashioned Kentucky welcome he received, Edward T. Breathitt, Jr. made a triumphant entry today, and captured the hearts of the thousands of 'Ned's neighbors'."

Breathitt's campaign song, "Hey Look Me Over" was being played everywhere even by the numerous high school bands marching in the parade.

Both Breathitt and fellow west Kentuckian Lt. Governor Harry Lee Waterfield had been sworn in just past midnight that day at the home of former Governor Lawrence W. Wetherby by Christian Circuit Judge Ira D. Smith. The ceremony was repeated on the platform before the huge crowd with his right hand resting on a 75-year-old Bible, a treasure of the Breathitt family.

"This is not a day of exultation," began Breathitt in his inaugural address as the sun shone down through a cold, brisk breeze. "This is not a day of triumph. This is not a day of unseemly rejoicing. This is a day of soul-searching."

In paying homage to the late president, Breathitt spoke of his commitment to civil rights. "For John F. Kennedy there were no races, no geographical sections, no inferior classes. For him there was no rest of body, mind, or spirit so long as the accidents of color, of geographical isolation, of economic heritage, served to isolate or to alienate individual Americans from the fullness, the richness, and vast opportunities of American life."

Just 11 months previously in his inaugural speech in Montgomery, Alabama, Governor George Wallace had promised, "Segregation now....segregation tomorrow...segregation forever."

These two young men, both born and nourished in the Jim Crow South, friends from their memorable time together in Minnesota as ambitious Young Democrats, charted the course of their respective states in opposite directions.

During his campaign against Nunn, Ned Breathitt had bent a little on the civil rights issue, particularly as to Combs' decree.

Philosophically, Breathitt agreed with Nunn that an executive order was not the best way to go about outlawing segregation and discrimination in Kentucky. It smacked at dictatorial power and was not in the spirit of representative government. Besides, it raised legal questions.

So, in order to help blunt some of Nunn's scathing political rhetoric, and to counter any possible court actions challenging the edict, Breathitt proclaimed that he too would rescind the executive order if elected. But in the same breath he promised that he would, with that action, propose a sweeping civil rights bill for the general assembly to enact.

The new governor of Kentucky faced a daunting task immediately after the inauguration. For within a month of

December 10, Breathitt had to get his staff aboard, and his legislative agenda set. The time called for a quick pulling together of the leaders of both the Senate and House in order to be ready to go by the second Tuesday in January, when the session began.

Upon taking office, he first called upon Burke Marshall, head of the Civil Rights Division of the U.S. Attorney's office to send someone to assist him in drafting the promised civil rights bill for the general assembly.

He had postponed carrying out his commitment to rescind his predecessor's executive order until a civil rights law looked imminent. So there was pressure on him from both the civil rights activists and those demanding the rescission to get the new law in place quickly.

The young governor struggled in that first session trying to find his sea legs. He lost two of his key legislative supporters before the session even began, one to political defeat and the other to death. The Chandler law makers and the anti-civil rights clique joined together to block Breathitt at every turn.

Civil rights bills were filed both in the House and in the Senate. Both bills languished.

On March 6, 1964 a giant demonstration in favor of the proposed legislation led by Martin Luther King, Ralph Abernathy, Jackie Robinson and other leaders from the NAACP and Southern Christian Leadership was held on the state capitol grounds. The popular folk music group of Peter, Paula and Mary were also there. Governor Breathitt's oldest daughter, Mary Fran, age 13, disobeyed her teacher at school and joined in the march.

In his office Ned warmly received a delegation from the march, including King and Robinson. It was the first time he met King. But it would be the beginning of a meaningful relationship.

The demonstrators also staged a sit-in in the gallery of the House from March 16-20. Black participants of all ages sat there in silence, placards around many of their necks proclaiming, "Give Me Freedom or Death!"

The lawmakers remained unmoved.

On March 12, in order to bring more pressure upon the legislators to do something, Governor Breathitt rescinded Combs' executive order.

The moved proved to be a disaster. Not only did it fail to cause the general assembly to act, it brought severe criticism upon the governor from civil rights groups and The Louisville *Courier Journal.*

In short, the 1964 legislative session came to an end without the civil rights legislation being passed. "There was just cold opposition to it in Kentucky," said Breathitt later, "especially in west Kentucky." Worse yet, now Kentucky did not even have the Combs order in place. The young governor had taken a licking in his first session. The general assembly would not meet again for two years.

While he threatened to call a special session to take up the matter, his informal polling of the legislators convinced him that it would be futile.

He would have to wait until 1966.

President Lyndon Baines Johnson lacked the television personality of his young predecessor, but there was no one more engaging and persuasive in person-to-person relationships than the tall Texan.

Johnson had been the master of the U.S. Senate, and was known for his overwhelming personal style. At six foot three, with ham-like hands, he was physical in his encounters. Hugging, patting on the back, grabbing by the arm, even by the lapels of the coat. Jabbing his finger into one's chest he would draw close to make special points, cajoling loudly at one point, whispering into the ear the next. His face could be kind and benevolent with the wide smile of a beloved uncle, or his eyes could narrow and his visage grow grim in a low rumble of suppressed anger.

Senator Johnson, now President Johnson, could take over a room. He was intimidating, and most always won his point.

Ned Breathitt first encountered the tall, powerful Texan at

the funeral of President Kennedy. Johnson had been masterful at taking charge right from the very start.

The night before the funeral the new president had called a meeting of all the governors who had come to Washington at the Executive Office Building. Breathitt was attending technically as governor-elect since he was still a few weeks away from being sworn in.

Johnson came into the room in shirt sleeves, grave and serious.

"We've got a constitutional crisis in this country now gentlemen," Johnson somberly drawled to the gathering of solemn faces. "There's going to be some people that I had him killed so I could be president. I'm appointing a top commission headed by the chief justice to investigate the whole matter." The president was typically direct and blunt. Turning to the more immediate crisis, "My presidency must be validated. Otherwise with emotions running as high as they are we could have some serious problems." His eyes narrowing, and his voice taking on a tough firmness, he declared, "To the Democrats in the room who supported Kennedy, I'm going to pass every piece of legislation that he had sent up to the Hill."

The Republican governors waited.

"And to all the Republicans, I need your support for the next 30 to 60 days simply to validate my presidency. After that, you can take your best shot, and if you can beat me that's fine. But we have to have a unified support of the presidency during these next few weeks."

After the meeting broke up governor-elect Breathitt broke the ice with the new president.

"Mr. President, Governor Bert Combs had been the leading fellow in getting the Appalachian Commission formed to fight mountain poverty and improve education there. President Kennedy had made a commitment to come to Kentucky and give a pitch for the poverty program. I hope you will carry out that commitment."

Johnson didn't blink an eye. "I will. Franklin Delano

Roosevelt was my political 'daddy,' and there is a lot of unfinished business from his administration because he died before the war was over and couldn't turn his attention to it. We'll have Kennedy's agenda passed by the August recess," the president assured confidently.

No doubt President Johnson was impressed with the new Kentucky governor's chutzpah and grit. LBJ was known for his keen assessment of men and their capabilities from his days in the Senate.

Ned Breathitt was a man who could be counted on.

Shortly before the National Governor's Conference met in Cleveland in June of 1964, Breathitt was summoned to the White House.

With all of his legendary charm the president pounced on the Kentucky chief executive in the awesome surroundings of the Oval Office.

Like a huge recruiting poster of Uncle Sam, Johnson made it clear that he wanted Governor Breathitt for a special mission.

Hovering together in a small room just off the Oval Office, just the two of them, Johnson asked Breathitt to co-sponsor a resolution at the Governor's Conference supporting the Civil Rights Bill of 1964, then pending in Congress.

The president wanted this Southern Democrat to be out front on the controversial issue.

Breathitt was impressed with the president's passion and sincerity.

Leaning in close to the governor, Johnson pressed the urgency of the moment, "It will take a Southern president and a Democrat to pass this thing," Johnson spoke of his civil rights bill, then caught up in a Senate filibuster. "It's going to mean that we're going to lose the solid South because the Republican Party will play the race card and we'll lose the South," he solemnly and prophetically told the Southern governor. "We are the leading nation in the world but we have no credibility because of the segregation of the races."

Staring the Kentucky governor square in the eye he proclaimed boldly, "We've got to pass this legislation."

Lyndon Johnson was, and remains, a great paradox in the struggle of civil rights. In his earlier years in the U.S. House and the Senate, he had been a strong segregationist in his votes. In his personal conversations, his language was coarse with racist slurs and references. Yet Johnson, from the poor hill country of Texas, bore in his heart of hearts a passion for the poor and the underdog. In 1957, his true bent began to show when he led the Senate to pass a mild civil rights measure. Meager as it was, it was the first positive measure of race equality since reconstruction.

Upon ascension to the presidency that past November, he took up the civil rights torch of the Kennedy administration with a vengeance. Civil rights became his most driving passion, and would remain as his greatest accomplishment of public life.

But for Vietnam, his efforts for the American Negro might well have landed him in heady company of Lincoln, Washington, Jefferson and Roosevelt among the country's greatest presidents.

Just four days after Kennedy had been gunned down in Johnson's home state, the new president stood before Congress and asked for passage of the sweeping civil rights legislation as a monument of the fallen president. The new law would assure equal rights to blacks in the fields of employment, public accommodations, as well as private hotels, restaurants, and movie theaters.

There had been another reason Johnson picked Ned Breathitt to carry the banner of civil rights to the nation's governors. Just that past January the Kentucky governor had been the first state executive south of the Mason-Dixon Line to attempt to pass a civil rights bill in the state legislature.

The legislation had failed but the effort had not been lost on President Johnson. Breathitt had been stung by criticism from the leaders of the NAACP that he had not done enough to have the measure passed. So he was committed to press the fight, not only at the next session of the Kentucky General Assembly in 1966.

And he was happy to have the chance to champion the

cause for the president at the National Conference of Governors.

"I got all the border state governors to support the resolution," Breathitt recalled, "but we lost every Southern governor of the old Confederacy. Carl Sanders of Georgia, and Terry Sanford of North Carolina told me they were for it, but it would end their political careers in their home states if they openly supported it."

Of course Breathitt had already narrowly survived that ring of fire.

Breathitt asked Oregon's Republican Governor Mark Hatfield to co-sponsor the resolution. On June 10, 1964 the governors passed a "statement of principle" urging the passage of the federal civil right's bill. It passed handily, bolstering and assisting Johnson in the passage of the country's powerful Civil Rights Act of 1964.

President Johnson continued to pay attention to the Kentucky governor.

After signing the nation's most broad-sweeping civil rights legislation since reconstruction on July 2, 1964, Johnson appointed a select commission to fulfill these rights. This committee was charged with the responsibility of overseeing implementation of the rights bill, as well as monitoring other areas of racial discrimination in American life. Its membership was made up of an impressive array of national human rights leaders. It included railroad executive Ben Heineman, Vernon Jordon, Roy Wilkins, Floyd McKissick, Whitney Young, Martin Luther King, Jr. and others. Breathitt was one of only three whites on the commission. The group met monthly in the Treaty Room of the Executive Office Building in Washington.

Martin Luther King was Breathitt's "seat mate" and they became personal friends through these meetings.

"During these regular gatherings we got to know each other pretty well," Breathitt would later recall of King, "and of course it wasn't all business. We had many personal conversations–family, personal interests, and so forth." The friendship forged between Breathitt and King would turn out to be pivotal in the future.

The intensity and substance of those monthly meetings made a deep impression on the Kentucky governor.

"It was a marvelous experience for a young governor from a small town in Kentucky with my kind of background to sit down as an equal with these men for two years. It was a great learning and growing experience for me," Breathitt recounted years later.

Breathitt was impressed by the sound wisdom and reason of these leaders of social change, some of which were highly successful men flying into D.C. in their private jets. Only McKissick, leader of CORE, would from time to time become a "little radical and strident."

In spite of Breathitt's growing reputation as a liberal advocate for equal rights for Negroes, it didn't seem to bother George Wallace at all.

The two had a warm and easy friendship. Neither ever mentioned to each other the topic of civil rights. Each knew it would do no good. They dwelled upon those things which they had in common. And they had much in common.

Both were of the same generation, World War II veterans, with Wallace only five years the senior. They both represented poor, rural states which had weathered similar hardships both politically and socially. Each knew what it was like to have their states stereotyped as backward and regressive.

In spite of their differences on the issue of civil rights, there was a mutual respect between them. Breathitt understood George Wallace and knew him when he was a liberal on civil rights. He knew his rhetoric was purely political. To Breathitt, the Alabama governor did not wear the horns of Satan. Most of the people Ned grew up with and still counted as friends and neighbors back home–otherwise good, decent people–believed the same way George did. George Wallace carried Ned Breathitt's home county in the 1968 presidential election.

They could have lived comfortably together as next door neighbors, sharing the same values on most things; maybe sharing strikingly similar values on race if they ever confided confidentially over the back fence

Had Ned and George Wallace ever seriously talked about the Negroes' plight in an emerging America, and had they been joined by another Southerner named Lyndon Baines Johnson, they would have all shared the same or similar experiences in their early race relations. Unlike northern or western politicians who grew up bereft of sizable minorities in their hometowns, these men had viewed from the cradle the injustices imposed upon the black men and women. They were undeniable.

These were different scales of justice, segregated housing and seating at public events, separate water fountains and rest rooms. They were exiled to the most impoverished and dilapidated neighborhoods in town, restricted to the most menial jobs and occupations, exposed to degrading—or at best paternalistic—treatment by whites. These were the same cultural roots from which all three men were nourished.

Did they all three notice and simply react in different ways? Had LBJ sympathized with the Negroes' plight, but harbored his feelings secretly until he became the most powerful man in America, buoyed on by the popular spirit of a martyred president?

Did George Wallace also notice early on, but soon learned after his speech in Minnesota, that he could not survive politically in the deep South by espousing such views?

Or was Ned Breathitt the only one of the three who both saw and felt their pain from his tender beginning? He was a unique Southerner. Most of that generation saw benignly, but most did not feel, nor even think, that there was anything wrong at all about this "peculiar institution" of post-slavery enslavement.

Wallace undoubtedly respected Breathitt, in part because of the latter's easy and gracious manner in disagreeing on issues. But most importantly, perhaps, because he knew that the Kentucky governor was right. In their relationship, George Wallace may have ever been mindful that Ned had heard and remembered what he said so many years before up North in Minnesota. He may have known that Breathitt was one of the few who knew George Wallace completely.

So they enjoyed each other's company and had fun together.

At the Governor's Conference in Texas, Ned and his wife, Frances, shared a car with the Wallaces' when they attended the Cotton Bowl game between Oklahoma and Texas. The car received a thunderous ovation as they circled the football field.

Frances was puzzled by the reception. "Ned," she turned to her husband, "How do they know you down here?"

"Hell, they don't know me," Breathitt laughed, "They know George."

Needless to say, President Johnson felt a deep sense of gratitude to the Kentucky governor. It was an easy choice for the president to fill the empty Federal Court of Appeals judicial chair with Breathitt's mentor, former Governor, Bert Combs.

In January of 1966, Breathitt was back to the drawing board in the gritty work of passing the South's first Civil Rights Act.

This time he was ready. Toughened by two years in office he also managed to get his people elected in the 1965 Senate and House elections. He had even talked former Democratic governor and strong ally, Lawrence Wetherby into oiling up his creaky political joints to get elected to the state Senate.

Breathitt was a man obsessed. He was still stinging from the criticism of civil rights leaders who said he had not done enough in 1964 to get the bill passed. King, the governor's new friend, was prodding Ned to push the bill through. And of course Breathitt knew that with the Constitutional restriction against consecutive terms, this would be his last chance.

Paul Oberst, law professor at the University of Kentucky helped draft the legislation. Through the strong assistance of the Speaker of the House, Shelby McCallum(from Marshall County with no blacks), and spell-binding orator and Representative, John Y. Brown, Sr., the bill rolled through the lower chamber on January 17, by a vote of 77-13. A little over a week later the Senate did even better by passing the act with only one dissenting vote. George Brand, senator from way down in the Jackson Purchase of west Kentucky cast the only negative vote.

Another west Kentuckian, Lt. Governor Harry Waterfield, who presided over the vote, later said, "We'll let ole George sing 'Dixie' at the signing ceremony."

There had been no marches this time. Two years had made a lot of difference. Integration was well on its way– the Brown Decision more than 12 years in the past. Johnson's Civil Rights Act was now a part of the political landscape.

Governor Ned Breathitt had many other reasons to be proud of his administration. His score sheet had included a monumental Reclamation Act which had required him to take on the deep pocket and powerful lobby of the coal industry, public utilities and the railroads. But his "team" had gotten it passed, and the moonscape appearance of the west Kentucky strip mines would soon be turning into rolling green hills and their brackish waters cleared.

But undoubtedly the proudest moment for the young governor was on January 27, 1966, when at the feet of the Lincoln Monument in the Capitol Rotunda, and in the presence of Rev. A.D. Williams King–Martin Luther's brother from Louisville–and others, he signed Kentucky's Civil Rights Act into law.

The Louisville *Courier Journal*, praised the passage and signing of the bill and deemed it "a tribute to Governor Breathitt's political skill and courage."

While Kentucky's 1966 Act was more inclusive than the national law passed two years before, and established the state's Commission on Human Rights, its most powerful good was symbolic.

As the first Southern state to enact a civil rights bill, Governor Ned Breathitt had struck the adamant segregationists of the deep South where it hurt the most. Most all of those opposing civil rights initiatives had done so under the respectable banner of "state's rights." That had been precisely the pretext used by George

Wallace when attempting to block the admission of black students at the University of Alabama.

Of course such specious posturing was exposed by the fact that none of these states below the Mason-Dixon Line had done anything on their own for their black citizens.

Until now, when Kentucky led the way.

Now Ned Breathitt–a card-carrying member of the Sons of Confederate Veterans–and the Kentucky legislators had effectively challenged their Southern brethren to flex their mighty muscles of statehood and do right by their people of color.

In effect, the governor of Kentucky had brought this heroic pilgrimage home to the states.

While the Kentucky Act of 1966 had passed the general assembly by a healthy margin, it had not been without political costs and rancor for Breathitt.

"The place where I was the most unpopular because of my stand, was in my own home county," Breathitt would recall many years later. "For a long time, I had a hard time there over it."

But his bold leadership won great praise in other circles. Following the passage of the Kentucky civil rights law, Governor Breathitt was one of ten American citizens to receive the distinguished Russwurm Award in 1966. The award was named in honor of John B. Russwurm, founder of the first Negro newspaper in the United States. Others receiving the award included Vice President Hubert Humphrey, Mrs. Lyndon B. Johnson and United States Attorney General Nicholas B. Katzenbach.

Louisville, Kentucky sits right on the rim of the Mason-Dixon Line. Geographically, Louisville and Richmond, Virginia are the two most northern cities in the South.

But its history is deeply embedded in the ways of the Jim Crow segregationist South.

This is especially true in the area of housing.

In 1954, just a few days before the landmark Supreme

Court decision in Brown vs. Board of Education was handed down, racial trouble erupted in the river city. A black man by the name of Andrew Wade purchased a house from Carl and Anne Braden, employees at The Louisville *Courier Journal* and known as "radicals" in the community. The house was located in the west Louisville blue-collar neighborhood. According to some, it was the most racist of all neighborhoods in that town, where segregation was still the prevailing way of life. Both the Bradens who were white, and Wade knew that the transaction would be controversial and they proceeded nevertheless with their cause celebre.

If they wanted attention, they were not disappointed.

When Wade moved into the neighborhood, violence erupted. Shots were fired at the house and the following month it was bombed.

Carl Braden was prosecuted and convicted under the state's "sedition" laws. What was considered to be Communist material–writings of Lenin, and Marx included–was found by law enforcement at the Braden home.

Eventually the appeals court overturned the Braden conviction, but not until he had served over 8 months in jail.

Fast forward to Derby time, 1967.

Again it was Louisville, Kentucky. Again the issue was race. And again the issue was housing.

And it was Governor Ned Breathitt's last year in office.

As the dogwoods exploded into white splendor across the emerald carpet of the Bluegrass and spring moved into Kentucky with all of its magnificent splendor, Governor Breathitt looked forward to his last Kentucky Derby as the state's chief executive.

It would be a time to relax, enjoy the festivities, the hoopla and grandeur which comes on the first Saturday of each May when Kentucky puts on its best dress and entertains the world. Celebrities from every possible field of human endeavor–politics, entertainment, the arts and sciences–would make appearances, if not at all of the balls and festivities leading up to the race, then at the "Run for the Roses" under the historic spires of Churchill

Downs in Louisville. There the media cameras would be smoking, capturing beautiful women in their wide-brimmed hats, and handsome men frocked out in their Derby best.

Kentucky's world renowned humorist from Paducah, Irvin S. Cobb, could not explain the magic of the Derby. "If I could do that, I'd have a larynx of spun silver and the tongue of an anointed angel. Until you go to Kentucky and with your own eyes behold the Derby, you ain't never been nowhere and you ain't never seen nothing."

At Derby time, Louisville, Kentucky tries to look as Southern as the rest of the state.

But the Derby on Ned Breathitt's last watch as governor would not be a walk through the mint julep patch. It would turn out to pose one of the major crises of his administration.

Neither the 1964 Federal Civil Rights Bill, nor Kentucky's version, adequately addressed discrimination in housing. So, an ordinance was introduced before the Louisville Board of Aldermen, which would outlaw discrimination based upon race in the sale of private homes in that city.

Immediately the proposal caused a firestorm.

Civil rights advocates and liberal politicians, of course, were strongly for it. Republican Mayor Kenneth Schmeid, supported by the local Landlord Associations and realtors drew the line in the sand, strongly opposing it.

On April 11, 1967 the Board of Aldermen rejected the ordinance.

A local civil rights group called the Committee on Open Housing went on the warpath.

This organization was led by prominent civil rights activists W.J. Hodge, president of the local chapter of the NAACP; Rev. A.D. Williams King, brother of Dr. Martin Luther King; and Rev. Leo Lesser.

For weeks after the board's rejection of the ordinance, violence and racial turmoil prevailed in Louisville's south end where civil rights demonstrators repeatedly clashed with open housing opponents and city police.

Over six hundred people were eventually arrested.

The unrest continued to simmer as the month wore on.

Governor Breathitt, strongly favored the passage of the ordinance and even went to Louisville to march in one of the peaceful demonstrations.

As Derby day approached with no solution in sight, the demonstrators began to think of disrupting the "Run for the Roses."

Ominously the demonstrators began to chant, "no housing ordinance, no Derby."

In an effort to use the governor's office to bring the matter to a peaceful and satisfactory resolution, Breathitt called Mayor Schmeid. He encouraged the 56-year-old mayor to agree to passage of a fair housing law.

While the conversation was civil, Schmeid did not attempt to hide his resentment of the governor's interference.

"You take care of the state of Kentucky, governor, and I'll take care of Louisville," said the city's chief executive.

"Louisville is in the state of Kentucky, Kenny," Ned quickly rejoined.

The conversation came to naught.

A shaky truce between the opposing forces, sewn together by the thin promise that there were already adequate state laws on the books to require fair housing, soon fell apart.

May 6, Derby day, drew nigh.

A growing tenseness gripped the city of Louisville as the civil rights leaders drew up the battle plans to shut down the Derby. The plan was simple. Hundreds, if not thousands, of the demonstrators would pay the standard $2 fare into the infield at the Derby. Once inside the track, they would go over the railing and sit down on the track just before the beginning of the big race. They would have to be bodily removed, one by one, by the police in full view of the nation through the eyes of television.

On Thursday night, March 4, Martin Luther King, Jr.

arrived in town to lend his support to the crusade.

"The Southern Christian Leadership Conference is 100 percent behind using every means of persuasion to get the city to pass a law banning racial discrimination in the sale or rental of housing property," King proclaimed.

Meanwhile over in Frankfort, Governor Ned Breathitt and his aides were not sitting by idly while watching with grave concern the gathering storm. He began to make plans for trouble.

Breathitt was determined that the 93rd Kentucky Derby would be run as scheduled, with no disruptions.

Said Breathitt early in the week, "I cannot believe that the cause of open housing or any other facet of civil rights could be helped by demonstrations at Churchill Downs."

He made a call to his friend Martin Luther King, Jr. beseeching him to halt their plans for disrupting the Derby.

The easygoing Breathitt, ever the gracious Southern gentleman, was direct with his old friend.

"Dr. King, I've always been on your side. I helped get the strongest state civil rights bill in the country passed," he recounted. "The Derby is our time. It's the one event when Kentucky comes into the national eye in a favorable light."

The implication was clear, "You owe me this one."

And then to bring it home to King's own people, "If you think Bull Connor was rough in Alabama, you wait 'till you see these drunken 2-dollar betters who are not allowed to see the race. They will kill your young people."

Ned Breathitt knew his people, both the rabble and the rude.

Still, King did not relent.

Marches continued in Louisville on Thursday and Friday, with thirty-five demonstrators being arrested the night before the Derby for staging a sit-in at the Churchill Downs ticket windows.

The National Guard activated under the governor's command for the Saturday confrontation. Every available state policeman was ordered to Louisville. Churchill Downs would become an armed camp.

Breathitt hovered with the state's Adjutant General Arthur Young Lloyd, Commisioner of Public Safety Glenn Lovern, and the head of the state police, Ted Bassett.

"The Derby will be run," he somberly directed, "but I don't want anyone injured."

To these seasoned old warriors it must have sounded like a Pollyanna approach. If there was a sit-in on the track, and the protesters had to be removed, it would be a miracle if no one was seriously hurt.

The plan was simple. The National Guard—numbering about 2,000—would be armed only with batons, no weapons. They would line the rail all the way around the track to block any entrance by the intruding demonstrators. The state police would be armed, in case disaster broke loose, but they would be hidden from public view in the stable areas.

Then, in a master stroke of imaging for the television audience he knew would be watching, Breathitt ordered each member of the National Guard to wear white gloves and carry white batons.

"They will march out, line up against the rail. They will look ceremonial," he assured Loyd and Lovern.

On Friday night, as Louisville and the Commonwealth of Kentucky braced for the following day, Governor Ned Breathitt had his plan in place.

But he still prayed for a reprieve.

Saturday morning, May 6, 1967 broke cloudy and threatening in Frankfort, Kentucky.

Ned was nervously entertaining guests at the governor's Derby Breakfast on the grounds of the mansion in Frankfort, mentally readying himself for the tough day ahead.

He was called to the phone.

It was Dr. King.

"Governor, we have decided to call off the sit-in at the Derby," King spoke softly on the other end. "We simply ask you to promise to keep the pressure on in your state for the cause of civil rights."

"Dr. King," Breathitt responded, "I would have done that anyway. And I assure you that I will. I must tell you that my prayers have been answered."

After the brief conversation, the Kentucky governor returned to his guests, a huge burden lifted from his shoulders.

"Proud Clarion," a 30-1 long shot, won the Kentucky Derby on that dark, damp Saturday afternoon.

The two dollar betters went wild.

Governor Ned Breathitt (right) meeting with Martin Luther King and Jackie Robinson in the governor's office in March, 1964. Photo compliments of Tim Tingle and Kentucky Department of Library and Archives

*Demonstrators pushing for the passage of civil rights legislation during the
1964 session of the Kentucky General Assembly.
Photo compliments of Tim Tingle
and Kentucky Department of Library and Archives*

Governor Ned Breathitt
Photo compliments of Ruth Murphy, Frankfort, Kentucky

Friends Ned Breathitt (seated second from the right) and George
Wallace (seated far right) at the Southern Governor's Conference
held at Kentucky Dam State Park in 1964.
Photo compliments of Governor Edward Breathitt Collection,
courtesy of Kentucky Historical Society

The Breathitts as
Kentucky's First
Family. Standing left
to right: Mary Fran,
Governor Breathitt,
Linda. Seated, left to
right: Edward, wife,
Frances and Susan.
Photo compliments of
Governor Edward
Breathitt Collection,
courtesy of Kentucky
Historical Society

Ned Breathitt never ran for another political office. In 1972 he wanted to run for the U.S. Senate when the incumbent Thruston Morton retired. However, Kentucky's Democratic Governor Wendell Ford was committed to Walter "Dee" Huddleston and asked Breathitt not to run for the sake of party unity. Being a good soldier, Breathitt obliged.

Huddleston would win, but would last only two terms.

Following his term as governor, Breathitt returned to Hopkinsville to practice law.

"One day I was governor of Kentucky living in the big mansion in Frankfort with all the servants," he would muse later. "The next day Frances and I were loading up the kids in the station wagon driving back to Hopkinsville."

He served on various boards and commissions during those years including acting as chairman on President Johnson's Commission on Rural Poverty. But his job as special counsel for the Southern Railroad would be the most pivotal as far as his future was concerned. In March 1972, he was appointed vice president of the Southern Railway System. He and his family moved to Washington where he worked as the railway's chief lobbyist until 1993.

It was in his position with Southern Railway that he renewed his friendship with George Wallace. Once again Wallace was governor of Alabama having made a strong run as a third party candidate in the 1968 presidential election. The Southern Railway was an integral part of the economy of Alabama, and Governor Wallace had reason to regularly confer with the former Kentucky governor and old friend.

In 1966, prohibited by law from running again, Wallace helped his wife, Lurleen become elected as surrogate governor. She died from cancer two years into her term. In 1971 Wallace married Cornelia Ellis Snively, a former Miss Alabama and niece of former Alabama Governor James E. Folson.

But in 1972, the life of George Wallace would change dramatically.

On May 15 of that year he was gunned down by Arthur

Governor Breathitt meeting with President Johnson at the
White House in the den adjacent to the Oval Office.
Photo compliments of Lyndon Baines Johnson Library

Bremer while campaigning for the presidency in a shopping center in Laurel, Maryland. He survived the attack but the bullet caused permanent paralysis from the waist down.

Confined to a wheelchair, Wallace made one last unsuccessful bid for president in 1976.

With his physical disability, slowly, but noticeably, Wallace began to change his personal and political viewpoints, especially in racial matters. It was as if his physical suffering mellowed him, made him less strident and more acceptable to the winds of change which were blowing across the South. He seemed to have returned to his more liberal views on race expressed so many years before when he and Ned Breathitt attended the national Young Democrats Convention. He recanted his racist views, and in 1982 was elected governor for the last time, receiving strong support from black voters.

His dramatic road to repentance and redemption came to a flourishing climax in 1974 at the Dexter Avenue Baptist Church in

Montgomery, Alabama. It was Martin Luther King's former church and Wallace was asked to speak by the pastor, Dr. Robert M. Dickerson. There, sitting in his wheelchair looking into a vast sea of black faces, Wallace told of how his own physical suffering since the shooting had helped him to better understand the suffering of all people. He asked to be forgiven.

Dickerson would later report, "He said some things people thought he would never say.....People stood–blacks and whites–and cried."

When he received a standing ovation from the congregation at the end, the emotional effect was overpowering. As James Russell Lowell proclaimed:

New occasions teach new duties; Time makes ancient good uncouth;
They would upward still, and onward who would keep abreast of Truth.

George Wallace, a national name, known and recognized by those who come and write the annals of the times. But he was a reed blown to and fro.

Ned Breathitt, a Kentucky governor from the Jim Crow upbringing of the old South–from the slow and happy ways of a land meaning much good, yet still counting race as a factor. Ned Breathitt, a good man who for much too long could not go home again without silent rancor and the loss of friends.

One who chose to stand and fight–lost to history.

Ned Breathitt well remembered that last visit with his friend during George Wallace's final term as governor.

Stylishly dressed and well-educated black aides and secretaries scurried in and around his office. He was assisted by a black state trooper. But Wallace himself was only a shell of the vigorous and dynamic individual he had once been.

"When I went to see him," Breathitt recollected, "he was

sick, in a wheelchair; his spirits were down and he spoke in a low voice. He was really dependent on his aides to govern. He still had his mental capacities to make decisions. George was a totally different and diminished figure. It was actually sad for me to see."

Two old friends who some thirty years before had shared the bracing Minnesota air. Two old friends who mingled with the hopes and dreams of their salad days of youth when they were green in judgment. Each staked out different paths to follow: one with the vision of the new, progressive South with racial harmony and justice and the other holding on to the old, only to find in the end that it was a way of life that had already died. That in the end it was a bucket of dust.

He that troubleth his own house shall inherit the wind.

Did George Wallace actually change his mind about race, or only return to his better self from when he was up North in the land of lakes so many years before?

"Of course by the time George changed, the blacks had begun to vote," Breathitt would later muse with a slight twinkle in his eye. "Besides, George was getting old. Maybe he was thinking of the next life."

A.O. Stanley and Ned Breathitt, their lives and times as governors linking up over a half century, in many ways were very different. Stanley was intemperate to the point of drunkenness. A story-telling, back-slapping, grandiloquent orator of the old style, he often shot from the hip in both his comments and decisions. In the way of many governors of that time he was undoubtedly, "tolerably corrupt."

Breathitt was a product of the modern age. Young, clean cut, with a button-down sense of decorum; ebullient in speech, but without flair; pleasant and upbeat, but not effusive.

But they were kindred spirits, of shared values and principles.

Both west Kentuckians, one from the top part, the other from the bottom part, of the far western enclave of a land often considered distant even exotic, of not only a different time zone but of a different culture from the Bluegrass.

Both were courtly and gracious in their dealings with others. They possessed a keen insight into the competitive nature of politics: that the furious battle over ideas and issues should not become personal.

Stanley maintained genuine love and affection for his arch political enemy, Edwin Morrow.

Breathitt, maintained and cultivated a warm and lasting friendship with George Wallace, even though the two represented opposite ends of the civil rights battle. Also, Ned Breathitt and his most ardent Republican nemesis Nunn, would become good friends.

"It was just talk," Ned would later say of Nunn's campaign rhetoric against the civil rights order, "fit for the mores and politics of the time. To his credit he never tinkered with the civil rights law once he became governor. In fact, Louie Nunn was a good governor."

Both Stanley and Breathitt were devout husbands and family men. And both adhered to the core value of social justice for all, regardless of color, or station in life. Both who had great confidence not only in people of wealth, brilliance and influence, but also in those whose fires might burn within the hovel of the wretched and dispossessed.

They both believed in the inherent decency of humanity. That from the darkest heart of the most villainous bigot, there was a reluctant chord which could be touched, if only men, good men, had the courage to stand and fight.

Each of these leaders possessed a clear sense of history. They understood from where we came and where we should go. Above the tug and pull of base influence and the contumely of the crowd, they could look out over the darkened waters and follow a distant light.

These two men—at the very heart of their souls—believed that America was man's last, best hope, and that every human being possessed a spark gifted by the gods.

So on that promising spring afternoon now so long ago, as Stanley and Breathitt shook hands and parted on that Frankfort Street, neither knew the Olympian nature of that farewell. The gods had ordained the passing of the torch, from a dying ember to the eager tender. As a young president proclaimed:

For the torch has been passed to a new generation of Americans, born in this century, tempered by war, disciplined by a hard and bitter peace, proud of our ancient heritage, and unwilling to witness or permit the slow undoing of those human rights to which this nation has always been committed...........

CHAPTER 15

TODAY

*A human life, I think, should be well rooted in some spot
of a native land, where it may get the love of tender
kinship for the face of the earth, for the labors of men
go forth to, for the sounds and accents that haunt it, for whatever will give that early home a familiar unmistakable, difference amidst the future widening of knowledge. The best introduction to astronomy is to think of the nightly heavens as a little lot of stars belonging to one's own homestead.*

George Eliot

Murray, Kentucky today is a town of over 15,000
people. Passenger trains no longer huff and puff into town.
The old passenger depot sits empty and abandoned.

Travelers coming to town from the north side,
enter the city on bustling Highway 641. It is a wide, four-
lane thoroughfare heavily developed with all the familiar
landmarks of interconnected America.

Holiday Inn Express, Burger King, Wal-Mart,
Captain D's, Chevron, Michelin Tires, Office Depot,

Applebee's, Pizza Hut, Taco John's, and Radio Shack mesh with a handful of local names such as Joe Smith's Carpet and car lots.

One could be approaching any small town in the country—Des Moines, Iowa or Rome, Georgia. We are becoming a nation of interchangeable parts. Until we draw closer to the core of the city, that is. Near Chestnut Street the harsh commercial landscape is softened considerably as one approaches the campus of Murray State University.

An attractive brick archway on the right marks the gateway to the campus, followed by white rail fencing bordering the highway on a field of green. The pastoral, horse-country look welcomes people to what *U.S. News and World Report* has ranked as one of the top regional universities in the South.

It had been A. O. Stanley's old friend, Edwin P. Morrow, who as governor in 1922, signed the legislation to establish two teacher-training colleges in the state, called "normal schools." Citizens of Murray and Calloway County, under the dynamic and driving leadership of another of Stanley's old friends, Rainey T. Wells, won out over numerous far western Kentucky counties by raising $117,000 for the purchase of the land and erecting the first building.

Wells served as second president of the college.

Murray Normal School grew and soon became Murray State College as the campus spread out over the western edge of town.

On a bright spring morning in 1966, Governor Edward T. Breathitt arrived on campus. To a full house of dignitaries, school officials and students in Lovett Auditorium, he officially christened the school as Murray State University.

Over the years it has increased its enrollment hovering now at 10,000 students. Its sound curriculum, growing academic reputation and nationally known athletic programs have drawn students from around the world.

Highway 641 turns into 12th Street at the busy intersection with Chestnut. If one turns left on Chestnut, the Cheri Cinema,

Monument of
Guthrie Diuguid
located in the
Murray cemetery.

soon arrives on the left, its marquee announcing the current showing. Mr. Gatti's Pizza comes and passes. Soon, to the left, the
rolling green acres of Murray Cemetery open up with an emerald
flourish. It has an impressive sweep of tombstones, granite markers
of a variety of shapes and sizes. There is even a mausoleum to welcome one to the city of the dead.

Wilson, Cook, McDaniel, Paschall, Ellis, Flood, Weatherly,
Lassiter, Beale, Grogan, Outland, Overby–old and venerated local
names mark the various stones.

And Diuguid.

Lying under an elegant stone with a Woodmen of the
World emblem are the remains of Guthrie Diuguid.

Not too far away is the "colored" section of the graveyard.
In an unmarked grave are the chalky and dusty remnants of Lube

Approximate location of the Guthrie Diuguid shooting as the site appears today.

Martin. Reportedly, the city had barred his burial there after his family claimed his body from the Kentucky State Penitentiary. It is believed that his brother, Chester, surreptitiously buried him there under the cloak of darkness.

So, at long last, after history has slapped its hands and walked away, the two bloody antagonists of the high-noon confrontation so long ago, rest in peace together.

The cemetery is only a short distance from the Diuguid farm from which Guthrie was walking to town on that fateful December day.

Soon old Curd Street, now Fourth Street, approaches. Here one moves into the geographical heart of the Lube Martin saga. It was toward this very spot, near the Rowlett Tobacco Factory that the four black men were headed on a dead run–north on Curd–after shooting Guthrie Diuguid. To go straight across Fourth Street is to head down the hill to the railroad track along which all trains enter town from the north–where A. O. Stanley entered town on that uncertain January morn. A crook to the right and one is in the middle of the Negro section of town. The majority of residents are still black. But this area today is a far cry from the tar-paper shacks and hovels of Lube Martin's day.

It's back on Fourth Street, however, where one can travel the same avenue where Diuguid was walking toward his death. Turning right off Chestnut, onto Fourth, one passes some of the same houses which stood on December 9, 1916.

At the approximate location of the shooting now stands the new Calloway County Judicial Building. On the west side of Curd, almost directly across from the Justice Center, is Imes Miller Funeral Home. Ironically, the approximate spot where the shooting took place is between the homes of death and justice.

Fourth Street bends downward into a broad dip before it heads back up to approach the court square. A massive, unseen subterranean system of culverts runs under the street at the spot where an old bridge had spanned the narrow creek.

The court square of Murray today is gallantly trying to

recapture the simple beauty and symmetry of its past through the recent streetscape reconstruction of streets and curbs under the federally funded Renaissance Program. Still, like most small towns in America, garish remnants of the modernistic architecture of the 50s and 60s still remain. Even the refurbishing is so neatly manicured and coiffed that it antiseptically resembles Renaissance streetscapes in a thousand other points on the map.

On the northeast corner of the court square stands the huge Union Planters Bank, now housed in a modern structure of drivet and glass. In a different time, in a more elegant and modest structure, it had been the Bank of Murray with its president, Edwin Diuguid, holding control of the financial plight of the rich and poor of Calloway County.

Unchanged through the years, is the majestic courthouse with its colonnaded entrance and its attractive cupola which hovers over downtown Murray.

The Southern writer William Faulkner knew such places well:

But above all, the courthouse: the center, the focus, the hub; sitting looming in the center of the county's circumference like a single cloud in its ring of horizon, laying its vast shadow to the uttermost rim of horizon; musing, brooding, symbolic and ponderable, tall as cloud, solid as rock, dominating all: protector of the weak, judicator and curb of the passions and lusts, repository and guardian of aspirations and hopes.....

Walking the street this day is a young, attractive Murray State coed. She is holding a small cell phone to her ear as she talks to.....it could be anybody from Paducah to New Delhi.

Long before cell phones and instant communication, the dreamer of worlds yet unknown and the eccentric inventor, Nathan B. Stubblefield, roamed these streets. It was here on this court square he was seen one day around 1904 with a little box taken from his pocket. He talked into it and then put it to his ear and listened. A curious friend, Ed Downs, asked him what he was doing.

"Talking to my son in Texas," was his calm reply.

"You know?" the astonished Downs reported later, "I almost believed him." One hundred years later and the impossible is a reality.

The clock atop the courthouse still tells the time above a hill worn down from history. It tolls the hours and days for a hamlet experienced with the tug and pull of civil strife and violence. Confederate and Union troops parried for control of this county seat. Night Riders of the tobacco wars walked the streets by day, rode under the flickering shadows of firebrand and torch by night.

The face of the ancient clock looked down upon the frantic street scene below on December 9, 1916. Its giant hands showed just a few minutes after noon as the livery rig of Curt Owen had hurriedly pulled up in front of the medical office of brothers Will and Rob Mason on the northeast corner of Curd and Main. Owen and bystanders had gingerly but urgently helped the mortally wounded Guthrie Diuguid up the steps into the attending hands of Dr. Will Mason.

It was to this square and intersection of crudely hewed roads that the capital of Calloway County had been moved in 1842 from Wadesboro after Marshall County was carved out of the top part of the county.

Murray—a settlement named for lawyer and Congressman John L. Murray—was at the geographical center of the newly divided county. The current courthouse of the Beaux Arts style was completed in 1913.

There is no longer any court in the courthouse. All judicial offices and courtrooms are in the new Judicial Center. This treasured old landmark now houses only county offices.

But, it remains known as the courthouse.

Inside on the first floor there is still that feel of a people's capitol. It has that worn look of public use like a lingering scent of humanity. Millions of feet, shod in a mind-boggling variety of footwear have traversed the worn terrazzo hallway floor. Down these same halls, on these worn and historic flagging, shuffled Lube Martin arm in arm with Patterson's men. Along this way charged A.O. Stanley on his dramatic mission. Men of the mob moved through these corridors guided by the unleashed and destructive passions of their worse selves. But mainly these ancient floors have given way to less dramatic, but essential chores: land transfers, licensing, road problems, feuding neighbors, car titles, and much, much politics.

Upstairs, the modern carpenter has taken his toll on the old courtroom, converting it into an office for the county court clerk—the long-standing registrar for deeds, car titles and other important businesses of the people.

It's a busy place.

The burial of the old historic courtroom has not completely covered the cadaver. Like a giant dinosaur partially covered with sand, identifiable parts—a joint here or a bone fragment there—stick above the surface.

The old stairways, especially the one to the rear, still have their steep and twisting pitch, guarded by the heavy, ornate railing. Behind the counter in the main room, where the deputy clerks scurry about their duties under the dropped ceiling, still stand the old metal columns which hold up the now enclosed balcony. Silently, like stubborn sentinels from the past, they stand to witness the frantic pace of a brave new world of neon lights and computer screens. The pressed tin ceiling on the underbelly of the balcony is still evident, so low one can reach and touch it.

Squarely above where the old bench set, above where A. O. Stanley stood and gave his dramatic oration in the tense and packed courtroom on that January morning, the pendulum of the Regulator clock swings back and forth, back and forth handing out time by the second. Time stops for no man or woman, whether governors, judges, or county court clerks.

Blessings on the people who at the funeral of the old room deemed to keep the windows open, where they still pour light into the work place. Around these windows had stood young soldiers, occasionally peering out on the downtown businesses, silently musing for home. Out of these windows Lube Martin must have certainly stared for some semblance of hope into the gray, winter sky. This is no ordinary or sanitized remodeled office, for framed faces from the past, lined up along the enclosed beam, give evidence of those county court clerks who served in that office back through the ages. One, H.C. "Clint" Broach, county court clerk 1914-18, stares on indifferently. He had made a cameo appearance in the Lube Martin trial reading from the county court record of the appointment of Guthrie Diuguid as deputy constable for the Murray magisterial district on August 12, 1916.

Those ghostly voices of Stanley, Bush, Holt and Smith can still be heard in this large room only by those who have a soulful ear to history and the spirit world.

But, from the friendly clerks who now ply their trade in this room of public service, the same distinctive accent lingers in the computer age.

"Rite hot out thare idnet Mr. Sullivan?" a pretty clerk welcomes an aging customer to the counter.

Narrow steps still lead up to the balcony of the old courtroom. But the space above has been cobbled into the office of the county treasurer.

In the northwest corner of the county clerk's domain, are the stacks and stacks of deed books and indexes. Entrance is still gained to this room through antique wooden doors. In this place, one can stand today, between the recordings of land deals and transfers, at the exact location where twelve, stern and unforgiving Christian County men decided to have Lube Martin die for his crime.

Back downstairs one moves out the doors into the spacious front yard of the courthouse. The oppressive heat of an August afternoon presses down and reminds one that air conditioning is another change to the old building. Sultry and languid courtrooms, where ceiling fans worked vainly to stir the air are no more. Gone

313

are the coatless men, sweating and pleading profusely to juries while open windows welcome in the noises of a summer afternoon along with barn swallows and wasps.

Sunshine filters through the trees as the visitor meanders from the door of the Calloway County Courthouse. Like a metal fragment to a magnet, one feels a pull to the northeast corner of the court square. There is a presence there, a person......no, not a person, but a replica of a person.

It's Robert E. Lee, here in the 21st century in Murray, Kentucky.

It's the monument.

Meet me at the monument.

In many Southern court squares, one knows what it means to meet "at the monument."

There, in hundreds of such squares, stand either General Lee, or another Confederate soldier. Or it may not be a soldier. In

Confederate Soldiers' monument today.

nearby Cadiz, Kentucky and many other towns–an elegant stone of some kind, commemorates those who fought and died in the lost cause.

But here in Murray, Kentucky it's the replica of Robert E. Lee. Standing atop an impressive colonnaded portico, he is still there after all these years. A world of change swirls around his head, a world of terrorists and strange new doctrines and ways.

Urinetown is opening on Broadway.

The U.S. Supreme Court has ruled that sodomy is a constitutional right.

But Bobby still stands, through the years.

Eighty-nine survivors of Calloway County's 800 Confederate soldiers who served in the Civil War stood at attention when General Lee was welcomed into town during the May 10, 1917 dedication. The oldest graybeard proudly saluting was 88-year-old P. D. Wicker.

Over eighty years later, on this summer afternoon, the trees droop in the simmering August heat. Traffic weaves around the square, seemingly in slow motion.

General Lee remains erect, unchanged.

By 4 p.m. offices begin to shut down as county employees head for their cars. The sun angles farther to the west, slipping fingers of sunbeams through the foliage onto the grounds. Downtown commerce winds down as shops and businesses wrap up their day and lock their doors.

On the west side of the court square historic Rudy's, a popular eating spot for over fifty years, closes out another day of country-style cooking and Southern hospitality. It was here where Lube Martin's only child, Queen, worked as a cook after her father's death. Customary for that time, her skin color dictated that she enter and leave through the back door.

The summer gloaming moves onto the square, crickets sing to mostly empty streets and vacant benches. Like dutiful sentinels, the street lights hum and come to life, faithfully appearing to arrest the encroaching darkness.

It's Emancipation Day, August 8, 2003, in Murray, Kentucky.

Just a few short blocks away from the courthouse, under the constant gaze of Robert E. Lee, is the old neighborhood of Lube Martin—known at one time as Darktown.

There along that same old railroad still resides most of the Negro population of the town. It is much different now however, than in 1917. All of the settlement which was located on the east side of the track has disappeared, swept clear by unsightly industrial growth. The area has given way to modern houses of varying types and sizes. It is a modest neighborhood, including some public housing, but one has to search long and hard to find any semblance of previous squalor.

The vibrant spirit of this race of people remains alive as families gather for reunions planned around this annual celebration. It is a yearly festival born of a date—August 8—that is of unknown origin, but which belongs uniquely to Kentuckians of color, just as the Passover belongs to the Jew. And, in a sense, it marks a similar point of departure—the freedom from slavery afforded by father Abraham through the Emancipation Proclamation on January 1, 1863. As the Hebrews rushed to exit the oppressive rule of Pharaoh and forever marked that day on their calendars, so do these sable-faced Americans pay homage to their liberation.

And they have much to celebrate for their long, hard journey to social justice. More American than most Americans; more Southern than most Southerners, their ancestors have paid an awful price in blood and tears—to live and thrive in the land of the free.

Still entrenched near the railroad, on the same piece of earth they have long claimed as their own, homes open up on this night for friends and relatives to come and go, greet and meet, embrace in that loving fellowship of kindred spirits. They come from far and wide, mostly from the North. There is food and drink, some of it strong, but mostly laughter and the enduring warmth of easy conversation. They are a people apart, yet so magnificently woven into the American fabric as to be inseparable from the grand tapestry of the whole. America would not be America without these undaunted souls. Brought to this country against their will, enslaved in dire servitude, they have in their liberation and rise to full citizenship raised America and all its people in the process.

On this evening as summer twilight engulfs the busy streets of Darktown, the 103-year-old son-in-law of Lube Martin sits at the home of his daughter, having arrived from far away Toledo, Ohio, perhaps the last pilgrimage of his life. The stealing steps of time have closed off most of the memory he has of those early days; the young light-skinned girl named Queen, with whom he fell in love and married when she was still a teen. The knowledge he has of the murder of Guthrie Diuguid, the trial and execution of his wife's father, the thunderous plodding of the lynch mob, all are gone behind the dark and merciful veil of time and dotage.

Beneath this benevolent and leathery old mahogany face is buried forever scenes and sounds of terrible deeds; forlorn cries of sadness and despair; and alas, the silent laughter and smiles of tender faces long loved yet forgotten.

Out on the campus of vibrant and effervescent Murray State University, the celebration goes on at the gleaming, modern student union center. After a reception, this gathering of smartly dressed, successful blacks enjoy the gospel music of the "Legionnaires" from Brownsville, Tennessee. The foot-stomping vocalist of this string quartet incites the listeners to hand-clapping enjoyment. There are a smattering of white faces in the crowd, thoroughly involved in the unrestrained mirth of rhythm and sound.

Finally, the concert comes to a close and everyone moves slowly out into the muggy August night. This crowd is a cross-section between old and young. Elderly black men and women are led away by younger generations of children and grandchildren. Many are from out of town, back in Murray to enjoy their heritage with their people.

Here is the recurring celebration of liberation—led by a generation of blacks who rushed through the portals of opportunity

317

once the gates were swung open by the heroes of the civil rights movement.

Among this group of well-educated, handsomely dressed black people is one of the first Negroes to enter Murray State, far back in 1955. His name is Bobby Brandon, whose broad shoulders and athletic physique belie his age.

He reminisces about that summer school so long ago as one of the only black faces on campus.

"President Woods told me not to go into the cafeteria or the swimming pool," he recollects. "I didn't want to go in those places anyway," he chuckles good naturedly without the slightest hint of bitterness or rancor. "All I wanted to do was go to class and go home."

It's as if he views his own history with a bemused detachment, hardly able to fully comprehend that strange world in which he had once lived.

Back downtown on this simmering evening of rejoicing and reunion, Bobby Lee stands still, representing heirs, past and present, of that second revolution. Stanley, Patterson, Holt, Young, Mason, Breathitt–all soldiers of the South, all gallantly struggled to exorcise the evil demon of slavery from the lost cause. All loved their Southland, its musical language, languid pace of life, earthiness in fervent worship, genuine friendships, touching and caressing and softening the sharp corners of life. There is a freedom from the oppressive decadence of northern prosperity whether it be the industrial blight of cities, or the homogenized and watered-down values of the internet age. It is a land of all who have sensed, if not spoken, a deep devotion to home, to land, to the religion of their fathers enlivened by gospel music and the haunting chants of Southern harmony singing, and an adulation of family.

....family instinct, the home, the sense of parents, the endless cousins, uncles and aunts, the nostalgia for one's own blood.....we defend certain qualities not because they belong to the South, but because the South

belongs to them.

And the Southern Negroes have all of this and more. For their souls carry the scars of our oppression and abuse, and these historical wounds give testimony that this ebony race was more of us than we ourselves, more real, more soulful, more Southern. For him and her, the pilgrimage has been far more painful, and in the end more prideful and robust.

There are many whites who both have lived and died in perpetual regret that time could not be erased, wrongs righted and the Negro liberated in time for the lost cause to have been remembered for what it was truly intended. The atrocities and debauchery of enslavement of their dark-skinned brethren had robbed all Southerners of that special bond which could have made them one; which may still be recaptured in those things the South was meant to be and which was lost to an institution then so ingrained, and now so despised and indefensible. Gray ghosts of an ancient feud still stalk this enchanting land, whose moderating voices saw two faces of slavery and who were betrayed by the firebrands of South Carolina—a state which should have been left to fight Massachusetts as proxies for their respective regions. Clarion and reasoned voices of state's rights were drowned by the Rhetts and the Yanceys who spewed the cause of slavery as paramount, assuring the eventual burial of redemptive virtues of the secession beneath the rubble and debris of defeat. There were Southern men even then who stood in the foggy field of ambivalence as to slavery. Men who secretly wondered, but publicly remained mute—Lee, Breckenridge, Stephens, Longstreet, and maybe in his heart of hearts, away from political reality, Davis himself.

For all of that and more, Bobby Lee in cold granite and his heirs in flesh and bone are condemned to an eternal pilgrimage to redeem the hidden virtues of the lost cause.

Not of the black man's bondage, but of the white man's soul. For freedom. Free to stand alone in a losing struggle against the cankerous byproducts of modernism—the grey skies of ambivalent values and decadence, loss of place, idolatry of tolerance, and a groveling obeisance to the gods of greed and consumerism.

Honor. To believe that the substance of a person is being what you say you are; where you say you'll be. Being, in essence, what you believe.

The voice is still unborn which can relieve the aching breast of the Southern white longing to be heard and the history of the South to be remembered for something other than the damning evil of slavery.

Values anchored to a sense of place. Family lines traced and cherished, hallowed in pictures on the wall where the wine of life may yet be poured by hands within the frame. Virtue rooted to the blackened earth: self-reliance and self-responsibility. The rushing torrent of change tempered in the quiet woods of reflection. Uniqueness in a shallow and homogenized land where no one knows where information ends and advertisement begins, all conveyed through the constant noise of the media which increasingly lobotomizes lonely millions. The disappearing art of storytelling, group gatherings and accents—a nation quickly becoming neutered and cloned: one dialect, one food chain, one attitude, and no soul. In the words of Norman Mailer, we are like "a potato molding in a plastic box."

Snow has fallen on the head of Bobby Lee. Winters have come and gone, summer heat has pressed against his brow—long summer afternoons, short winter days, on and on.....hour after hour, generation after generation.

So let us bend ear to them in this hour of lateness,
And what they are trying to say, try to understand,
And try to forgive them their defects, even their greatness,
For we are their children in the light of humanness, and under
the shadow of God's closing hand.

In the summer of 1917 when the Murray Chapter of the

Daughters of the Confederacy was raising funds for the final payment of the monument, they approached the president of the Murray Bank, Mr. Edwin Diuguid.

He, and his bank, would fund the balance of the project on one condition. The monument must not only stand upon the northeast corner of the square, but the distinguished visage of Bobby Lee must face his bank.

The deal was struck. So even today, he stands there, true to that commitment to Ed Diuguid, neither looking south–as most stony veterans do–nor north, or west.

But east.

And behold, the glory of the God of Israel came from the way of the east; and his voice was like a noise of many waters and the earth shined with his glory.

Looking eastward across the neighborhood of former slaves and the tracks upon which A. O. Stanley arrived on that cold January morning.

Eastward, to Trigg County, the home place of Alexander Cunningham where his descendants, including biracial children, and those of his slave, Rose now live, work and laugh together.

Eastward to Eddyville where Lube Martin died…

To Hopkinsville where Charles Bush sleeps peacefully near Ned Breathitt…

Eastward past the obelisk marking the birth of Jeff Davis at Fairview, and to Frankfort where A.O. Stanley sleeps upon capitol hill.

Across a state shot through with nature's bounty of resourceful rivers, fertile grounds, timbered highlands and soft, rolling hills; drenched in a violent and noble history of duels, feuds, violence and master spirits.

After all the years, these anxious eyes still await the first streaks of dawn.

Forever searching for that distant light

A Distant Light

Bibliography

Foote, Shelby. *The Civil War*. New York: Random House, 1958, 1963, 1974.

Harrison, Lowell and Klotter, James C. *New History of Kentucky.* Kentucky: University Press of Kentucky, 1999.

Hooks, Malinda Cunningham. *Memoirs of Malinda Cunningham Hooks*, 1930.

Kleber, John E. *The Kentucky Encyclopedia*. Kentucky: University Press of Kentucky, 1992.

Clark, Thomas D. *A History of Kentucky.* The John Bradford Press, 1960.

Caught in the Middle; The Civil War Years on the Lower Ohio, Cairo, Illinois to Henderson, Kentucky.

Lucas, Marion B. *A History of Blacks in Kentucky Volume 1 From Slavery to Segregation 1760-1891*. Kentucky: Kentucky Historical Society, 1992.

Egerton, John. *Speak Now Against the Day.* New York: Alfred A. Knof, 1994.

Waldrep, Christopher. *Night Riders Defending Community in the Black Patch 1890-1915.* North Carolina: Duke University Press, 1993.

Jennings, Kirby and Jennings, Dorothy. *The Story of Calloway County 1822-1976.*

Shuffett, Chuck. *Montage Magazine.* May 2000 to March 2001.

Ramage, Thomas W. *Augustus Owsley Stanley Early Twentieth Century Democrat.* Doctoral Thesis, University of Kentucky.

Eaton, Clement. *Jefferson Davis.* New York: The Free Press, 1977.

Klotter, James C. and Sehlinger, Peter J. *Kentucky Profiles; Biographical Essays in Honor of Holman Hamilton.* Kentucky: The Kentucky Historical Society, 1982.

Cunningham, Bill. *Flames in the Wind An Inspiring Collection of Stories about Courageous West Kentuckians.* Kentucky: McClanahan Publishing House, Inc., 1997.

Blyton, Gifford and Capps, Randall. *Speaking Out: Two Centuries of Kentucky Orators.* New Jersey: Hunter Publishing Company, 1977.

Cunningham, Bill. *Castle The Story of a Kentucky Prison.* Kentucky: McClanahan Publishing House, Inc., 1995.

Carter, Dan T. *The Politics of Rage.* Louisiana: Louisiana State University Press, 1995.

Brenner, Marie. *House of Dreams The Bingham Family of Louisville.* New York: Random House, New York, 1988.

Brinson, Betsy and Williams, Kenneth H. *The Register of the Kentucky Historical Society,* Vol. 99, No. 1, Winter 2001.

Interview with Governor Ned Breathitt. Kentucky: The Kentucky Historical Society, 2001.

Cooper, William J. *Jefferson Davis: The Essential Writings.*
New York: Modern Library, 2003.

Southerners, Twelve. *I'll Take My Stand The South and the
Agrarian Tradition.* Louisiana: Louisiana State University Press,
1977.

Memorial Record of Western Kentucky. New York: The Lewis
Publishing Company, 1904.

People

All nonfiction books are a team effort.

This book could not have been written without the assistance of many people.

Chuck Shuffett of Murray, Kentucky, is at the top of the list. His excellent series of articles in his historical periodical, *Montage*, was the starting point for this book. Also, he has served as a faithful assistant and provided much help to me there on the ground in Murray.

My good friend, Sid Easley of Murray, has also been a most valuable helper for me. Sid and his paralegal, Max Dodd, have turned into part-time investigators of the Diuguid shooting and have provided me with the results of their dogged research. Because of them I feel very comfortable with the information related in this book about the tragic event. We have worked together as a team, trying to get it right.

Glenn Martin of Princeton, Kentucky, has been a very congenial consultant on the history of the railroad in west Kentucky.

Others who have contributed in varying ways and for all of which I am grateful are as follows:

Lon Carter Barton, Mayfield; James M. Prichard and Tim Tingle, Kentucky Department for Libraries and Archives; Michael Walker, Paducah; Barbara Diuguid Mason (daughter of E.S. Diuguid, Jr. and granddaughter of E.S. Diuguid, Sr.), Paducah; Eleanor Diuguid (wife of James Diuguid, son of Herman Diuguid who was brother of E.S. Diuguid, Sr.), Murray; Gene Thurmond (grandson of Guthrie Diuguid), Murray; Professor David Beito, History Department, University of Alabama, Tuscalossa, AL; Rev. Charles Blair; Caroline Keaton, Spartanburg, SC; Randall Patterson, Hazel; Robert O. Miller, Murray; Wells T. Lovett, Owensboro; Governor Edward T. Breathitt, Jr.; Shannon

McFarlan, Paris, TN; Dr. Thomas D. Clark, Lexington; Ruth Murphy, Frankfort; Hon. Walter A. Baker, Glasgow; Karen Lyman, Lexington; William T. Turner, Hopkinsville; Jennie Gordon, Murray; John Ed Scott, Murray; Jane Melusin Henry, Jonesboro, AR; Wimpy Jones, Murray; Christian County Court Clerk Mike Kem, Hopkinsville; John David Hudspeth, Toledo, OH; Kathryn Hudspeth, Murray; Eugene Blanton, Murray; Talmadge Tutt, Murray; Kenny Imes, Murray; Betty L. Spratt, Daviess County Public Library; Charlene Smith, Kentucky Historical Society; Stacey Beans, Paducah; Gladman Humbles, Paducah; Betty Dobson, Paducah; Andrea Moore, Murray; Don Henry, Murray; Barron White, Paducah.

There are quotes throughout the book which have been placed in italics with no name given for the source. The italics indicate that they are not words of the author, but for stylistic purpose credit was not given at the time. Any such quotes in this work came from the Bible, Robert Penn Warren or Shakespeare, with the exception of John F. Kennedy's inaugural address.